ISBN 978-1-332-34773-5
PIBN 10317114

1 MONTH OF
FREE
READING

at

www.ForgottenBooks.com

By purchasing this book you are eligible for one month membership to ForgottenBooks.com, giving you unlimited access to our entire collection of over 700,000 titles via our web site and mobile apps.

To claim your free month visit:

www.forgottenbooks.com/free317114

Recollections of Seventy Years

AND

HISTORICAL GLEANINGS

OF

ALLEGHENY, PENNSYLVANIA

BY

JUDGE JOHN E. PARKE

BOSTON

RAND, AVERY, & COMPANY

Franklin Press

1886

47437

INTRODUCTORY NOTE.

SOME years previous to his death, Judge Parke commenced writing the history of Pittsburg and Allegheny; learning that his friend, the late Dr. Jonas R. McClintock, was engaged on a similar work for the first-named city, he generously desisted from that part of his self-imposed task, and confined his labors to a preparation of the early history of Allegheny. Except a couple of trips to California, his entire life was lived in these cities; and it extended almost from the commencement of settlement here, for three-quarters of a century. The many papers he read before the Historical Society of Western Pennsylvania, evinced his ability to perform this work; and it is greatly regretted that he was not permitted to complete it.

The papers here offered to the public were found among his manuscripts; and his earnest and frequently repeated desire to give the people of this city and vicinity a history of their city, has induced his family to undertake the publication. It is the request of his widow, that they be printed precisely as he left them; and with the exception of a few slight alterations, absolutely necessary, her request has been complied with.

J. L. F.

BIOGRAPHY OF JOHN E. PARKE.

JOHN E. PARKE was born Dec. 12, 1806, on what is now the South Side, Pittsburg, in a small log house that stood near the end of the Point Bridge. His father, John Parke, was born in Belfast, Ireland, and died in Pittsburg, in 1808. The son attended school in a house near his home, and received such an education as that early period afforded. Influenced by an elder sister, he entered upon the study of medicine, and prosecuted it until he obtained the degree of M.D. ; but his physical strength not being equal to the labors required, he abandoned the practice. He, however, availed himself of the advantages of a knowledge of medicine, by engaging in the drug business, in partnership with his brother-in-law, Dr. Henry Hannen. Their store was on a corner of Market and Liberty Streets. After continuing in this trade for several years, they abandoned it, and engaged in the manufacture of glass-ware. Their factory was in what was then Bayardstown, now the Ninth Ward, Pittsburg ; and their storehouse was on Wood Street, opposite the First National Bank building.

Subsequently he became a member of the firm of Phelps, Parke, & Co., wagon-makers. Their large factory was located on Beaver Avenue, Allegheny, between Greenwood and Locust Streets, on the west side of the avenue. During the war, they furnished the government with a large number of wagons. When this firm was dissolved, he retired from business. During his long and successful business career, sagacity and integrity were his prominent characteristics.

In the establishment and carrying on of beneficent enterprises, Mr. Parke was always interested, active, and liberal. He aided in the establishment of the Second Presbyterian

Church, was one of the first managers of the House of Refuge, and secretary of the Society of Old Residents.

He obtained the title of judge by being chosen to the honorable office of Associate Judge of the Civil Court.

In the "Hesperus" (N. Ruggles Smith, editor), issue of Dec. 20, 1828, the following notice is found : —

"HYMENEAL.

"Married, on Tuesday evening, Dec. 8, by the Rev. Joseph Stockton, Dr. John E. Parke to Miss Jane, daughter of John Hannen, Esq., of Allegheny town."

His death occurred April 22, 1885, at his residence, No. 77 Page Street, Allegheny. His body was buried in Mount Union Cemetery.

At this writing, June, 1886, Mrs. Parke is still living, to enjoy the affection of their family and the esteem of many friends.

The following anecdote, clipped from one of our city papers, is given a place here, because it illustrates the early life of Judge Parke : —

EDITOR MAIL, — In the column of your paper of the 2d inst., I noticed a terrible account of the death of a youth on Long Island, a victim of misplaced confidence in the friendly disposition of a pet bear, the reading of which called to my recollection a similar case, which occurred to the writer in the year 1816 or 1817, which very nearly terminated with a like fatal result.

On the east side of Third Street, Pittsburg, about midway between Wood and Smithfield Streets, the tan-yard of the Poyntz Bros. was located. They were the owners of a pet bear, which they kept chained to a post firmly set in the ground, in close proximity to the street. Being a lad of about ten years, I frequently had occasion to visit the premises, and pass it almost daily on my route to and from school. I consequently became somewhat familiar with bruin, and on many occasions filched from my mother's larder such articles of food as old Dan (named after the Kentucky hunter, Daniel Boone) was fond of. I often played with him ; and, although he was at times rather rough in his demonstrations, our relations heretofore were of the most friendly nature. A change, however, soon came over the spirit of our dreams. The facts recorded below are so vividly photographed on my memory, that the lapse of over sixty years has failed to erase them.

On the day the occurrence took place, some boys had, by some means, made old Dan cross; and, not being aware that there was any thing wrong, I approached him as usual with my friendly offering of food. When sufficiently near, he seized and drew me within his crushing embrace; and with one despairing cry, I became oblivious of all surroundings. The cry having attracted the notice of the proprietors and workmen in the yard, they hastened to the rescue, armed with the implements of their trade. Mr. John Poyntz, by a well-directed blow, delivered with force with a currier's shaving-knife, directly behind the ear, stunned the enraged beast, and enabled them to withdraw me, limp and unconscious, from my perilous situation. Judging from my delicate physique and the angry condition of the animal, they feared I had received internal injuries which would render a return to life almost hopeless. The external wounds were a few unimportant scratches, evidently from his claws. The position of the bones of the chest were horribly out of shape; they were, by careful manipulation, however, restored to their original position; by the adoption of this and other prompt means, I was thus ushered back to life.

Old Dan, after recovering from the effects of the blow, and still smarting under the treatment received, became perfectly frantic with rage, and in his fury broke the chain that bound him, and fled towards the Point. The people who happened to be on the streets at the time, fled in terror, in every direction, leaving him free to go where he list. He finally invaded an orchard near Ferry Street and First Avenue; and, after amusing himself in demolishing the apple-crop, he was with difficulty captured by the Messrs. Poyntz and their employees, and safely taken to his old quarters, secured in such a manner that the like should not occur again. In conclusion, permit me to say, that, having attained and passed the threescore years and ten of man's allotted life, when I gaze around me, I find but few living who stood with me in the great battle of life; and as one by one drops out of the friendly circle, I am yet spared, a monument of the mercy of an all-wise Creator, and have the melancholy consolation to say of my departed companions, "Though dead, they are not forgotten."

> "I've wandered o'er my native place, I've sat beneath the tree,
> Upon the schoolhouse playground that sheltered them and me;
> But none are here to greet me, but few are left to know,
> That roamed with me upon the green o'er fifty years ago."

JOHN E. PARKE.

ALLEGHENY, Jan. 4, 1879.

CONTENTS.

EARLY HISTORY.

HISTORICAL PAPERS.

INSTITUTIONS.

HISTORY OF THE ALLEGHENY OBSERVATORY.

FACTORIES.

CEMETERIES.

FAMILY RECORD.

BIOGRAPHICAL SKETCHES.

EARLY HISTORY

PREFACE AND DEDICATION.

To write a history of past events, is a task both difficult and tedious. So much research is necessary, so much care has to be exercised, and labor performed, in the examination, comparison, and digesting of various statements, in order to avoid error, that the author's progress is painfully slow.

Prejudice and lack of interest in persons, and inaccurate and imperfect records, have to be encountered.

In compiling the miscellaneous history of Allegheny, the author has endeavored, to the best of his ability, to elaborate the several subjects introduced in the work, in a plain and comprehensive manner, relying upon his own recollection, and data obtained from others whose age and experience well qualify them to impart the desired knowledge.

Materials for a work of this kind are exceedingly difficult to obtain, and frequent disappointments were encountered after considerable time and labor consumed in the endeavor. This will account in some degree for the apparent delay in the issue of the work.

There are many other interesting events in the history of Allegheny which should have been introduced into the work, the memory of which, however, has become so faded, that the efforts made to obtain the facts have proved abortive.

His especial aim has been to elaborate incidents and events from his own recollection, and that of others, and has spared no pains to render the work complete, and interesting to the public generally, and especially to the citizens of Allegheny.

Being fully aware of its many imperfections, he confidently submits it to a discerning public, and trusts they will recognize in the effort an earnest and honest endeavor to supply a void, — to rescue from oblivion the memory of 'events and scenes of the receding past.

To the early settlers of Allegheny, and their descendants, this work is respectfully dedicated, by the

AUTHOR.

INTRODUCTION.

WRITTEN history is the record of memorable events; and writing it is grouping together facts, gathered from authentic sources, in language free from speculation or prejudice, so that those who follow after "may know and live the truth."

It is not the province of man to manufacture history; he possesses no creative power to do so; he is but a plagiarist at best; he merely compiles from statements of "others gone before," and can only claim originality for his own construction of language, and the details of the subject of which he treats, and the elaborations of events from his own recollections: the materials are the common property of all.

The records of the past, if truthfully written, are worthy of preservation: every thing appertaining thereto is more or less interesting and valuable to the present and to the coming generations.

We can scarcely realize the wonderful changes which have occurred in our midst, even within the compass of our own recollections. The Indian war-whoop, the midnight howl of the wolf, and the light of burning cabins, have been superseded by the scream of the steam-whistle, the light of glowing furnaces, the sound of the ponderous engine and clang of machinery, and the whir and clatter of tens of thousands of spindles.

The author's object in preparing these miscellaneous sketches of the past, is to collect together such important facts and statistics as relate principally to Allegheny and the "Reserve Tract" opposite Pittsburg, arranging the same, as far as possible, in their chronological order, commencing with the date of

their survey and early settlement, and bringing them down
to the present day : they have been carefully gleaned from
reliable sources, and every effort made to render them correct
in every particular. He does not expect to offer much that is
new, especially to those who possess the opportunity to examine
for themselves the records which have from time to time been
written on the prolific subject of the early settlers of the country around the " Forks : " his aspirations are of a more humble
nature, and he trusts that his efforts in this direction will not
be considered valueless. His object is to furnish information
to those who have not the facilities to investigate such matters,
nor the spare time necessary for such investigation.

He will aim to treat his subject in a plain and simple manner,
with the hope that his efforts will enable the reader to form
some conception of the change in the country, from a savage
and uncultivated condition to its present advancement in civilization and the useful arts.

HISTORY OF THE TOWN OF ALLEGHENY AND RESERVE TRACT.

THE written history of the town of Allegheny and Reserve Tract opposite Pittsburg, is exceedingly meagre and unsatisfactory. Subsequent to the date of its survey, and opening for sale of lots, but little is known, except what may be gleaned from newspaper scraps, and a few antiquated directories published in the neighboring city of Pittsburg. There has been scarcely an effort made to redeem from oblivion the history of a locality fraught with so many dangers "by flood and field," and rich in scenes of other days.

"The Reserve Tract opposite Pittsburg," as it is called, together with the town of Allegheny, was ordered by the Supreme Executive Council of the Commonwealth of Pennsylvania to be surveyed and laid out as a manor, or reserve, Sept. 11, 1787, and was fully accomplished the following year. (*Vide* Colonial Records, vol. xv. p. 509, etc.) The town, as originally laid out, contained 144 lots, each 60 feet by 240 feet, in blocks of 240 feet square. Four of these blocks, in the centre of the town plan, were reserved and designed for public buildings, etc. The whole surrounded by the common ground, which is 60 feet wide on the south, 250 feet on the north and east, and 1,400 feet on the west, containing an area of 102 acres, and was designed for a common pasturage for cattle. It was respectively named East, West, North, and South Commons.

The grants, however, to the Western Penitentiary, Theological Seminary, and the Ohio and Pennsylvania Railroad, have reduced the area to about eighty acres. It is now laid out in beautiful "parks," ornamental walks and drives, and filled with trees, shrubbery, flowers, fountains, lakes, monuments, etc., alike conducive to the health and happiness of the inhabitants of both cities.

Up to the year 1788, the jurisdiction of Westmoreland County extended over a large portion of the territory now embraced in the county of Allegheny: the seat of justice was then established at Hannah'stown, thirty miles east of Pittsburg.

In the fall of 1788, it was ordained by supreme executive authority to erect a new county out of parts of Westmoreland and Washington Counties, to be called Allegheny. By the provisions of the Act, the seat of justice was temporarily established at Pittsburg until certain trustees named therein should construct suitable public buildings on the Reserve Tract "opposite Pittsburg" on the public square in the town of Allegheny.

The following report of the surveyor, D. Redick, to the Supreme Executive Council, clearly indicates his estimation of the propriety of laying out a town in this locality : —

"I went with several gentlemen to fix on a spot for laying out the town opposite Pittsburg, and at the same time took a general view of the tract, and find it far inferior to my expectation, although I thought I had been no stranger to it. There is some pretty low ground on the rivers Ohio and Allegheny; but there is but a small proportion of dry land, which appears any way valuable, either for timber or soil, but especially for soil: it abounds with high hills and deep hollows, almost inaccessible to a surveyor. I am of the opinion, that if the inhabitants of the moon are capable of receiving the same advantages from the earth which we do from the world, — I say, if it be so, this same famed tract of land would afford a variety of beautiful lunar spots, not unworthy the eye of a philosopher. I cannot think that ten-acre lots on such pits and hills will possibly meet with purchasers, unless, like a pig in a poke, it be kept out of view. Would it not be of more advantage to the State if the Legislature would alter the law, — that a town and a reasonable number of out-lots for the accommodation of the town be laid out, the remainder of the lands be laid off in two-hundred-acre lots, fronting on the rivers when practicable, and extending back so as to include the hills and uneven ground, which might be of some use to a farm?

"I cannot believe but that Col. Lowry and Col. Irwin will on consideration be of opinion with me, that small lots on the sides of those hills can never be of use for any purpose but as above mentioned. Perhaps council may think proper to lay the matter before the Legislature. I shall go on to do the business as soon as the weather will admit; and before I shall have proceeded further than may accord with the plan here proposed, I may have the necessary information, whether to go on as the law now directs, or not.

"WASHINGTON, Feb. 19, 1788."

The project of locating the county-seat on the north of the Allegheny River having met with a determined opposition on the part of the citizens of Pittsburg, the section in reference to location was deemed inexpedient to carry out : in view of which, a supplementary Act was passed early in the following spring repealing this feature, and authorizing the trustees to purchase ground on the Pittsburg side of the river for public buildings, etc., thus fixing the seat of justice for Allegheny County.

The Reserve Tract, as laid out by the authority aforesaid, contains an area of over 3,000 acres, divided into 10-acre lots more or less, numbered from 1 to 276 inclusive, except the tract containing 312 A., 3 R., 15 P., patented to James O'Hara, May 5, 1789, consideration £234, 12s., 6d., located in 'the Butcher-run district, and is described as high, rough land, embracing the rugged hillsides of the Allegheny Valley.

It is bounded on the north by a line commencing at a point on the Ohio River near the mouth of Wood's Run, thence north $87\frac{1}{2}°$ east 972 P. to a hickory, thence north $2\frac{1}{2}°$ west 80 P. to a sassafras, thence north $87\frac{1}{2}°$ east 229.5 P. to a maple, thence north $2\frac{1}{2}°$ west to Keystones, thence north $87\frac{1}{2}°$ east 85 P. to a point near where Girty's Run empties into the Allegheny River ; on the south and east by the Allegheny River, and on the west by the Ohio River.

It commences with No. 1 on the west, and follows the meanderings of the rivers, No. 70 being the extreme eastern number: the balance of the numbers are somewhat erratic in the order of numbering ; the highest, being No. 276, is located on south-east corner of Western and Irwin Avenues.

All this territory is hallowed by the memory of the past : over it the merciless Indian roamed, the undisputed master, and claimed the country lying between the Ohio and Allegheny Rivers and the great lakes of the north, bidding defiance to his indomitable Anglo-Saxon foe.

The startling war-whoop, and no less appalling cry of the panther, struck terror into the hearts of all who had the temerity to venture within the depths of its gloomy forests.

Westward from Smoky Island the great Indian trail led through this territory to the mouth of the Big Beaver, thence in a north-west direction to Sandusky and Detroit ; following the ridges, it passed through Trumbull and Portage Counties, Ohio ; it is clearly defined by stone piles and trees, the bark of which had been carefully removed from one side, and rude figures cut thereon. Near the junction of the Mahoning and the Shenango, forming the Beaver, another trail crossed this one, following a more westerly course to the Tuscarawas branch of the Muskingum. Over these trails, the wild nomads made their periodical raids upon the settlements, unchecked, except when opposed by the *avant-courier* of civilization, — the venturesome pioneer, and brave and hardy scout. Notwithstanding the important *treaty* made with the Six Nations at Fort Stanwell, in the State of New York, in 1784, by which their title to the country above described was extinguished, they still continued their atrocities upon the defenceless pioneer who had the hardihood to brave the dangers consequent upon the settlement of an unknown country.

BOROUGH OF ALLEGHENY.

THE town of Allegheny was created a borough by the Act of
the General Assembly approved the fourteenth day of April,
A.D. 1828, with the following described boundaries: Beginning on the bank of the Allegheny River, corner of East Lane;
thence by the north-east line of said lane to the north-west
line of the Butler Turnpike; thence along the same to the line
between out-lots Nos. 140 and 145; thence north 14° west by
the line between lots Nos. 140, 145, 141, 144, 142, 143, to the
high, rough tract granted by patent to James O'Hara, May 5,
A.D. 1789; thence by the same 76° west to lot No. 148;
thence north 14° west by the line of out-lots Nos. 148, 149,
and 150 to the north-east corner of out-lot No. 150; thence
south 76° west by the line dividing out-lots Nos. 150, 151, 174,
175, 182, and 183 to the north-east line of Pasture Lane, now
Irwin Avenue; thence by the same south 14° east to the
north-west corner of Water Lane, now Western Avenue;
thence by the same south 76° west to the south-west corner
of Ferry Lane, now Beaver Avenue; thence by the same south
to the Ohio River; thence by the various courses of the Ohio
and Allegheny Rivers to the place of beginning.

By the Act of the 14th April, A.D. 1838, the foregoing was
repealed, and the boundaries were established as follows, to
wit : —

Beginning at a point on the Allegheny River, where "Saw-
mill Run" empties into the said river; thence by the centre of
said run northwardly to the point where it strikes the northern
line of out-lot No. 142; thence west by the said line of out-lots
Nos. 142 and 143 south 76° to out-lot No. 148; thence north

14° west by the east line of out-lots Nos. 148, 149, and 150 to the north-east corner of the latter ; thence south 76° west by the dividing line between out-lots Nos. 150, 151, 174, 175, and 183 to the north-east line of Pasture Lane, now Irwin Avenue ; thence by the same northwardly to Island Lane, now Washington Avenue ; thence westwardly by the north line of said Island Lane to a street running southwardly between out-lots Nos. 251, 250, 257, and 256 (Sedgewick Street) ; thence south by the west line of said street to Ohio Lane, now Pennsylvania Avenue ; thence by the north line of said lane to Fulton Street, the dividing line between out-lots Nos. 261, 262, 270, and 269 ; thence by the west line of said street to Water Lane, now Western Avenue ; thence by the northern line of Water Lane to the south-west line of Ferry Lane, now Beaver Avenue ; thence by the same south 14° east to the Ohio River ; thence by the same and the Allegheny River by the several courses of the same to the place of beginning.

One of the items connected with the history of the north side, and of which there is no particular record, is only here adverted to with the hope that it may prove of sufficient interest to those whose long associations with the locality justify them for the time spent in its perusal.

During the year 1835, Stephen Colwell and Charles S. Bradford, for themselves and others, purchased about 150 acres lying east of Ferry Lane, which was then embraced within the limits of Reserve township. This purchase was made with a view to lay out a town : it was surveyed and laid out in lots in the following year, and was called Chatham in honor of Sir William Pitt, Earl of Chatham, who, upon his accession as Premier of England, evinced his friendship, and became the sturdy defender of the infant colonies. His appeals to the British nation in their behalf from the aggression of France and the cruel red men are matters of history, and need not be repeated here. The town project, however, proved a failure, situated, as it was, between Allegheny and Manchester ; and when about to rise into some importance, the extension of the boundaries of Allegheny, and subsequently Manchester, absorbed all the land embraced in its survey.

AN ORDINANCE

CREATING THE OFFICES OF FIRE WARDENS AND BELL RINGER.

SEC. 1. *Be it ordained and enacted by the Burgess and Council of Allegheny*, That annually hereafter each of the different Fire Companies of Allegheny, shall on or before the *15th day of January*, in each year, report the names of *eight* persons to the Council, of whom *four* shall be elected at the election of the other Borough officers, for each company, to serve for *one year*, and until others be elected; and in failure of the Fire Companies recommending individuals for Fire Wardens, then the Council shall proceed, without such recommendation, to elect the said Wardens, four for each Company; and the Wardens so elected shall wear on their hats a distinguishing badge, and also a staff of office; they shall be present at all fires in the Borough, & preserve the apparatus from wilful injury, direct the protection of private property, and remove the crowd, or any other obstruction that may impede the successful operations of the Firemen.

SEC. 2. That annually hereafter, at the time of electing Borough officers, the Council shall elect one suitable person as *Bell Ringer;* whose duty it shall be to ring the Bell at such times as the Council may direct, sweep the rooms, and light fire and candles in the Council Room, at such times as the Town Clerk may direct. He shall, also, take charge of the Engine and Hose belonging to the Borough, and shall carefully preserve and clean the apparatus, or any part thereof, as often as he may be required so to do by the Captains of the different Fire Companies; — for all of which duties he shall be entitled to the yearly compensation of *Sixty Dollars*, to be paid in quarterly payments.

Ordained and enacted into a law this 26th day of January, A.D. 1838.

JOHN TASSEY, *President of Council.*

Attest. GEO. R. RIDDLE, *Town Clerk.*

Approved; In Testimony Whereof I have hereunto set my hand, and caused the seal of the Corporation to be affixed, January 26, 1838.

HUGH DAVIS, *Burgess.*

LIST OF OFFICERS OF THE BOROUGH OF ALLEGHENY SINCE ITS ORGANIZATION.

BURGESS.

JOHN IRWIN, 1829 to 1834.   HUGH DAVIS, 1835 to 1838.
JOHN MORRISON, 1839 to 1840.

COUNCIL.

JAMES BROWN, President, 1828, 1829, 1834.
ISAAC LIGHTNER, President, 1830, 1831.
JOHN TASSEY, President, 1832, 1833, 1835–1837, 1839.
JOHN HANNEN, President, 1838.
S S. SHIELDS, President, 1840.

JOHN MEASON, 1828
ROBERT CAMPBELL, 1828 to 1831.
WILLIAM SAVORY, 1828.
WILLIAM LECKY, 1828, 1829, 1837, 1838.
E. G. NELSON, 1829.
DAVID MACLEAN, 1830, 1831.
JOHN HANNEN, 1830, 1831, 1837.
ROBERT McELHENNY, 1830.
JAMES BROWN, 1831, 1833, 1835, 1836.
A. H. HARVEY, 1832.
HUGH SMITH, 1832, 1833.
CHARLES PLUMB, 1832.

JACOB GEYER, 1832.
JOHN KEOWN, 1833, 1834.
J. J. CARPENTER, 1834, 1835.
NATHANIEL MOLONEUX, 1834.
WILLIAM A. IRVINE, 1835, 1838, 1840.

ROBERT DAVIS, 1836.
SAMUEL S. SHIELDS, 1836, 1838, 1839.
R. A. CAMPBELL, 1837, 1838.
WILLIAM H. CLARKE, 1837, 1838.
WILLIAM A. CHARLTON, 1839, 1840.
PETER BAIRD, 1840.

ROBERT STEWART, 1828, 1829, 1839, 1840.
RICHARD GRAY, 1828 to 1831, 1836.
FOSTER GRAHAM, 1828, 1829.
ISAAC LIGHTNER, 1828, 1829, 1833 to 1835.
ENOCH WRIGHT, 1829.
JOHN TASSEY, 1830, 1831, 1834, 1838.
JAMES CORREY. 1830
JOHN PATTERSON, 1830, 1831.
SAMUEL B. McKENZIE, 1831.
THOMAS J. PEARSON, 1832.
WILLIAM HERRON, 1832, 1833.
THOMAS BARNETT, 1832, 1833, 1836 to 1839.
WILLIAM FITZSIMMONS, 1832 to 1835.
SYLVANUS LOTHROP, 1833.
JAMES DAWSON, 1834, 1835.
JOHN MORRISON, 1834 to 1836.
WILLIAM ROBINSON, Jun., 1835, 1839, 1840.
ARCHIBALD LAMONT, 1836, 1837.
NICHOLAS VOEGHTLY, 1836.
HENRY IRWIN, 1837 to 1840.
H. NIXON, 1837 to 1839.
G. E. WARNER, 1839.
JAMES A. GRAY, 1840.

LOT O. REYNOLDS, 1840.

CLERK OF COUNCIL.

R. A. CAMPBELL, 1828.

JOHN MORRISON, 1829–1833.

GEORGE R. RIDDLE, 1834–1838.

THOMAS L. McMILLAN, 1839–1840.

TREASURER.

HUGH DAVIS, 1828, 1829.

WILLIAM ROBINSON, Jun., 1830–1835.

JOHN PATTERSON, 1836.

JOHN MORRISON, 1837, 1838.

JOHN HANNEN, 1839, 1840.

HIGH CONSTABLE AND COLLECTOR.

JACOB SLOTERBACK, 1828–1834.

THOMAS FARLEY, 1835.

ANDREW BARCLAY, 1836.

WILLIAM SKYLES, 1837.

ARCHIBALD MONTGOMERY, 1838–1840.

STREET-COMMISSIONER.

THOMAS SAMPLE, 1828.

ROBERT BRYAN, 1829.

ROBERT STEWART, 1830, 1831.

ANDREW ERWIN, 1832.

JAMES DAWSON, 1833.

WILLIAM LIGHTNER, 1834–1836.

SYLVESTER TYLER, 1837.

ARCHIBALD MONTGOMERY, 1838–1840.

ASSESSOR.

THOMAS SAMPLE, 1828 -1831.

WILLIAM ROBINSON, JUN., 1832, 1833.

THOMAS L. McMILLAN, 1834.

SAMUEL CARR, 1835.

THOMAS FARLEY, 1836.

WILLIAM DAVIDSON, 1837, 1839, 1840.

ALEXANDER CAMERON, 1838.

COLLECTOR OF TAXES.

JACOB SLOTERBACK, 1828.

R. A. CAMPBELL, 1830, 1831.

THOMAS FARLEY, 1833, 1834.

ALEXANDER CAMERON, 1838.

HUGH FLEMING, 1829.

DAVID WHITE, 1832.

JOHN GORMLEY, 1835–1837.

WILLIAM DAVIDSON, 1839, 18;0.

RECORDING REGULATORS.

1828.	ROBERT BOWMAN,	JOHN ORR,	JOHN STODDART.
1829.	ROBERT BOWMAN,	THOMAS SAMPLE,	JAMES GILCHRIST.
1830.	ROBERT BOWMAN,	THOMAS SAMPLE,	JAMES GILCHRIST.
1831.	ROBERT BOWMAN,	THOMAS SAMPLE,	JAMES GILCHRIST.
1832.	JAMES GILCHRIST,	JOHN STODDART,	JAMES STERRITT.
1833.	JAMES STERRITT,	JOHN STODDART,	GEORGE A. KURTZ.
1834.	JAMES STERRITT,	THOMAS BARNETT,	GEORGE A. KURTZ.
1835.	JAMES STERRITT,	THOMAS BARNETT,	H. NIXON.
1836.	JAMES STERRITT,	JOSEPH TURNER,	H. NIXON.
1837.	JAMES STERRITT,	JOSEPH TURNER,	JOSEPH IRWIN.
1838	JAMES STERRITT,	JOSEPH TURNER,	JAMES RICHEY.
1839.	JAMES STERRITT,	RICHARD DEWHURST.	JOSEPH IRWIN.
1840.	JAMES STERRITT,	RICHARD DEWHURST,	JOSEPH IRWIN.

FIRE-WARDENS.

1840. *Phœnix Engine Company.* THOMAS FARLEY, S. S. SHIELDS, WILLIAM M. DAVIS, H. DEHAVEN.

1840. *Columbia Engine Company.* PETER BOISOL, THOMAS BARNETT, WILLIAM DAVIDSON, J. GEYER.

BOARD-MEASURERS.

1828. ROBERT BOWMAN, DAVID WILSON, WILLIAM FRAZIER.
1829. ROBERT BOWMAN, DAVID WILSON, WILLIAM FRAZIER.
1830. FOSTER GRAHAM, J. C. DOWNER, JOHN DOWNING.
1831. JOHN DOWNING, WILLIAM D. CRAWFORD, WILLIAM H. CLARKE.
1832. JOHN DOWNING, L. O. REYNOLDS, WILLIAM FRAZIER.
1833. JOHN DOWNING, H. NIXON, J. B. MCKEOWN.
1834. JOHN DOWNING, H. NIXON, WILLIAM H. CLARKE.
1835. JOHN DOWNING, GEORGE A. KURTZ, WILLIAM H. CLARKE.
1836. JOHN DOWNING, GEORGE A. KURTZ, WILLIAM H. CLARKE.
1837. WILLIAM HUTCHISON, JAMES RICHEY, THOMAS FARLEY, NATHAN CARLISLE
1838. NATHAN CARLISLE, WILLIAM KNEPPER, JAMES RICHEY, GEORGE A. KURTZ.
1839. NATHAN CARLISLE, HENRY HINE, GEORGE A. KURTZ, JAMES RICHEY.
1840. JAMES L. MORRIS, BENJAMIN PATTERSON, GEORGE A. KURTZ, JAMES RICHEY.

INSPECTOR AND MEASURER OF COAL, ETC.

JOHN MCGREW, 1830–1833.
JOHN STREET, 1834.
DAVID ADAMS, 1835.

WILLIAM DAVIDSON, 1836–1838, 1840.
NATHAN CARLISLE, 1839.

WEIGH-MASTER.

JAMES MUNDEN, 1838–1840.

CLERK OF MARKET.

JAMES MUNDEN, 1831, 1834, 1835, 1837–1840.
JOHN STREET, 1832.

WILLIAM LIGHTNER, 1833.
JAMES MILLER, 1836.

BOARD OF HEALTH.

Drs. DALE, HENDERSON, and SMITH.
1st Ward. Messrs. GEYER and SMITH.   2d Ward   Messrs. TASSEY and HERRON.
3d Ward. Messrs. PEARSON and FITZSIMMONS.   •
4th Ward   Messrs. PLUMB and BARNETT.
Commissioners, Rev. JOSEPH STOCKTON and DAVID WHITE.

BELL-RINGER AND MESSENGER.

THOMAS GRIFFITHS, 1836, 1837.   WILLIAM McDONALD, 1838.
GEORGE McINTYRE, 1839, 1840.

SOLICITOR.

WILLIAM O. H. ROBINSON, 1836–1840.

ORGANIZATION OF THE CITY OF ALLEGHENY.

———

ON the thirteenth day of April, A.D. 1840, it was enacted by the Senate and House of Representatives, in General Assembly met, that the inhabitants of the borough of Allegheny, in the county of Allegheny, be constituted a body politic, by the name and style of " the Mayor, Aldermen, and Citizens of Allegheny."

In pursuance of the Act of the General Assembly of the Commonwealth of Pennsylvania, approved the thirteenth day of April, A.D. 1840, incorporating the city of Allegheny, the election for city officers to be held at the following places : to wit, —

> 1st Ward, at the house of HARMON DEHAVEN.
> 2d Ward, at the house of JOHN GHOERING.
> 3d Ward, at the house of CHARLES VICK.
> 4th Ward, at the house of HUGH SWEENEY.

The following members of council were appointed to hold the election on the second Tuesday of July, A.D. 1840.

> 1st Ward, HENRY IRWIN, WILLIAM A. CHARLTON.
> 2d Ward, ROBERT STEWART, PETER BEARD.
> 3d Ward, L. O. REYNOLDS, WILLIAM H. IRVINE.
> 4th Ward, WILLIAM ROBINSON, Jun., JAMES A. GRAY.

The borough council adjourned finally, to meet the mayor and city councils elect on the 17th of July, at ten o'clock A.M., to partake in the ceremonies of inauguration, etc.

LIST OF OFFICERS OF THE CITY OF ALLEGHENY SINCE ITS
ORGANIZATION.

MAYORS.

Gen. WILLIAM ROBINSON, Jun., 1840.   HEZEKIAH NIXON, 1844, 1845.
THOMAS SAMPLE, 1841.   R. S. CASSETT, 1846.
WILLIAM B. FOSTER, 1842, 1843.   HENRY CAMPBELL, 1847, 1848.

JONATHAN RUSH, 1849.
H. S. FLEMING, 1850–52.
R. W. PARK, 1853.
WILLIAM B. ADAMS, 1854–1856.
HARMON DEHAVEN, 1857.
JACOB STUCKRATH, 1858.
JOHN MORRISON, 1859, 1860.
SIMON DRUM, 1861, 1862.
A. C. ALEXANDER, 1863, 1864.
JOHN MORRISON, 1865–1867.
SIMON DRUM, 1868, 1869.

A. P. CALLOW, 1870–1874. Died during 1874.
DAVID NEELY, elected by councils for 30 days.
H. S. FLEMING, for unexpired term of A. P. CALLOW.
O. PHILLIPS, 1875–1877.
THOMAS MAGRAW, 1878–1880. Term expires April, 1881.
L. PETERSON, Jun., April 1, 1881.
I. G. WYMAN, April 1. 1884.

PRESIDENTS OF SELECT COUNCIL.

JAMES BROWN, 1840, 1841.
H. NIXON, 1842.
E. W. STEPHENS, 1843, 1844.
JOHN TASSEY, 1845, 1846.
R. S. CASSETT, 1847, 1848.
WILLIAM ROBINSON, Jun., 1849 to 1856.

JACOB PAINTER, 1857, 1858.
JAMES MARSHALL, 1859 to 1865.
JAMES McBRIER, 1866 to 1874.
JOSHUA PATTERSON, 1875 to 1878.
A. D. ARMSTRONG, 1879 to 1883.
JAMES H. LINDSAY, 1883.

PRESIDENTS OF COMMON COUNCIL.

HENRY IRWIN, 1840 to 1844.
G. E. WARNER, 1845 to 1849.
WILLIAM BOYD, 1850 to 1852.
JAMES PARK, Jun., 1853.
WILLIAM CHAMBERS, 1854.
JAMES MARSHALL, 1855.
JOHN ATWELL, 1856.
JOHN W. BARR, 1857.
J. GARDNER COFFIN, 1858.
H. S. FLEMING, 1859.
JOSEPH KIRKPATRICK, 1860.
A. D. SMITH, 1861, 1862.
JOHN BROWN, Jun., 1863.

JAMES McBRIER, 1864.
SIMON DRUM, 1865.
GEORGE D. RIDDLE, 1866, 1867.
JOHN S. SLAGLE, 1868.
ALFRED SLACK, 1869.
HENRY WARNER, 1870.
ALFRED SLACK, 1871–1873.
HENRY M. LONG, 1874.
WILLIAM P. PRICE, 1875.
J. O. S. GOLDEN, 1876.
JAMES HUNTER, 1877.
GEORGE W. SNAMAN, 1878–1880.
JAMES HUNTER, 1881.

CLERKS OF SELECT AND COMMON COUNCILS.

SELECT.

GEORGE R. RIDDLE, 1840 to 1842.
J. J. CARPENTER, 1843 to July 17, 1851.
H. J. LEMON, July 17, 1851, to Jan., 1854.
DAVID MACFERRON, Jan., 1854, to Jan., 1868.
J. R. OXLEY, Jan., 1869, to Feb., 1873.
R. T. WHITE, Feb., 1873.

COMMON.

C. PLUMB, 1840 to 1842.
H. J. LEMON, 1843 to 1846.
J. W. KENNEDY, 1847 to 1848.
M. McGONNIGLE, 1849 to 1865.
ROBERT DILWORTH, 1866 to 1880.

TREASURERS.

JOHN HANNEN, 1840–1842.
THOMAS H. STEWART, 1843 to 1847.
JOHN H. STEWART, 1848, 1849.

JONATHAN RUSH, 1850–1853.
HENRY CAMPBELL, 1854–1857.
DAVID MACFERRON, 1858.

CONTROLLERS.

R. B. FRANCIS, 1865 to 1869. Re-   WILLIAM M. PORTER, 1870, 1871   Resigned.   signed March 1, 1872.

JAMES BROWN, March 1, 1872.

RECORDING REGULATORS.

	CHIEFS.	ASSISTANTS.
1840.	JAMES STERRITT.	JOSEPH IRWIN, RICHARD DEWHURST.
1841.	JAMES STERRITT.	CHARLES PLUMB, RICHARD DEWHURST.
1842.	JACOB STROOP.	JAMES RICHEY, RICHARD DEWHURST.
1843.	RICHARD DEWHURST.	JAMES RICHEY, JOHN STODDART.
1844.	RICHARD DEWHURST.	JAMES RICHEY, JOHN STODDART.
1845.	JAMES RICHEY.	JOSEPH IRWIN, JOHN STODDART.
1846.	JAMES RICHEY.	S. ALEXANDER, JOHN STODDART.
1847.	JAMES RICHEY.	WILLIAM BROWN, JOHN STODDART.
1848.	JAMES RICHEY.	N. CARLISLE, JOHN STODDART.
1849.	JAMES RICHEY.	WILLIAM BROWN, JOHN STODDART.
1850.	W. A. P. EBERHART.	JOSEPH IRWIN, JOHN STODDART.
1851.	W. A. P. EBERHART.	JOSEPH IRWIN, JOHN STODDART.
1852.	JAMES RICHEY.	JOSEPH IRWIN, JOHN STODDART.
1853.	JAMES RICHEY.	T. J. MOORE, JOHN STODDART.
1854.	JAMES RICHEY.	JOSEPH IRWIN, JOHN STODDART.
1855.	JAMES RICHEY.	HUGH MCCORMICK, JOHN STODDART.
1856.	ALEXANDER HAYS.	WILLIAM WILSON, JOHN STODDART.
1857.	ISAAC MORLEY.	ROBERT R. RAY, JOHN STODDART.
1858.	ISAAC MORLEY.	ROBERT R. RAY.
1859.	WILLIAM MCHENDRY.	ROBERT R. RAY.
1860.	WILLIAM MCHENDRY.	ROBERT R. RAY.
1861.	WILLIAM MCHENDRY.	ROBERT R. RAY.
1862.	WILLIAM MCHENDRY.	ROBERT R. RAY.
1863.	WILLIAM MCHENDRY.	ROBERT R. RAY.
1864.	WILLIAM MCHENDRY.	ROBERT R. RAY.
1865.	WILLIAM MCHENDRY.	
1866.	WILLIAM MCHENDRY.	
1867.	CHARLES DAVIS.	

CITY ENGINEER.

CHARLES DAVIS, 1868 to 1876.   N. M. MCDOWELL, 1877 to Nov., 1879.

CHARLES EHLERS, Nov., 1879.

BOARD OF SCHOOL CONTROLLERS.
Organized June 1, 1854.

PRESIDENTS.

Rev. John T. Pressly, D.D., from June 1, 1854, to February, 1861.
James Brown, M.D., from February, 1861, to February, 1865.
Rev. J. B. Clark, D.D., from February, 1865, to February, 1870.
Rev. Joseph King, from February, 1870, to March, 1877.
David B. Oliver, from March, 1877, to 1885.
J. A. Emery, March, 1885.

SECRETARIES.

James T. Sample, from June 1, 1854, to February, 1857.
David Macferron, from February, 1857, to June, 1863.
Matthias McGonnigle, from June, 1863, to February, 1864.
R. B. Francis, from February, 1864, to February, 1870.
C. W. Benney, from February, 1870.

SUPERINTENDENTS.

Professor John Davis, from Sept. 2, 1873, to May 7, 1878.
Professor L. H. Darling, from May 7, 1878, to May 7, 1881.
Professor John Morrow, May 7, 1881.

LIBRARIANS.

C. W. Benney, from 1872[1] to 1876.
James W. Benney, from 1876.

The first post-office in Allegheny was established in 1836, under the administration of Andrew Jackson. It was located on the west side of the diamond, between Ohio Street and Gay Alley; from here it was removed to the south side of the diamond, between Federal Street and Middle Alley; thence to the north-east corner of Federal Street and the canal. From this point, it was removed to the west side of Federal Street, between Lacock and the canal; from here to the east side of Federal Street, between South Common (now Stockton Avenue) and Water Alley (now Park Way). It was next removed to the north side of Park Way, between Federal and Sandusky Streets; subsequently from Park Way to the north-west corner of Federal and Lacock Streets; and in 1865 it was finally removed to City Hall.

---

[1] The public library having been turned over to the Board of Controllers, they assumed the control of the same in 1872.

POSTMASTERS.

1. Dr. E. HENDERSON. Appointed under Jackson's administration. He died soon after his appointment; his wife appointed to fill vacancy.
2. GEORGE R. RIDDLE. Appointed under Van Buren's administration; resigned during the year 1840, and was succeeded by
3. G. L. DOANE. Appointed under Van Buren's administration.
4. R. C. FLUSON. Appointed under Harrison's administration.
5. WILLIAM KARNS. Appointed under Polk's administration.
6. JOHN McGREW. Appointed under Taylor's and Fillmore's administration.
7. THOMAS FARLEY. Appointed under Pierce's administration.
8. WILLIAM M. STEWART. Appointed under Buchanan's administration.
9. SAMUEL RIDDLE. Appointed under Lincoln's administration.
10. A. L. ROBINSON. Appointed under Johnson's administration; appointment not confirmed.
11. HUGH McKELVEY. Appointed under Johnson's administration.
12. JOHN A. MYLER. Appointed under Grant's administration; still in office.
13. JOHN SWAN, Jan. 1, 1886.

STREET-COMMISSIONER.

ARCHIBALD MONTGOMERY, 1840 to 1842.
JAMES MILLER, 1843 to 1848.
SYLVESTER TYLER, 1849, 1851 to 1853.
ARTHUR HOBSON, 1854 to 1865.
THOMAS MEGRAW, 1866 to 1873.

W. W. TYSON (eastern district), 1874, 1875.
ALEXANDER HANNA (western district), 1874 to 1880.
H. NESMITH (eastern district), 1876 to 1880.

BOARD-MEASURERS.

JAMES RICHEY, 1840 to 1847.

JAMES P. MORRIS, 1840.
JOSEPH BLACK, 1841, 1842.
ISAAC PATTERSON, 1841.
JOHN STODDARD, 1843, 1844.
THOMAS BARNETT, 1849.

JOHN EVANS, 1845.
JAMES RYND, 1848.
JAMES SCOTT, 1849.

E. WELLEVER, 1850.
JACOB SPRINKLE, 1851.
JAMES H. LOGAN, 1852 to 1858.
SAMUEL W. McGINNIS, 1852 to 1866.
A. BUNGY, 1854.
HENRY PRICE, 1855.
ERNEST FAULHABER, 1856, 1860 to 1862.
JOHN FRANCIS, 1859, 1865.
C. F. INGHAM, 1864, 1866.

GEORGE A. KURTZ, 1840, 1842, 1844, 1853.
BENJAMIN PATTERSON, 1840.
ALEXANDER MOORE, 1841.
JOSEPH IRWIN, 1842, 1843.
E. DERBY, 1843, 1845 to 1851.
ANDREW DAVIDSON, 1845 to 1848, 1866 to 1880.
JOHN McGREW, 1846, 1847.
ROBERT BROWN, 1848, 1849, 1863.
WILLIAM MURDOCK, 1849 to 1851, 1856 to 1860, 1862 to 1870.
LEONARD WALTER, 1850, 1852.
JAMES TODD, 1851.
BENJAMIN RANDLETT, 1852.
DAVID BLACKSTOCK, 1853.
A. GRAY, 1854, 1859 to 1863.
R. M. REED, 1855.
HUGH McNEIL, 1857, 1858.
ALFRED SLACK, 1861.
JAMES McCORMICK, 1864.

ROBERT WHITE, 1865, 1867 to 1874, 1876 to 1880.

FRED BECKER, 1867.

MICHAEL SEIMON, 1868, 1869, 1871 to 1877.

ROBERT M. PARKE, 1868 to 1880.

ALEXANDER CAMPBELL, 1868, 1875.

JOSEPH LOFINK, 1868.

THOMAS H. GILSON, 1869 to 1874, 1877, 1879.

MARTIN LEY, 1869.

WILLIAM S. OAKLEY, 1869, 1870, 1872 to 1878, 1880.

W. P IFFT, 1870.

F. ERCK, 1870 to 1873, 1876 to 1878.

JOHN McDOWELL, 1870 to 1873, 1875.

JAMES G. DOWNIE, 1871.

JAMES McVEIGH, 1871, 1874, 1876, 1877, 1879, 1880.

SAMUEL DOEBALL, 1871.

JOHN DONALDSON, 1872.

R. DONALDSON, 1874 to 1879.

CHARLES H. PHILLIPS, 1872.

CHARLES P. STREIGHT, 1873.

GEORGE FINK, 1873 to 1877, 1879, 1880.

GEORGE KREBS, Jun., 1874, 1875.

JAMES DOUGLASS, 1874.

WILLIAM FINCHER, 1874.

F. COMMERFORD, 1875.

SAMUEL BENNETT, 1875, 1878, 1879.

M. BAIRD, 1875.

WILLIAM F. TRIMBLE, 1876, 1878, 1880.

WILLIAM BEECHER, 1877.

B. F. BIBER, 1877.

GEORGE SNYDER, 1877.

WILLIAM MILLER, 1878.

JOHN WILLIAMS, 1878.

MICHAEL WOODS, 1878.

A. JOHNSTON, 1878-1880.

WILLIAM PHILLIPPI, 1878, 1879.

P SAUER, 1878.

E. KENNA, 1879.

PETER STREIPEKE, 1879.

THEO. STREIPEKE, 1880.

JOSEPH DIERSTEIN, 1879.

WILLIAM BARCLAY, 1879.

LEONARD STEINBRUNER, 1879, 1880.

GEORGE W. DAY, 1880.

JOSEPH SPRAGUE, 1880.

F. STAHLE, 1880.

J. HILLANGASS, 1880.

CLERK OF MARKETS.

JAMES MUNDEN, 1840, 1841.

DAVID HARTZ, 1842.

WILLIAM SCOTT, 1843 to 1851.

M. McGONNIGLE, 1852 to 1862.

DUNCAN DALLAS, 1863 to 1872

D. HASTINGS, 1873 to 1880.

MEASURERS AND INSPECTORS OF COAL, WOOD, AND BARK.

WILLIAM DAVIDSON, 1840.

CHARLES PLUMB, 1841 to 1846.

THOMAS L. McMILLAN, 1847 to 1851. SCHOUPE, 1853.

BENJAMIN LUKER, 1852.

JOHN STODDART, 1854.

S. W. McGINNIS, 1855 to 1857.

ALEXANDER MAXWELL, 1858 to 1868.

WILLIAM BODEN, 1869.

C. ACKERMAN, 1870.

A. HAZLETT, 1871.

WILLIAM GREENAWALT, 1872 to 1880.

WEIGH-MASTER.

JAMES McVICKER, 1842 to 1849.

THOMAS L. McMILLAN, 1850, 1851.

JOHN CHAMBERS, 1852 to 1858.

JOHN MOON, 1859, 1860 (Diamond).

JOHN CHAMBERS, 1860, 1861 (2d ward). ROBERT ENIS, 1861, 1862 (Diamond).

JOHN A. WHITE, 1862, 1863 (2d ward).

WILLIAM F. ANDERSON, 1864 to 1866 (2d ward).

HUGH LARIMER, 1867 (2d ward).

JOHN D. McCALLISTER, 1868 (2d ward).

JAMES HUNTER, 1869 (2d ward).

R. T. WHITE, 1870 to 1872 (2d ward).

D. J. BODEN, 1873 to 1877 (2d ward).

G WITTACH, 1878 to 1880 (2d ward).

WILLIAM SCANDRETT, 1863, 1864 (Diamond).

JOHN S. EDGAR, 1866, 1867 (Diamond).

GEORGE B. McNULTY, 1868 to 1878 (Diamond).

THOMAS WARD, 1879 (Diamond).

A. J. CHAMBERS, 1880 (Diamond).

ISAAC HIPSLEY, 1874, 1876 to 1878 (4th ward).

VICTOR PAULINE, 1875 (4th ward).

THOMAS MALLEY, 1879, 1880 (4th ward).

WHARF-MASTER.

JAMES RICHEY, 1841, 1842.

A. MONTGOMERY, 1843, 1844, 1846 to 1848.

JAMES SMITH, 1845.

WILLIAM WILLS, 1849.

R. M. PARKE, 1868 (West).

GEORGE B. GIESINGER, 1869 (East).

S. R. DAVIS, 1869 to 1876 (West).

A. DUFFNER, 1870 to 1875 (East).

S. TYLER, 1874, 1877 (East).

ALEXANDER JOHNSTON, 1850 to 1853.

J. HUESTON, 1854 to 1860.

ALEXANDER MAXWELL, 1861, 1865.

GEORGE HUTCHISON, 1866, 1867.

JOHN BLAIR, 1868 (East).

A. L. FAUST, 1876 (Eastern District).

D. F. JACKSON, 1877 to 1880 (Western District).

W. H. H. TYLER, 1878, 1879 (Eastern District).

SUPERINTENDENT OF WATER-WORKS.

ROBERT MOON, 1850.

JAMES RAY, 1851 to 1856.

JOHN ALSTON, 1857 to 1864.

WILLIAM SCANDRETT, 1865.

WILLIAM D. FAULKNER, 1866.

GEORGE N. MILLER, 1867.

WILLIAM PAUL, Jun., 1868 to 1874.

H. C. RICHMOND, 1875 to 1880.

WILLIAM H. FAULKNER, 1878.

SALT-INSPECTOR.

A. MONTGOMERY, 1844.

JOHN STODDART. 1845 to 1857.

JAMES WILSON, 1846.

THOMAS H. SMITH, 1858, 1859.

ALEXANDER MAXWELL, 1860 to 1868.

C. ACKERMAN, 1869, 1870.

N. HAZLETT, 1871.

WILLIAM GREENAWALT, 1872 to 1880.

CITY ASSESSOR.[1]

THOMAS I. PEARSON, 1841.

JAMES McVICKER, 1842.

ANDREW ALEXANDER, 1843 to 1846.

THOMAS L. McMILLAN, 1847 to 1851

E. DERBY, 1852, 1853.

Z. PACKARD, 1854.

WILLIAM WILSON, 1855.

ABRAHAM DAVIS, 1865.

M. McGONNIGLE, 1866.

R. R. RAY, 1867 to 1872, 1874.

JOSEPH OXLEY, 1873.

THOMAS WARD, 1875 to 1877.

WILLIAM P. HUNKER, 1878 to 1880.

[1] This office was abolished March 15, 1855, and re-established again in 1865.

ASSESSOR OF WATER-RENTS.

JONATHAN RUSH, 1851, 1852.
E. DERBY, 1853.
Z. PACKARD, 1854.
WILLIAM WILSON, 1855.
ABRAHAM DAVIS, 1856, 1858 to 1867.

ANDREW DAVIDSON, 1857.
DAVID CORNELIUS, 1868 to 1873.
JAMES NICHOLS, 1874 to 1878.
SAMUEL C. GRIER, 1879 to 1880.

MEAT INSPECTOR.

WILLIAM ZEHNDER, 1873, 1874.

JOSEPH A. DREXLER, 1875 to 1880.

CITY PHYSICIANS.

W. W. COLE, 1876, 1877.

THOMAS G. HERRON, 1878 to 1880.

PARK-COMMISSIONERS.[1]

MEMBERS OF COUNCILS APPOINTED.

JOHN S. SLAGLE, 1868.
J. C. PATTERSON, 1868, 1871, 1873, 1875.
ALFRED SLACK, 1869 to 1873, 1876.
HUGH McNEIL, 1870 to 1873.
H. M. LONG, 1874.

JOSEPH WALTON, 1875.
J. D. STROUSE, 1874.
WILLIAM P. PRICE, 1875.
J. O. S. GOLDEN, 1876.

APPOINTED FROM THE CITIZENS AT LARGE BY THE COUNCILS.

ROBERT LEA, 1868 to 1876.
JAMES PARK, Jun., 1868 to 1876.

JONATHAN GALLAGHER, 1868 (resigned).
A. M. MARSHALL, 1869 to 1876.

BELL-RINGER AND MESSENGER.[2]

GEORGE McINTIRE, 1840 to 1850.

AUGUSTUS M. HUSSELBAUGH, 1851 to 1854, 1858 to 1873.

J. R. LUPTON, 1874 to 1880.

MESSAGE CLERK.

R. T. WHITE, Jun., 1881 to 1884.

MARSHALL W. WHITE, 1885.

CITY GAUGER.

WILLIAM BROWN, 1862.

JANITOR.

JOSEPH MARSHALL, 1865 to 1873.
MATTHEW KERR. 1874 to 1875.

D. L. KEPHART, 1875.
FRANK WADLOW, 1884.

ASSISTANT STREET-COMMISSIONER.

ISAAC STEWART, 1868.

[1] Abolished in 1876.
[2] The office of bell-ringer was abolished Jan. 16, 1855.

The fire-alarm telegraph was organized and put in working order in the month of July, 1867. Number of signal-boxes in the original line, 36 ; in the present line, 57.

FIRE-DEPARTMENT.

The ordinance creating the office of Chief Engineer of the Fire-Department was enacted by councils on the 27th of February, 1868.

James E. Crow was elected chief engineer, March 12, 1868, and has been continued in office to the present time. Dec. 9, 1869, councils passed an ordinance creating the paid fire-department, which was inaugurated on the first day of February, 1870, under the auspices of the following committee : —

J. E. B. DALZELL, *Chairman.*	GEORGE F. COMLEY.
ORMSBY PHILLIPS.	JAMES CALLERY.
ALEXANDER PATTERSON.	ALFRED SLACK.
SAMUEL HASTINGS.	

The present force of the department consists of fifty-five men, including the Chief Engineer and Superintendent of Fire-Alarm Telegraph.

There are nine first-class steamers, one of which is always held in reserve to take the place of any that may be undergoing repairs. The hose-carriages are ten in number, two of which are held in reserve in case of accidents. There are also thirty-six head of horses, two of which are held in reserve to supply the place of any that may become sick or disabled.

CHIEF ENGINEER OF FIRE-DEPARTMENT.

JAMES E. CROW, from 1869.

SUPERINTENDENT OF FIRE-ALARM TELEGRAPH.

L. D. McCANDLESS, from 1870 to 1874 inclusive.
G W WINN, from 1875.

MANCHESTER.

THE original town of Manchester was laid out in 1832, by John Sampson, C. L. Armstrong, Thomas Barlow, Thomas Hazelton, and Samuel Hall. It was bounded on the north by Island Lane, now Washington Street; on the east by Ferry Lane, now Beaver Avenue; on the south by the division line of out-lots Nos. 19 and 20; and on the west by the Ohio River. It was incorporated as a borough by the court of Quarter Sessions, Nov. 2, A.D. 1843, under the Act of the Legislature approved April 1, A.D. 1834. And subsequently, to wit, on the eighth day of April, A.D. 1854, upon application of the citizens, the court granted and decreed to said borough all the rights and privileges under the Act of the Legislature approved April 3, A.D. 1851, entitled, " Act for the incorporation of boroughs, and repealing the provisions of the former Act as far as they may conflict with the provisions of said Act." The boundaries are as follows : viz., Beginning at the intersection of Pasture and Strawberry Lanes; thence by Pasture Lane and the boundary of the city of Allegheny 514° east $106\frac{7}{10}$ P. to the intersection of Pasture and Island Lanes ; thence by Island Lane and the boundary line of the city 576° west 120 P.; thence by the dividing line of out-lots Nos. 250 and 257 from Nos. 251 and 256, being also a boundary line of the said city; thence 514° east 80 P. to Ohio Lane, now Pennsylvania Avenue ; thence by said lane and the boundary line of Allegheny 576° west 40 P.; thence by said boundary and the eastern boundary of out-lots Nos. 261 and 270 to Water Lane, now Western Avenue ; thence by said Water Lane and the boundary of said city aforesaid south 76° west 80 P. to Ferry Lane, now

Beaver Avenue ; thence by said lane southwardly to the Ohio River ; thence down said river by the several courses of the same to the dividing line between out-lots Nos. 11 and 12 on the bank of the Ohio River ; thence by said dividing line north 76° east 50 P. more or less to Ferry Lane, now Beaver Avenue ; thence by the same northwardly to its intersection with Strawberry Lane ; thence by Strawberry Lane north 76° east 242 P. to the place of beginning.

One of the provisions of the Act approved April 3, A.D. 1851, makes it obligatory to record all proceedings in such cases, in the proper office for the recording of deeds, etc.; and only when complied with, shall the same be deemed a body corporate, entitled to the several powers, rights, privileges, and immunities conferred by the Act.

By gross negligence on the part of those having the matter in charge, the proceedings were not recorded until the 17th of March, A.D. 1860. Immediately upon ascertaining the fact, and in order to avoid the troubles looming up in consequence of the neglect to record, a petition was presented to the Legislature, setting forth the facts in the case, whereupon they passed an Act, to wit, on the second day of April, A.D. 1860, confirming and making valid, and of the same force and effect, all acts done in the premises, as if the said proceedings of court had been regularly recorded within the time prescribed by law, etc.

In view of the common interest existing between the citizens of the city of Allegheny and the borough of Manchester, the councils of the said city and borough, having met together in general meeting, in consideration of such community of interest, and for other good and sufficient reasons, agreed together upon a plan for a union or consolidation of the same, in pursuance of which an Act of consolidation was enacted by the Legislature, approved March 12, A.D. 1867, extending the boundaries of the city of Allegheny so as to embrace all the territory constituting and forming the borough of Manchester ; and all the powers conferred upon said city by the several Acts of the General Assembly are extended over the inhabitants and territory embraced within the limits of said borough, together with all ordinances now in force in said city, except such as prohibit the erection of wooden buildings.

ANNEXATION OF THE BOROUGH OF MANCHESTER WITH THE CITY OF ALLEGHENY BY ACT OF THE LEGISLATURE APPROVED MARCH 12, 1867.

By the Act of consolidation of the borough of Manchester with the city of Allegheny, all the territory embraced in the former, together with that embraced within the limits of the latter lying west of Allegheny Avenue, was divided by a line running from east to west from Allegheny Avenue through the centre of Locust Street to the Ohio River, into two wards, respectively named Fifth and Sixth Wards ; the southern portion constituting the Fifth, and the northern the Sixth, Ward.

By the same Act, the city was authorized to extend her northern boundaries by a direct line from the north-east corner of the borough of Manchester to a point of intersection with the northern boundary of the borough of Duquesne so as to include the Troy-hill District, and from said point of intersection to the eastern terminus of the line of said borough of Duquesne, whenever the council of said borough shall consent to the extension of said boundary line. *Provided*, the said borough of Duquesne shall be annexed on the same terms and conditions as the borough of Manchester. The territory here described to constitute the Seventh Ward.

Also, by the Act of the General Assembly approved March 18, 1868, the boundaries of the city were further extended so as to embrace all that portion of the borough of Duquesne lying south-west of a line drawn from the head of Herr's Island to the run at Willow Grove, thence by said stream to the boundary line of said borough and Reserve township : this, including the island, constitutes the Eighth Ward.

Also all the territory embraced within the limits of McClure and Reserve townships, lying south of the following line, commencing at the north-east corner of the borough of Manchester, thence eastwardly by a direct line to Wickline's Lane in the township of Reserve, thence due east until said line intersects the line of Duquesne Borough, was annexed to the city by the Act of the General Assembly approved April 9, A.D. 1867, out of which the Ninth, Tenth, Eleventh, and Twelfth Wards were subsequently formed.

HISTORICAL PAPERS.

THE PITTSBURG BLUES.

The following is a paper read before the Historical Society of Western Pennsylvania: —

Mr. President, Ladies and Gentlemen.

Many of the startling events which have rendered Western Pennsylvania conspicuous in the history of the past, leave their impress on the mind of every American citizen. "The Forks of the Ohio" was among the first points selected by the hardy pioneer to commence the work of civilization in the Western world.

The interesting events connected with the early history of Pittsburg and Allegheny, and the regions in and about the "Forks," are well calculated to excite an interest in the minds of every citizen of the county, especially those "to the manor born." Feeling assured that those who spend time and labor in gathering up the threads of the almost forgotten past will certainly be interested, with your permission I here present for your consideration the following elaboration of memoranda, jotted down from time to time, as the scenes and events transpired.

Previous to the declaration of war, June 19, 1812, between the United States and Great Britain, the Pittsburg Blues were organized under the military laws of the State. Immediately upon the commencement of hostilities, filled with becoming zeal and patriotism, they unanimously tendered their services to the General Government, which were accepted; and the Blues at once were ordered into active service, to join the North-western troops, commanded by Gen. William Henry Harrison.

The company having been, previously, thoroughly drilled in the science of military movements, by officers well qualified by experience and education, were fully prepared to take the field at a moment's notice. Preparatory to their departure for the seat of war, they went into camp on the 10th day of September, 1812, on Grant's Hill, near where the Court House now stands. On the 20th they were ordered to the north side of the Allegheny River, and there went into camp, on the commons, on the ground afterwards occupied by the Western Penitentiary. On the 21st they again struck their tents, and went into camp on the bank of the Ohio River; their white tents extending westerly from Belmont Street, to a beautiful grove of sugar-trees, where Ferry Lane (now Beaver Avenue) enters the Ohio River.

All this territory, hallowed by the memory of the past, is now embraced in the Fifth Ward of the city of Allegheny. Under the shadow of these magnificent trees, the officers' headquarters were established.

The writer of these reminiscences has a vivid recollection of the scenes on this occasion : although but a youth of a few years, the impression made upon his memory was of an enduring kind.

Having been reared upon the land occupied by the encampment, and having been permitted to roam with the utmost freedom at all times through it, gazing with rapt amazement on the "pomp and circumstance of war," and being witness to the affecting parting scenes between the soldier and his friends, memories as lasting as life itself were made.

When arrangements had been fully completed, the Blues broke camp, and on the 23d of September embarked on keel-boats moored in the river opposite their encampment, and departed for a point on the Ohio River, whence they were to proceed over-land to join the troops concentrating under Gen. Harrison, on the Maumee, to meet the combined forces of the British and Indians, under Gen. Proctor and the redoubtable Tecumseh.

I have no doubt there are many citizens of the cities and county, now living, who have a distinct recollection of this gentlemanly and well-organized body of soldiers, whose valor was fully and satisfactorily attested on the battle-fields of Meigs and Mississinewa, and who, on several occasions, received the earnest commendations of the commander-in-chief. They were the first military organization in the county of Allegheny; were composed of the best material, and made up of members of the best families in the city and county. Many of their descendants are still living. The following authentic list of the officers and men composing the organization, was copied from the official roll of the company, and can be relied upon as correct : —

OFFICERS.

JAMES R. BUTLER, Captain.
MATTHEW MAGEE, 1st Lieutenant.
ELIJAH TROVILLO, 1st Sergeant.
ISAAC WILLIAMS, 2d Sergeant; wounded at Fort Meigs, May 5, 1813.
JOHN WILLOCK, 3d Sergeant; wounded at Fort Meigs, May 9, 1813.
GEORGE HAREN, 4th Sergeant.

NATHANIEL PATTERSON, 1st Corporal.
JOHN W. BENNY, 2d Corporal.
SAMUEL ELLIOT, 3d Corporal; wounded at Mississinewa, Dec. 18, 1812.
ISRAEL B. REED, 4th Corporal; wounded at Mississinewa, Dec. 18, 1812.
JAMES IRWIN, Ensign.

PRIVATES.

Robert Allison, Daniel C. Boss (wounded at Fort Meigs, May 5, 1813), Isaac Chess (wounded at Mississinewa, Dec. 18, 1812), John Deal, John Davis, John D. Davis, Andrew Deemer, Joseph Dodd (wounded at Mississinewa, Dec. 18, 1812; died June 16, 1813), Thomas Dobbins (wounded at Fort Meigs, May 5, 1813), J. Elliot, Oliver English, Enoch Fairfield, Samuel Graham, Nathaniel Hall, Samuel Jones, John Francis Lonsong (killed at Mississinewa, Dec. 18, 1812), Jesse Lewis, Peter S. Lewton, George McFall, Thomas McClernin, Robert McNeal, Norris Matthews, John Maxwell, Oliver McKee (killed May 28, 1813), Nathaniel McGiffen (discharged for disability), John Marcy (discharged for disability), Moses Morse, Joseph McMasters, Pressly J. Neville (promoted to sergeant), James Newman (killed at Fort Meigs, May 5, 1813), William Richardson (killed at Fort Meigs, May 5, 1813), John Park (wounded at Fort Meigs, May 5, 1813), Matthew Parker, John Pollard, Charles Pentland, Edward F. Pratt, George V. Robinson, Samuel Swift, Thomas Sample, Henry Thompson, Nathaniel Vernon, David Watt, Charles Weidner, Charles Wahrendorf (wounded at Fort Meigs, May 5, 1813), George S. Wilkins (promoted, May, 1813).

It should also be understood that two colored men, Frank Richards and William Sidney, went with the Blues in the capacity of servants to the officers, who, when necessity required it, handled muskets, and gained a reputation for coolness under fire, and unflinching bravery in time of danger.

It is stated that James Newman and William Richardson were killed by one and the same bullet. It seems that Newman was standing erect; while Richardson, just in his rear, was in a stooping posture, picking his flint. An Indian, concealed in the branches of an oak-tree, fired at Newman; the bullet passing through the latter's body, and thence into that of Richardson, killing both men.

As an illustration of the material of which the Blues were composed, permit me here to relate the following incident, as told by a member of the company on the occasion of one of their anniversary meetings, at which the writer was an invited guest : —

One morning, during the memorable siege of Fort Meigs, Sergeant Trovillo, being possessed of some rare bit not furnished in Uncle Sam's daily rations, in order not to excite undue envy on the part of his messmates during the preparation of his morning meal, wandered off into the woods, a short distance from the fort, but within the picket-line. There he built his fire, and commenced his preparations for breakfast. During the process, and near its completion, a hungry messmate was attracted to the sergeant's *cuisine* by the savory smell emanating therefrom, and of which he hoped to be invited to partake. Here was a quandary of a very embarrassing sort. The worthy sergeant's supply would scarcely justify a tender of hospitality; as his breakfast was pretty much in the category of a celebrated Methodist minister's turkey, — quite enough for one, but hardly enough for two.

The difficulty, however, was speedily settled in the following manner. Whilst engaged in conversation, the peculiar *ping* of a rifle-bullet saluted their ears, and the missile struck in close proximity to where they were standing. "Hallo, Lige, what in thunder does this mean?" For an explanation, his attention was quietly directed to an oak-tree, upon the upper branches of which was perched an Indian.

"That infernal Indian has been pegging away at me ever since I commenced cooking my breakfast!" The prospect of enjoying a quiet meal not being very encouraging, the visitor departed, to seek a breakfast under more favorable circumstances.

During the great and exciting Presidential contest of 1840, the few remaining members, in conformity with their usual custom, assembled at the house of Mr. James Lambie, corner of Federal and Robinson Streets, Allegheny. Mr. Lambie being a gentleman of fine education and polished manners, an old soldier of France, under Napoleon the First, possessing a genial disposition, was well qualified to act the host, and contribute to the general good feeling. Let it be understood that politics were never permitted to intervene. A want of knowledge of this fact, on the part of one of the invited guests, led to a very unpleasant state of feeling, and bade fair to result seriously. An eminently gifted attorney of the Pittsburg bar, a warm and enthusiastic supporter of the Democratic nominee, was introduced by the host, and cordially welcomed by all present. Quiet being restored, the president, John D. Davis, suggested the resumption of business. At this point, the health of Gen. Harrison was proposed. The guest, not understanding the condition of affairs, like a flash, and before he could be prevented, commenced a philippic reflecting severely on the moral, military, and political character of the Whig nominee. If a bomb-shell had suddenly exploded in their midst, they could not have been more surprised. The excitement for a while was intense, and boded no good to the vilifier of their revered chief. President Davis, however, in a very eloquent manner, administered a scathing rebuke to the disturber of their peace, and feelingly explained the object and nature of their time-honored custom of meeting once a year, to drop a tear to the memory of departed comrades, as an outward manifestation of the inward truth, "though dead, they are not forgotten," thus calming the troubled waters. The guest then arose, and in a very feeling and eloquent manner made the *amende honorable*, by protesting his entire ignorance, and begged the forgiveness of all present for the untimely part he had taken. Good feeling was at length restored, and the parties left for their respective homes.

A REMINISCENCE OF THE WAR OF 1812.

IN answer to my inquiries, Capt. Robert Beer, one of our eldest and most respected citizens, a soldier of the war of 1812, gave me the following account of his trip from this city to Upper Sandusky, O., in the winter of 1812–13 : —

"About the 1st of November, 1812, the government advertised for volunteer teamsters, having some thirty cannon-carriages (without cannon) and forty covered wagons to supply with drivers. As soon as a volunteer would sign the roll, he was ordered to go into a large yard on Garrison Alley, and bridle four horses. I was among the volunteers, being then an unsophisticated country boy of twenty years. (You will observe that I am now old enough to vote.) I was directed to hitch a team to a cannon-carriage, and drive over to the ground where the Western Penitentiary stood. Here we were encamped for three weeks before we were ready to start. The road-wagons were loaded with cannon, powder, clothing, and all kinds of government stores. These wagons were drawn by five, and sometimes by six, horses. All being in readiness, we started for Gen. Harrison's winter headquarters at Upper Sandusky, O. Col. James Anderson was wagon-master; James McHenry, a brick-layer of our city, assistant wagon-master; Paul Anderson, forage-master; Samuel Oliver, assistant forage-master; and Capt. Gratiot had command of the train. To guard the teams and property, we had Capt. Johnson and his company from Greensburg, now called Darlington, and half a company from Beaver County, under command of Lieut. Walker, who was subsequently killed by the Indians.

"The journey was through an almost unbroken wilderness,

and its difficulties cannot be appreciated by the people of to-day. Ten miles were considered good travel for one day; and when the route was bad, as was frequently the case, we did not make more than six miles. It took us three days to get through Hahn's Swamp, and had hard work to do it in that time. We would often stop for a day, and, mounting our horses, go miles away along paths, there being no wagon-road, and return with our horses loaded with forage.

"At Canton we lay a whole week, repairing the wagons, shoeing the horses, giving them much needed rest, and procuring a supply of forage.

"From Canton to Wooster was thirty-five miles. At the latter place we found the first picketed fort. Mansfield ended the settlements in this direction. The only buildings were a fort, one tavern, one store, and one private house. We remained three days in Wooster, to recruit our animals, repair damages, and gather forage. Between Wooster and Mansfield, we had a good deal of new road to cut, the old one being impassable for the train. This was slow work, as you can judge.

" We were about two months on the road, and finally reached Upper Sandusky on New-Year's Day, as cold a day, by the way, ás I ever experienced. We never saw a fire from sunrise till sunset; and to make the matter worse, we were but thinly clad at best. On our arrival, we were ordered to ungear our horses, and start with them for a small town on the Sciota River, called Franklinton, just across the river from Columbus. Corn was plenty and cheap in that neighborhood, and they wanted their horses to recruit there for the spring service.

"Next day we started back to Upper Sandusky, to get our money, and be discharged from the service. There was no money to pay us with, — not a dollar in the treasury, — so they furnished us with tents and rations. We pitched our tents just outside the military lines, and for three weeks had nothing to occupy our time but eating and sleeping. At the end of this time, Col. Piatt of Cincinnati, who was treasurer of the army, gave us our discharge, and an order for our pay at the barracks in Pittsburg. We hadn't a dollar towards paying our way home.   They gave us rations to put in our knapsacks ; but they soon became stale, and unfit for use.

"Of course, after we left our horses at Franklinton, we did all our travelling on foot.   I cannot now tell the distance from Franklinton to Upper Sandusky, but from the latter place to Mansfield was thirty-five miles.   We all arrived in Pittsburg safe and well, after a very fatiguing journey.

"The Captain Gratiot I have mentioned was one of the engineer corps of the regular army, and an officer of high standing.   Capt. Wheaton was the paymaster, and a cross old chap he was.   He carried a canteen of brandy slung round his neck, and sometimes he absorbed the brandy too freely.

"I suppose I am entitled to a pension for my services in 1812, but have not yet applied for one.   I observe that some are drawing pensions whose term of service lasted but fourteen days.   In 1856 I got a land-warrant for 160 acres of land."

A LEGEND OF THE "SHERTEE."

A FEW years ago the writer, in hunting through a hetero-geneous mass of musty old papers, the accumulation of years gone by, and so demoralized by time and the corrosive action of the elements as to render their further preservation impracti-cable, was prompted by curiosity to preserve as far as possible the subject-matter contained in a fragment of what he supposed to be some magazine published in early time. It is without date, and much impaired, evidently by the action of fire. In copying the manuscript, the author's language is faithfully quoted, as far as it is practicable, only supplying the voids as they occur from the causes above referred to.

LEGEND OF CHARTIERS.

On the north bank of Chartiers Creek (vulgarly called Shertee), which empties into the Ohio a short distance below the Forks (now Pittsburg), there resided, anterior to the Rev-olution, a stalwart farmer, a native of England, who, in the ab-sence of written history, tradition has styled Oliver Harris. Of his birth, parentage, early history, and other matter of no less importance, no authentic memorials are ·known. Tradition avers that he descended from a respectable family, who fled, on account of religious intolerance, from his native home, to one of the New-England colonies, there to enjoy the blessings of reli-gions liberty so generously promised to all. Possessed of a roving disposition, he was early induced to leave the paternal home, and brave the dangers " by flood and field," in seeking for fortune in a far Western land. On his arrival at the Forks, after a careful examination of the country, he selected as his

future home the locality above described.[1]   His rude surroundings, by indomitable energy and perseverance, were soon made
to blossom as the rose, and gradually assume the appearance
of comparative comfort.   In a few years his humble log cabin
was encompassed by well-cultivated fields, from which, by his
untiring industry, he derived annually a bountiful harvest, the
revenue from which afforded him a sufficiency for all his humble wants.

In the midst of this agreeable condition of affairs, he became
seriously impressed with the importance and wisdom of the
scriptural declaration, " That it is not good for man to be
alone," in view of which he straightway prepared himself to lay
siege to the ruby-checked daughter of a neighboring farmer,
wooed and won her.   The nuptials were consummated in a
much shorter period than is thought necessary by the belles
and gallants of the present day.   In the due course of time, a
son, their only child, was born, whom they named Philip, and
who was destined to act a prominent part in the event here
described.

When the scene of our tale opens, he had attained his majority, and was as comely a young farmer as six feet stature,
fair proportions, and black eyes, could make him.   On a clear
and calm, but piercing cold, morning in the month of Decem-

---

[1] There was very little improvement at this point until after the close of the Indian
war, in 1764. The only authentic account we have of its settlement, is the grant to
Alexander McKee, assistant Indian agent, to improve the lands at the mouth of Chartiers
Creek. The following is a copy of the same, taken from the original, and is in the hand-
writing of the commanding officer at Fort Pitt : —

" By Henry Bouquet, commanding his Majesty's forces in the Southern District, permission is hereby granted to Alexander McKee to occupy and build upon the land at the mouth
of Shertee creek, on the south side of the Ohio. In consideration of which, he is to pay
five shillings yearly, if demanded, and also to be subject to such regulations as his Excellency, the Commander-in-Chief, may order for the good of his Majesty's service.

" Given under my hand, at Fort Pitt, this 25th day of November, 1764.

" HENRY BOUQUET, *Col. Commanding.*"

The above fails to specify the amount of land granted. I learn, however, from other
sources, that the survey included an area of about fourteen hundred acres, a large portion of
which is still in the possession of, and occupied by, some of the descendants of the grantee.

The original document covering this grant is now in the possession of Gen. Joseph
Browne, who owns and resides upon a portion of the land conveyed.

J. E. P.

ber, succeeding a tempestuous night, the sun rose in unclouded splendor upon the romantic highlands that overlook Chartiers. The damaging effects of the storm were visible wherever the eye fell upon the scene surrounding the home of Oliver Harris. On every hand were mighty forest trees that had succumbed to its fury, and lay in confused heaps. Along the margin of the river, as far as the eye could reach, extended a line of ice, which the violence of the storm and waves had massed, exhibiting a rare spectacle of ruin and desolation.

At an early hour of the morning above referred to, young Harris set out on a hunting excursion. As the country was harassed and disturbed by the frequent inroads of the Indians, who held dominion over all the country north of the Allegheny and east of the Ohio, extending to the great lakes, it was considered dangerous for hunters to venture alone far from home, in view of which fact he joined a party of eight or ten of his associates, who expected to be absent for several days. Their course lay along the west bank of the Ohio, as near to the same as the rugged nature of the ground would permit, never relaxing the wariness acquired by experience and knowledge of the intentions of a bloodthirsty and insidious foe. Owing to the ruggedness of the course traversed, they reached a point but a few miles from whence they set out. As the evening shades approached, they gained a locality well adapted to afford them both shelter and rest. Here they went into camp for the night. At this point, the steep and rugged rocks presented an almost unbroken wall, varied at short intervals by deep indentations and bold, projecting crags. Under one of these the hunters chose their shelter for the night. Having started a large fire, and posted guards at a convenient distance to prevent any sudden attack from lurking foes, they drew near the cheerful blaze, and, taking from their haversacks a portion of the food which they had provided for the occasion, ate with appetites becoming men of their vocation. The wild loneliness of the place, the bright glare of the fire falling upon the river, and reflected back upon the rocks and on the guards who kept watch on the shore, and the group of hunters assembled around the fire, presented a scene of romantic interest and beauty. The air, which during the day had been clear and elastic, had now become dark and misty, indicating a fall of snow. Through the gathering vapors, that floated in agitated waves above the surface of the river, the silvery moon, now in her first quarter, shed doubtful rays, that gambolled upon the waters, and glimmered through the forest. The brightest stars twinkled with a dull, sickly gleam, and the increasing western wind rushed in sudden gusts through the naked woods, whilst the angry waters of the Ohio in heavy surges were hurled against its shores. Silently the white, fleecy clouds rolled onward, until they formed a compact body, through which the faint rays of the queen of night could hardly penetrate. Soon the snow began to descend, at first in feathery flakes, which soon changed into more condensed particles, denoting a change of temperature.

"I thought," said one of the hunters, breaking the profound silence hitherto observed, "that we should have a fall of snow ere long; and I'm not often mistaken in my predictions of the weather."

"What reason had you for thinking so?" asked one. "You are one of the prophets, who, for want of spectacles to extend their vision far enough forward, wait until time has brought them alongside of events, and then look back to see how they might have happened." This sally against the would-be weatherwise hunter brought a general laugh from the party, one of whom exclaimed, —

"Ah! you're right, Philip. Peters has his prophesying eyes in the back of his head. He can see things clear enough after they have come to pass. Only let him get on the top of a hill, and he will soon tell you what the country is like beyond it."

"Every bird has its own song," retorted the other. "I haven't followed the woods, man and boy, for good thirty years, not to be able to tell an owl from a turkey-buzzard. The air was sharp enough in the morning to shave like a razor; but for the last three hours the air hasn't been near so keen, and the haze has been gathering along the tops of the hills; and that's always, to my mind, a sure sign of falling weather. Since the setting of the sun, I've been watching the constella-

tion of the Bear, as Phil calls it, to the north yonder. I don't
know what he calls it that for; for I have shot many a bear, and
them stars look no more like such an animal than like a stack
of corn-fodder. Howsomever, people have different names for
things; and, as I was going to say, I've been noticing that con-
stellation getting dimmer and dimmer for some time, till at last
I couldn't see it any longer."

" You've heerd, maybe," said one of the circle, changing the
subject, " the report they have up at the creek in regard to
Luke Purdy and Watty Hughes."

" What is that ? " asked Philip.

" Why, they say that when they left home, without bidding
good-by, they went on to Canada. One of my neighbors had
the whole account from an Indian trader that stopped with him
all night. He says they went first to Detroit, where Luke,
hearing an alarm of pursuit, mounted his horse in haste, swam
across the Detroit River, and rode full speed to Malden. He
made a desper't leap from the high bank into the water, they
say; and it was well for his bones that he had a soft place to
light on."

" He's a bold fellow, that Luke Purdy," says one. " But
where are he and Watty now ? "

" Somewhere about the Upper Sandusky, I hear," replied
the other.

" They're both living with the Indians there, and pass for
great men among 'em."

" Well," continued one, " Watty Hughes was always a nice,
clever sort of a man: I'll say that much for him. But as for
Purdy, why, I don't know; but, somehow, I never thought
much of him. You mind when he was arrested as an enemy of
the country, and imprisoned in Fort Pitt, and how he walked
across the parade-ground, past the sentry, into the barracks,
went out of the back-door, jumped over the wall, and was
gone a good hour before he was missed. He was a fool,
though, to give himself up again, when he might have got clear
without any trouble. I reckon he didn't like to be called a
runaway as well as a traitor, and so thought it best to come
back and stand his trial."

During the conversation, the dogs that attended the hunters, by their whining and restlessness, appeared to have discovered some object, to which they endeavored to direct the attention of their masters. They kept in continual motion to and from a part of the rocky cliff that projected considerably beyond the range to which it belonged, and beneath which the dim fire-light that gleamed upon it, showed a deep excavation, apparently the entrance of a large cavern.

"Come in, Hector! Back, Ponto, I say! Why, what possesses the creatures?" exclaimed Peters, to two of the dogs that were more unruly than the others. "Hec has as good a nose as any dog in the settlement, and Pont's as knowing a slut as there's any 'casion for. But I wonder what the plague makes them so busy now. I don't believe there's a fox or coon about these rocks, for I was here the other day, and couldn't find the sign of a living thing. Be quiet, you whelps! none of your howling! There's no scent here for you worth a decent dog's trouble."

This expostulation was unheeded by the animals to whom it was addressed, and was instantly followed by the sharp report of a rifle, evidently discharged within a short distance of the hunters. The flash was distinctly seen by them all; and the bullet, striking the rocky wall near them, rebounded, and fell at their feet; while the echo of the report resounded along the rocky bank, until it died away in low, dull murmurs among the hills. The hunters instantly sprang to their feet, and seized their rifles that reclined near them against the cliff. Scarce had the sound that had occasioned the alarm reached the ears of the vigilant hunters, when a man leaped with a light, agile motion, to a position within a few paces of where they stood. The instant he appeared, every rifle was brought to bear upon him.

"Who dares," exclaimed the intruder, "call Luke Purdy a runaway and a traitor? Lower your rifles, you cowardly braggarts! or, if one man is enough to terrify you all, fire upon me, like dastards as you are, and then boast of having sent your bullets into the body of a single enemy."

Instinctively, all obeyed the order thus authoritatively given, b d pressing the muzzles of their rifles.

"We're no more cowards than you, Luke Purdy," exclaimed Tom Peters. "It's not just the fair thing to call us so, when you've seen our courage tried in many encounters with the redskins. But I reckon you were in a sort of a passion and flustration of spirits like; and so here's my hand, and it's all well again; but you may thank Philip, there, that your carcass isn't as full of holes as an orchard in locust-time."

The matter being thus adjusted, Philip inquired of Purdy the cause of his sudden departure from his home, and his unexpected re-appearance.

"It would profit you but little," replied Purdy, "to know what you pretend to be ignorant of. I did not leave Chartiers without good reason. Was I not an object of suspicion and reproach throughout all the settlement? Was I not persecuted and vilified by every malicious settler on the Western frontier? And for what? Because it was reported that I was the secret enemy of the whites; that I was the instigator of the Indians in their attacks upon your people: as if they had not sufficient provocation for revenge, without needing any persuasion from me! I would have lived quietly enough at my home, had not the senseless clamors of the settlers about the creek forced me to leave it, and seek refuge among the savages. And Walter Hughes, too, who so often kept back infuriated tribes from vengeance, and watched over the whites like a father, even he was not spared by his slanderous enemies. They thought to persuade him they did him honor by confining him in his own house; while I, who was looked upon as a more contemptible· traitor, was imprisoned in your fort, like a felon, among drunken vagabonds and soldiers. But my time of vengeance is coming. The mean, cowardly treatment I have received, the insults I have borne from the craven churls, — I have marked them all in my memory; and when the day of reckoning comes, I will wash the infernal record out with the blood of all who would have made me the victim of their malice. I will "—

Philip interrupted the enraged Purdy, and endeavored to mitigate his indignant feelings.

"I acknowledge, Luke, that you have been treated rather harshly. But you must admit that the whites had reason for severity, when the frequent massacres and burnings by the Indians had exasperated them, and compelled them to provide, by prompt and vigorous measures, for their safety."

"Massacres and burnings!" exclaimed Luke. "Who set the example of massacres and burnings? Did not your cream-faced, black-hearted crew murder in cold blood the unsuspecting Indians, even when they were professing friendship for them, and perjure themselves by swearing to treaties they never intended to observe? Are not your lazy surveyors and land-pirates even now entering upon the lands of the natives, and driving them from their homes, under pretence of titles purchased with rum and gew-gaws, or asserted without even a show of right? It was but a few months ago that Dunmore led his cut-throats against the tribes on the Western rivers, and killed, burnt, and ravaged wherever he set his foot. And you talk of massacres and burnings! And I suppose the dastardly assassins, Cresap and Greathouse, were only providing for *their* safety, when they treacherously slew the family of Logan at Grave Creek, and the women and children at Yellow Creek! What think you of massacres and burnings now?"

"The conduct of these men," replied Philip, "was as cruel and unjust as it was unauthorized. But, surely, the wanton acts of a few individuals" —

"A few individuals!" echoed Purdy. "A few individuals! I tell you, Philip Harris, they did not act for themselves alone. They were but the unfeeling tools of those who set them on, and who kept themselves concealed until they should discover how their plot would work. No, no! all are alike, dark, murderous, butchering ruffians; and may I burn in the flames of perdition, if I do not drench my knife in their hearts' blood! And you," he continued, addressing the others, "you, who think yourselves secure, and laugh at the words of one whom you call a traitor, and believe to be powerless as he is oppressed, — dearly shall you recompense me for the wrongs which you and your abetters have made me suffer. Ay, scowl at me, and point your rifles against me! I fear you not. I defy your malice, as I have escaped your snares. And mark me! Though I stand among you alone, I am not the friendless wretch that you would make me. One word of mine can rouse more warriors, and better ones, than all your white settlements west of the Allegheny can muster. And when you think me a solitary fugitive, I will be in the midst of men who are as able and ready to avenge their injuries, as myself. I will be near you, though all your bloodhounds shall not be able to track my course ; and when you suppose that I am hundreds of miles distant, you shall see me at your doors, and hear my battle-cry, that shall be the signal for blood, death, and conflagration."

Having thus vented his vindictive feelings, he left the astonished hunters as suddenly as he had come among them, and disappeared among the recesses of the rocks.

"That's a queer chap," said Peters. "But he's a plucky fellow, and I've often heard Watty Hughes say that he is a capital interpreter to explain the lingo of the Indians. But he needn't think to scare a body so easy, or he will find his match about Shertee."

"I wonder," said one of the men, "where in the thunder that bullet came from. It whistled past my ear as sharp as the whizzing of a scared pheasant."

"It came out of my rifle, as true blue as ever shot forty-five to the pound," replied another, who had acted as one of the sentinels. "It was a pretty good miss, too; but the fellow came in such a hurry that I hadn't time to draw a sure sight."

When the day dawned, the sky was again clear, and the ground was covered with a thick mantle of snow. A short consultation was held by the hunters, the result of which was a resolution to proceed no farther on the contemplated hunt, but to return to the settlement, and warn the inhabitants of the danger which might be anticipated from the machinations of Purdy.

The time and events comprised in the period allotted to this legend, were favorable to the development of the character of this vindictive traitor. Cast by destiny in a sphere of life where his fortunes and his hopes depended for their success on his own unaided efforts, he had only divested himself of the diffidence which the mutual dependence consequent upon a refined state of society occasions, and assumed the bold, reckless bearing which he supposed was adapted to his condition. He resolved to act only for himself, and to live among his fellows without sympathy in their happiness or sorrows. In thus separating himself, mentally, from the rest of mankind, he was, perhaps, insensibly impelled to the extreme, which is the invariable result of a course such as he had chosen for himself.

His opinions of self-dependence produced a fierceness of disposition and an unconciliating tone of expression which had an effect directly opposite to that which he had expected from them. Instead of making him out one who was careless and fearless of human power, only when it crossed his rightful path, they exhibit him as a man intent upon his own interest, regardless of the claims of others, as a stern, overbearing despot, who would make his way to authority over all the human rights and feelings by which he might be opposed.

The occupation of a hunter inured him to peril and hardships; and the frequent combats in which he was engaged with hostile parties of savages on the Western frontier, taught him the alertness and skill so requisite in a partisan leader.

He had for several years been employed by the Superintendent of Indian Affairs on the Ohio, as an interpreter, for which situation his intimate knowledge of several aboriginal languages well qualified him. The dissatisfaction of the colonies with the Government of England, which now foreboded a speedy resort to arms, extended to every individual having the most remote relation to its cause. Purdy, from his known attachment to the interests of the British crown, and his familiar intercourse with the Indian tribes of the Western and North-western frontiers, became an object of suspicion to those of the colonists who were intimately acquainted with his character. He was, together with Walter Hughes, the Indian superintendent, arrested, and placed in confinement, himself in the fort at the "Forks," and Hughes in his own house. By a bold and decisive movement, he effected his escape, and joined a tribe of savages,[1] by whom he was chosen a leader in their contemplated raids on the colonial territory. His originally ferocious disposition was aggravated by his supposed wrongs, inflicted on him by the settlers on Chartiers, among whom he had lived, and against whom he swore deep and lasting hostility.

Only a few days had elapsed after the return of the hunters to the settlement, when rumors began to circulate among the settlers, that the hostile Indians had made formidable preparations for a general attack upon the whole line of the Western frontier, and that a large force would soon assail the people who resided at Chartiers and its vicinity. Alarms had hitherto been so frequent that they no longer created the sensation which they at first excited. But the report of impending danger was now so often repeated, and so well sustained, that the most careless and intrepid were induced to give it credence, and to join with the more timorous in recommending prompt measures for defence. All who were able to bear arms were enrolled, and placed themselves under officers of their own selection. Guards were detailed by lot, who assumed, in alternate parties, the duty of patrolling at night; and even during the day, a small number of the most confidential among the inhabitants were constantly stationed as sentinels near the settlement.

A line of defence was hastily thrown up, consisting of a rude stockade, bastions, and blockhouses. In the walls of the blockhouses, as well as in those of the dwelling-houses within the temporary fort, loop-holes were opened, through which those within might fire upon the assailants. All the cattle were driven within the stockade; and provisions, ammunition, and arms were collected, sufficient to enable the little garrison to make a long and determined resistance. A representation of the expected attack having been made by a committee to the commandant at Fort Pitt, that officer immediately detailed a party of ten soldiers, under the orders of a sergeant, to assist in the defence. It was usual for the inhabitants who resided on this part of the frontier, and who, from their exposed situa-

[1] Wyandots.

tion, were liable to sudden attacks from the Indians, to retire for safety to the fort on the " Point." But so many inconveniences resulted from removal from their farms, which in their absence were subjected to devastation by the invaders, that on this occasion it was resolved to provide for their own defence, and to contend with whatever force they could command against the attack which they anticipated.

The intimation of menacing danger, which so frequently came to the people who resided on our Western borders, at this early period, when communicated at night, generally consisted in a tap at the door or window of one or more of the houses which composed the settlement. This signal was so usual, that all who were accustomed to hear it, were readily aroused from their deepest slumbers whenever it was given.

One of the calmest days of midwinter was succeeded by a night of unusual inclemency. The wind howled in loud and furious gusts through the forest; and the snow descended in dense showers, drifting before the blast; while the Ohio and Chartiers, excited by the fury of the tempest, were raging with unwonted violence, bearing upon their swollen tides the immense masses of ice which had been broken up by a recent thaw. In accordance with the system of strict vigilance and discipline which had been established by the settlers for their defence, every precaution had been adopted to secure them from sudden surprise by a treacherous foe. Scouts were moving in all directions around the exterior of the defensive lines, and wary sentinels walked the circuits appropriated to them immediately without the stockade. It was past midnight, and the storm continued with unabated violence, when, by the dim gleam of light which at intervals broke through the clouds, one of the sentinels discovered an object moving towards him slowly, and apparently anxious to escape observation. He kept his eye steadily upon it for several minutes, and his finger on the trigger of his rifle, in readiness to resist whatever peril might ensue. The object approached until it came within a few paces of him, keeping close under the stockade, and advancing with cautious and hesitating movement, when it rose suddenly from the recumbent posture which it had held, and the sentinel distinctly saw the figure of a man, wearing the costume of an Indian warrior. "Stand, or die!" he exclaimed in a loud voice. The intruder instantly became stationary.

"Who are you, and on what errand?" the guard inquired.

"A friend of the pale-faces, come to open their ears, that they may hear the war-whoop of their enemies," was the reply.

"Advance, and give the countersign!"

"Before my brother strikes, let him listen: the red man has not learned the strange words that the pale-faced warriors whisper into each other's ears. I am a friend to your people; and I come to tell them that evil birds are flying around them, watching for prey. I am an Indian brave, a friend of the white man, and will speak the truth. Guide me to the wigwam of my friend Oliver Harris. He knows that I am a good man, and I will tell him how to drive the bad birds away."

After a further conference of a few moments, the sentinel gave a preconcerted signal, and two others of the guard joined him. It was agreed that the Indian who had caused the alarm, and who was recognized as one of the most steadfast friends of the whites, should be conducted, agreeably to his request, to the house of Oliver Harris. He was, therefore, taken thither by one of the sentinels, while the others resumed their duty. When the sentinel and his Indian companion arrived at Harris's residence, the former tapped lightly at the window.

"Who is there?" inquired Harris.

"Here's our friend, Guyasutha,"[1] answered the sentinel, "come to bring us news from our red neighbors, that intend to pay us a visit without giving us notice."

Harris knew Guyasutha to be worthy of the confidence which the whites had long reposed in him. He therefore, without hesitation, opened the door, and invited him to enter.

---

[1] According to Craig's history, the name of this celebrated chief is spelled in various ways: the same sound, however, is preserved in all variations; viz., Guyasutha, Guy-as-ootha; Guyasudy, Keyasutha, Kiasutha, and Kaishuta. In the war between France and Great Britain, he early espoused the cause of the latter, and afterwards the Americans. He acted a very prominent part in several important treaties with the various Indian tribes: he also accompanied Gen. Washington on his journey from Logstown to Fort Le Bœuf, in 1753. He died about the close of the last century, in his humble wigwam, on the West Penn Railroad, situate on the farm owned and occupied by William M. Darlington, Esq.

" Guyasutha will not rest in the wigwams of his friends, the pale-faces, while the evil redskins are on the warpath to do them harm.   Tell your warriors to wake from their slumbers, to open their eyes, and look towards the setting sun, before the tomahawk strikes them, and the keen scalping-knife severs the bloody trophies.   I have listened to the wicked chiefs and warriors, and heard them speak angry words against my white brothers.   I have seen the war-fires kindled, and the dark wampum circulate among the tribes.   Rank weeds cover the path that was once smooth between my white and red brothers ; and the bright chain of friendship, that they held in their hands, is now broken.   Listen to the words of Guyasutha, for they are true.   I have seen the big eagle sitting on the rock, while the hawk seized the little bird, and carried it away in its claws, and the eagle pretended not to look that way, and did not tell the little bird to fly away quick, and hide itself in its nest, till the hawk was no more in its path.   I have spoken to my brother. He will open his ears wide, and listen to my words."

Guyasutha was a chief of the Seneca tribe of Indians, which formed a part of the powerful confederacy of the Six Nations. His daring but cautious character, his intelligence and fidelity to the interests of Great Britain, and his knowledge of the English language, had secured for him the respect and confidence of Sir William Johnson, the superintendent of Indian affairs in North America, by whom he was often employed on important embassies to different tribes and to his subordinate agents. Firm in his adherence to the English cause, he never meanly betrayed that of his tribe, or degenerated from that lofty dignity of character which distinguishes the aboriginal inhabitants of North America.   It was ascertained from this friendly chief, that an alliance had been consummated between the several hostile tribes in the North-West, that frequent war-councils had been held among them, and that the black wampum of war was freely circulating among the tribes to invite a speedy invasion of the settlements.   He said that he had obtained correct and minute information relative to the whole plan of operations that was to be pursued.   Simultaneous attacks were to be made upon the entire line of the settlements, from the Canadas to

the Mississippi; and a numerous party, and especially chosen
for the enterprise, was now within a short distance of Chartiers,
under able leaders, among whom the notorious Luke Purdy
held a principal command, and who was represented to be particularly exasperated against the settlers who resided in and
about the Forks of the Ohio, and was urging on the savages to
take prompt and bloody revenge upon them, denouncing special
vengeance against some, whom he named as his most active
and relentless persecutors.

On the day ensuing the visit of Guyasutha at Chartiers, a
meeting was convened to consider measures adapted to the
perilous condition of the country. The conference was earnest
and brief. Few speeches were delivered. There was evidently
little disposition to indulge in florid and verbose declamation:
the informal but sage counsel of Oliver Harris and one or two
other experienced advisers was all that was deemed necessary
to present the importance of maintaining the strict vigilance
which had hitherto been observed for the security of the settlement.

The respective posts and duties of all composing the garrison
were assigned; and they were enjoined, by a regard for the
public welfare and their personal security, to be strenuous and
unremitting in the observance of discipline, and performance of
their allotted services.

Guyasutha, who was a warrior well tried and intrepid, was
charged with the duty of collecting the few friendly Indians
who were at Fort Pitt and in the immediate vicinity of the settlements; and at his suggestion it was determined that under
his direction they should constitute a reconnoitering party, to
harass the enemy, and impede their approach, or form an ambush
in the rear, and complete their rout, should the garrison succeed in repelling their assault.

The attack, which had been awaited with so much anxiety,
was not long delayed. A large body of Indians, after rapid
marches, prosecuted with all the wariness incident to their
mode of warfare, on the evening of the day succeeding the
meeting referred to, was within a mile of the little fortress.
The scouts brought the intelligence of the enemy's arrival; and

each individual of the garrison braced himself for the encounter, as if its happy issue depended solely on his personal exertions.   Shortly after midnight, the discharge of a rifle, by one of the sentinels stationed at a distant outpost, warned the garrison that the conflict was about to commence.   In a few minutes the report of fire-arms and the war-cry of several hundred savages broke in wild and loud peals upon the stillness of the night; and the vivid flashes that incessantly came from the surrounding forest, glared through the darkness like sheets of electric fluid.   The scouts and sentinels were driven within the stockade, and took their posts among the defenders.

"Now, my brave friends," said the elder Harris, to those who were stationed with him in one of the blockhouses, "stand fast for your homes and all that makes them dear to you. Reserve your fire until the foe is within good point-blank distance, and let each bullet give a good account of its errand."

The word was passed rapidly through the fort, until it came to the post which young Harris superintended.

"Prime well, my lads," he said, "and pick your flints, so that your pieces shall not hang fire.   When you see the flash of their rifles at fifty yards distance, give them a volley.   Remember what we fight for, and let us fight like men."

The assailants rushed forward with eagerness, to obtain the easy triumph they so fondly anticipated.   Peal on peal of their rifles and their shrill war-whoops resounded through the woods, and were echoed back by the rocks and hills.   They approached the palisades which formed the external defence of the garrison, and attempted to tear them away, or leap over them, to gain nearer access to their devoted prey.   They were met by a regular and general discharge from the rifles of the besieged, which, as it was entirely unexpected, created surprise among them, and for a few moments arrested their advance.

One terrific and shrill yell arose from the living mass that crowded before the stockade, indicating the astonishment which the resistance of the defenders occasioned.   The compact body of the invaders, who had thus incautiously exposed themselves to the bullets of the besieged, was instantly broken; and each of the assailants betook himself to the shelter of a tree, from which he could more securely continue the assault. But again, after the interval of a few seconds, the powerful voice of one of their leaders was heard, giving orders to renew the attack; and the entire force of the enemy, extended so as nearly to surround the works, dashed onward, and were endeavoring to surmount or remove the pickets, when another united and effective volley compelled them to recoil. Their yells and shouts now became louder and more furious. Their thirst for blood had been inflamed by the shame of ·a momentary discomfiture. The orders of their chiefs became more audible and distinct as the combat thickened; and mingled reproaches on the timid, with encouragement for the more resolute, were heard rolling in deep and sullen mutterings among the scattered and disconcerted enemy. The onsets were renewed in frequent and quick succession; the savages, impelled by their native ferocity and the instigations of their leaders, making desperate efforts to leap over or remove the palisades, and always driven back by the well-timed, steady fire of the besieged, aimed in the direction indicated by the shouts of the assailants or the flashes of their rifles. The conflict grew every moment more fierce and terrible; the yells, shrill and deep-toned, of the Indians uniting with the loud and mutual exhortations of the men within the lines, and the irregular discharges of rifles from both sides. A few of the assailants, led on by Purdy, after a furious struggle, succeeded in entering the stockade; and the combat was sustained for a considerable time hand to hand, with desperate effect.

A large barn within the fortified enclosure was occupied by a party of the whites, whose repeated and deliberate fire was delivered with deadly effect: the attempts of the savages to dislodge them were often renewed, but without success. At length, Purdy, seizing a burning torch which one of his band held, darted forward, followed by several Indians, and entered the building. The fight within and around it was maintained man to man; and the knife and tomahawk were substituted for the rifle, which was less effective in the closeness of the *mêlée.*

Purdy, making his way to the upper part of the building, applied the torch to the thatch-roof; and in a few minutes a column of flame burst into the air, casting through the darkness a vivid light, which extended far over the surrounding forest, and brought into distinct view the scene of battle that raged in and near the fort. The incendiary himself was seen rising from the midst of the smoke and flames that ascended from the top of the building, his long hair fluttering in the breeze, his face begrimed with blood, waving his ensanguined tomahawk above his head, with features convulsed by the tempest of his passions, his demoniac yell betraying at once the deep malignity of his soul, and the joy he felt from his triumphant achievement.

"Down with the traitor!" vociferated Peters, when he beheld the fiend-like apparition. "Down with him! Now, my boys, take a sure sight. Give the Devil a few leaden pills to put him to sleep, and then honest people may have a chance to die in their beds."

In an instant he was the mark for a dozen bullets; and he disappeared within the burning pile, now rapidly yielding to the fury of the conflagration. It was supposed that the charge had taken effect; and Peters exultingly cried, "Huzza, my heroes! we've done for the bloody villain. Load and prime, and let us send his red imps to keep him company." Purdy had, however, escaped the peril, and, emerging for an instant from the flaming roof, uttered a demoniac yell, shook his tomahawk in defiance at his enemies, and then sped from the building, which the next moment fell to the ground.

As the burning mass crashed and roared in its fall, a dazzling sheet of flame suddenly flashed upwards, and then all was lost in profound darkness, except when a faint and unsteady light was thrown off from smouldering embers that marked the place of the recent conflagration. The enemy still persevered in their efforts to gain possession of the little fortress, but it was bravely and successfully defended against an infuriated and a superior force.

Day dawned, and the cheerful beams of an unclouded sun lit up with unusual splendor the romantic prospect of forest, rock, and stream, that lay around the scene of sanguinary warfare.

The assailants, discouraged by their repeated repulses, made a precipitate retreat. They had fallen back but a short distance, when Guyasutha, with a small body of friendly Indians under his order, rose from their ambuscade, and, shouting their fierce battle-cry, fell upon them in their disorder, and while they were unsuspicious of an enemy lurking in their rear. The rout rendered by this unexpected attack proved fatal, and was completed by a chosen party from the garrison, who, on hearing the battle-cry of Guyasutha and his chosen band of warriors, hastened to their aid, thus placing the retiring foe between two fires, who, becoming panic-stricken, broke, and sought safety in flight, from a force, which, had they remained unbroken, they might have overwhelmed by their superior numbers. The sortie was led by Philip Harris, and Tom Peters was one of the most eager in the pursuit. Purdy was seen in the midst of his savage allies, brandishing his bloody tomahawk; and his strong, sonorous voice was distinguished clear above the clamor and general commotion, calling upon them to arrest their flight, to renew the combat, and to wreak vengeance on their mutual foes. His efforts, however, to stay the living tide that was ebbing in impetuous torrent, were unavailing. He was left almost alone by his dismayed and flying associates.

The sallying party led by Philip Harris were close upon him, and the intrepid warriors led by Guyasutha were pressing rapidly towards him. Finding all his efforts to rally his disorganized force ineffectual, he stood for a moment, attended by a few of the most resolute of his band, like a lion encircled by the hunters, raving with the wildness of a maniac, and imprecating curses, both on his foes and those who had pusillanimously deserted him in his utmost need. Death or prompt flight were the only alternatives left him; and even his ferocious and daring spirit did not, in this extremity, restrain him from adopting the latter discretionary measure. He therefore sought safety by flight, with a speed unequalled by the fleetest of his savage allies, which promised him an escape from all his pursuers. But these were all as brave as himself, and several of them were well qualified to compete with him in speed and lightness of foot. The pursuit was ardent, and continued unabated for some time, until several of those engaged in it became so weary, that they were compelled to relax their exertions, and lag behind their less exhausted comrades.

The long and vigorous chase had, after a winding and intricate course through dense forests, deep ravines and swamps, urged Purdy to a point on the Ohio, several hundred yards below the mouth of the creek. A gradual elevation of the ground, terminating in a considerable eminence, the side facing the stream, presents a bold, precipitous, and rocky bluff, at whose base rolls the river, which at this particular point is of more than its usual depth. This singular elevation presents toward the stream a rude and wild aspect. It was generally known by the specific appellatives of "The Rocks," "Rock Hill," and is now called "McKee's Rocks," from the name of the family who have owned and occupied the premises since the time of the grant to their ancestor, Alexander McKee, by Henry Bouquet, colonel commanding his Majesty the King of Great Britain's forces at Fort Pitt, in 1764. On the summit of this height is a level piece of ground,[1] on which may be traced the vestige of a rude fortification, evidently constructed at a very remote period, and which is covered with trees, of a size confirmatory of the opinion that the embankment from which they rise is of great antiquity.

Purdy, having exerted himself to the utmost of his speed, called into requisition all his ingenuity to baffle his implacable pursuers, and gain the margin of the river immediately above the rock bluff, with the intention, probably, of concealing himself in one of the recesses, which, from his intimate knowledge of the locality, he knew existed in the rocks that at intervals formed a part of the river-bank. Hemmed in by his indefatigable pursuers, and reduced to extremity of peril by their persevering efforts to overtake him, he was compelled to ascend the "rocks" on the southern side, and rely upon

---

[1] Within the circle of the earthworks is the burial-place of many of the families residing in the vicinity. South of this, immediately on the top of the rocky bluff, is one of those mysterious tumuli so frequently met with in the West, evidently the work of the ancient mound-builders. It is about twenty feet at the base, and about twelve feet high; and on its summit grows an oak at least three feet in diameter, attesting its ancient origin.

stratagem for the means of final escape. In his left hand he still retained his trusty rifle with a firm grasp, while his right was left free to aid him in clambering over any obstacles that might present themselves in his onward progress. Philip Harris, Tom Peters, and two or three more of those who had engaged in the pursuit, were all who were able to continue the chase, the others having dropped behind from weariness and inferiority of speed. Purdy, having gained the brow of the rocky declivity, anxiously cast his eye around, seeking for a place of shelter from his pursuers: failing to discover one, he had either to turn back upon his course, surrender himself a prisoner, or risk the descent of the rocky precipice. He determined at once to adopt the latter alternative.

Midway to the Ohio lay a beautiful island,[1] the lower extremity of which was directly opposite to the point he had gained. He was a bold and expert swimmer, and had frequently, during his life of peril and vicissitude, been compelled to cross over some of the widest and most impetuous streams of the West. With a cautious but hasty movement, he commenced the descent from the top of the precipice, holding on to bushes and roots of the trees that grew out of the interstices of the rocks: he reached the base of the bank just as his pursuers had arrived upon its summit. Dashing into the stream, which was now clear of ice, he buffeted the waves with "lusty sinews," and safely arrived at the foot of the island.

While crossing from the main-land to the island, he contrived to keep his weapon above the surface of the water. The powder, therefore, retained its capacity of explosion undiminished; and the hand that held it was unaffected in its steadiness by the coldness of the element in which it had been immersed. The instant Purdy obtained a footing upon the firm ground, he cast his eye towards the fearful height which he had so lately descended, and perceived one of the

---

[1] Brunot's, in early times called Charteer, after Peter Chartier, a treacherous half-breed trader and French spy: it also bore the name of Alliquippa, after the celebrated Queen of the Delawares, who during her life resided at the mouth of the Youghiogheny. This island originally contained 136 acres, 21 perches, including a small island on the south side, now entirely washed away.

pursuing party, making his way slowly down the precipitous cliff. It was one towards whom he retained a feeling of especial hostility, from the knowledge that he had been particularly active and malignant in exciting against him the hatred and prejudices of the settlers by whom he had been proscribed. A vindictive smile of delight pervaded the countenance of Purdy, as he now saw himself enabled to wreak his vengeance on at least one of his implacable and detested persecutors. The distance between the spot where he stood and the point where his enemy was cautiously moving, was not greater than his trusty rifle had often carried a bullet, with unerring certainty, to the object of his aim. Springing behind a large tree that stood near, he drew a quick but deliberate and sure sight upon his victim, whom he observed, as soon as the discharge was made, to pause suddenly in his course, and place his hand on his right side. Immediately the wounded man relinquished his hold of the branch of the tree to which he had clung for support, reeled, fell, and, rolling rapidly down the rocks, was precipitated into the deep water at their foot, which whirled and plashed as it received the lifeless body, spread into successive rippling circles, and then became smooth and silent, as if its surface had not been disturbed. A loud and fiendish whoop sent forth by Purdy, attested the ferocity of the joy which he felt in having thus partially appeased his vindictive spirit by the sacrifice of a human victim: and, continuing his retreat along the northern shore of the island, he again plunged into the chilly waters of the Ohio, and swam to the main-land opposite, where he arrived in safety; here he briefly paused, and, feeling that with two such indomitable foes as Harris and Peters on his track, it would be unsafe to remain in the neighborhood, fled precipitately. When next heard from, he had joined a tribe of savages far to the West, whose warriors he often led on the warpath, and dyed his knife and tomahawk in the blood of the defenceless settlers on the frontier borders; and where, it is said, from his vindictive spirit and overbearing manners, he became embroiled in a quarrel with one of the chiefs, resulting in the fate he so often meted out to others, — a bloody death.

PONTIAC'S PLOT.—THE GREAT INDIAN UPRISING OF 1763.

A PAPER read by Judge Parke at the celebration of the one hundred and twentieth anniversary of the battle of Bushy Run, Penn., Aug. 6, 1883.

We have been called together this day to celebrate one of the most important and interesting events connected with the history of our country. On this spot, sacred to the memory of the past, one hundred and twenty years ago the gallant and accomplished Col. Henry Bouquet, with his heroic little band of Highlanders and Anglo-Americans, having passed the rugged and dangerous defiles of the Allegheny, arrived at Bushy Run, Aug. 5, 1763.

The description of the prominent events connected with Bouquet's expedition, and the subsequent development into permanent settlements, the knowledge of which is of the highest importance in perpetuating the fame of these gallant men, who left the confines of civilization to brave the dangers of an unknown country, — I will leave to others more competent to do justice to the subjects.

The imagination fails to conceive incidents more romantic than those which sober truth reveals in the career of the men who penetrated the Western wilds in order to create new homes for themselves and families, impelled by those powerful motives of human action, — ambition and a love of liberty.

In the career of many of the early adventurers, we see these passions overruling all others. These men stand out in bold relief as grand heroes worthy of a representation in the annals of the country. In the delineation of their deeds, and of those who follow after them, who occupied what they had won, faith, courage, and indomitable perseverance are prominent features in the picture. These were the necessary elements of success in the wide and dangerous fields of adventure, and were ever present in great abundance, when required in laying the foundation of their future homes.

Many of the events which have rendered Western Pennsylvania conspicuous in the history of the past, leave their impress on the mind of every American citizen. They pass before us as a mighty vision, making us feel the poverty of language, and weakness of eloquence, when startling realities are to be described.

Old Westmoreland, whose vast boundary at an early day extended so as to embrace nearly all the territory lying westward from the foot-hills of the Alleghenies to the Virginia borders, may be justly styled the Mother of the Western Counties; and her soil was among the first points selected by the hardy pioneer and venturesome scout, on which to commence the work of civilization.

Here all the embarrassments of a new settlement were encountered. The terrible conflicts with the cruel and treacherous red men, isolation from society, cut off from aid and intercourse with the Atlantic seaboard, were evils of no ordinary magnitude.

The rugged passes of the Alleghenies then presented a formidable barrier; and the traveller who passed them found himself, as it were, in a new world, where he was compelled to defend himself or perish. A continual conflict was waged between the sturdy pioneer and his implacable Indian foeman. These conflicts were for life, and all that made life dear, and were, however, only marked by individual acts of heroism, which produced none of those events affecting national greatness, which it is the province of the historian to record. They will, therefore, find no place in the annals of our country; yet it is to be hoped, nevertheless, that the indomitable reporter will start out in quest of traditionary lore, listen patiently to the reminiscences of hoary-headed men, and laboriously glean the frail and fragmentary memorials of other days.

Then will the hardy pioneer and gallant conqueror of the country of which we are so proud, find a place, if not with heroes of history, at least with heroes of romance.

The exploits of the explorers of Westmoreland County, of which there is no authentic record, are well calculated to excite an interest in the breast of every American citizen.

The memorable struggle between the legions of France and the battalions of England for supremacy in the great North-West, during which time the gorgeous *fleur-de-lis* and the royal banner of St. George waved successively over the battlements of old Fort Duquesne, was happily terminated by the peace of 1763. Negotiations with this view were entered into during 1762, and were finally consummated early in the following year. By the condition of the treaty, France agreed to surrender absolutely all her possessions in North America to England. Anticipating an early peace, the former made a secret covenant with Spain, ceding to that nation the territory of Louisiana (in the year 1800 it was re-ceded to France, and in 1803 was purchased by the United States for fifteen million dollars), which at the time embraced a large portion of the South-West. The object of this secret covenant was evidently to keep from under the control of their hereditary enemy, the free navigation of the waters flowing through the Mississippi and Ohio valleys within the ceded territory. This deception was not apparent during the negotiation : it was only discovered at the time of the execution of the treaty. This covert disposition of the territory which they failed to maintain by the prestige of arms, was a diplomatic trick, seriously involving their national honor, and which came near defeating the object. In view of the prostration of the country by the recent war, England resolved to accept the situation, trusting in her ability to acquire in the future the peaceful possession of the disputed territory.

The restoration of peace, it was confidently hoped, would forever end the troubles and difficulties with the Indians, who were, with a few exceptions, the allies of France.

This, however, was a fatal mistake ; as it proved the prelude to a most cruel and devastating war, destructive alike to life and property throughout the entire Western frontier. The contemplated and simultaneous uprising of the several hostile tribes was so unexpected, that the outposts were in a great measure unprepared to repel successfully their murderous on-slaughts, except in the instances of the attacks on Forts Pitt, Detroit, and Ligonier.

Hitherto, the Indians, who had been held in subjection by the French, had been won over by a doubtful diplomacy and ap-parent kindness, so that the relations existing between them were of the most friendly character.

When, however, they discovered that they were to be handed over, under the treaty, to their foe, they indignantly re-fused to consent thereto. The onward and steady progress of civilization carried forward by the indomitable Anglo-Saxon race, assured them that submission on their part would end in extermination : to prevent such a calamity, then was the time to act, while the forts were feeble and wide apart, and the set-tlements scattered and thinly populated.

The war familiarly known as the Pontiac war, was so called because this great war-chief was the genius who devised, inau-gurated it, and carried it on with that relentless cruelty so characteristic of the North-American Indian. Pontiac's per-sonal efforts, however, were confined chiefly to the neighbor-hood around Detroit and the lakes ; while the operations on the borders of the Ohio were intrusted to warriors equally fierce and unrelenting.

As far as the English and colonists were concerned, the contests were principally confined to Forts Pitt, Detroit, and Ligonier. All the frontier forts, except these three and Niagara, fell without an effort at defence : the latter was con-sidered too well fortified to be molested, so that the three former were the only ones that successfully resisted the ad-vancing tide of savage vengeance : whilst there was nothing left of the unfortunate garrisons and the settlements around them but a mass of smouldering ruins. Immured within the gloomy depths of a mighty wilderness, isolated from all inter-course with civilization, these gallant defenders not only main-tained their posts, but actually carried the war into the heart of the enemy's country, and, at the point of the bayonet, wrung from them an unwilling peace.

The movements, therefore, on these three forts, and the expedition that subsequently went out from them against the savages, comprise the entire history of the war as far as it relates to our own military movements. The sparse frontier defences scattered through the vast wilderness lying between the great northern lakes and the Ohio and Mississippi valleys, were but rude log enclosures, principally located on the lines of water communication, but occasionally met with in the heart of the forests, garrisoned by a mere handful of soldiers; and the emblem of sovereignty floating above them seemed more of a burlesque than the distinguishing mark of a mighty nation. These forts, situated so distant from each other, were but mere dots in the interminable wilderness.

The presence and maintenance of these isolated outposts inflamed the spirits of the haughty chiefs, who had the sagacity to believe, that, if the struggle for the supremacy was maintained and accomplished by their foes, it would be the foreshadowing of the red man's coming fate.

To resist this encroachment on their rights, the head chiefs of the various tribes who inhabited the country, then only known and travelled by their own hunting and war parties, determined to crush out at once the power of their foes.

The Shawnees, Delawares, Senecas, Wyandots, and Miamis, who considered themselves the exclusive masters of the territory, being moved by their hatred and fear of their Anglo-Saxon foemen, joined together in a common cause, in order to wipe out at once, by a simultaneous movement, the further progress of civilization.

Although rumors of this confederation occasionally reached the military authorities, they did not wholly ignore them, but rather treated them with a cool indifference highly discreditable to their military education; for, if prompt measures had been carried out on the first intimation of alarm, the sacrifice of life and the destruction of the outposts might have been prevented.

It was in consequence of this fatal indifference, that, when the storm burst upon the forts and defenceless settlements, it came like the mighty tornado, carrying terror and destruction as it sweeps its irresistible course.

The period of time selected by the tribes to carry into effect their purposes, evinced their profound knowledge and sagacity Operations were delayed until the harvests were safely garnered, so that their foes, with the provisions provided for their sustenance, might be destroyed at the same time.

Fort Le Bœuf, on French Creek; Venango, on the Allegheny; Presque Isle, on Lake Erie; La Bay, on Lake Michigan; St. Joseph, Miami, Sandusky, and Michilimackinac, — went down in gloom one after another, with scarcely any resistance. Many of them fell by stratagem, and their garrisons were cruelly massacred; others capitulated, and shared the same fate; out of all, only one, Le Bœuf, escaped. The defence of the latter proved futile, the Indians having succeeded in firing the adjacent buildings. The garrison took refuge in the woods, and ultimately escaped.

The royal banner of St. George, wherever it floated over mountain, prairie, and stream, within these vast domains, was stricken down. Forts Pitt, Niagara, Ligonier, and Detroit still remained intact; and the hardy settlers who had escaped the murderous tomahawk and scalping-knife, fled for safety within their protecting walls. The intrepid trapper and venturesome trader were followed up with untiring zeal, and, when taken, were horribly tortured and ruthlessly butchered in cold blood in a manner only known to and practised by these human sleuth-hounds.

The stout pioneer in the clearing, and the loved ones in the log cabin, fell alike before the rifle and tomahawk.

The sound of the woodman's axe and the boom of the morning and evening gun of the lonely forts went down in silence together; and the fires of civilization, whose smoke gracefully ascended above the tree-tops, were extinguished with blood. Those who escaped the murderous raid, left their rude homes to the torch of the foe, and sought safety in flight, carrying with them a tale of blood and cruelty, the bare recital of which filled the border settlements with terror and dismay. In the midst of these scenes of gloom and desolation, the indomitable defenders of Forts Pitt, Detroit, and Ligonier watched with vigilance the movements of their treacherous assailants, thus assuring the safety of the forts, their flag gallantly spread to the breeze, the only emblems of Anglo-Saxon power and civilization in a land now covered with teeming cities, girdled by the wires of the electric telegraph, and traversed by a mighty network of railroads.

STRUGGLING AGAINST MISFORTUNE.

In gathering up the threads of the history of departed days, many of the incidents interwoven therewith are of a sad and melancholy nature, the truth of which is strongly exemplified in the following narrative of David Morgan and his wife Hannah, whose exemplary life and Christian character endeared them to all their acquaintances. In writing the memoirs of this excellent family, my intention will be to record such events as may be considered of interest to the general reader.

"Nothing extenuate, or aught set down in malice."

With this object in view, I will endeavor, to the best of my ability, to give a faithful record of those friends of my early youth, whose many acts of kindness and affectionate regard still remains a bright spot, "to memory dear."

There are many citizens of Allegheny, now living, who will doubtless remember this family and the sad calamity that befell them.

On a pleasant evening in the year 1817, returning from a visit to Pittsburg, in company with my mother, and being detained in crossing the river, we did not reach the landing at Federal Street until the dusky shades of night began to appear. It must be remembered that this was long before the era of bridges and street-railways, and also anterior to the opening of streets from Federal through to what was then called the "Bottoms," situate south of the base of Seminary Hill to the Allegheny River. The facility for getting to and from Pittsburg was quite a different matter from what it is to-day.

The only highway (if it may be called such) leading west from Federal Street to the Bottoms at that early day, was the erratic Bank Lane, which owing to the natural unevenness of the ground upon which it was located, and total neglect of the authorities of Ross township to put it in a condition for travel, it was for many years only accessible for foot-passengers.

The usual and most convenient route for pedestrians was along the bank of the Allegheny River to the bank of a slough bordering the lands formerly belonging to the estate of the late William Robinson, jun., thence northerly along the bank to its junction with the water of a stream having its source in what was called Snyder's Hollow, now known by the more euphonious name of Pleasant Valley. Over this stream, near the junction above referred to, a giant sycamore had fallen, forming a narrow bridge convenient and easy of access. Over it the road led to Bank Lane, now South Avenue. At this point the slough took a westerly direction. The onward march of improvements, however, and the busy stream of dump-carts, will soon obliterate the few remaining landmarks so dear to the memory of those who in early youth sported upon its banks under the shade of its magnificent sycamores. Where now arethese mighty giants of the forest? Echo takes up the melancholy refrain, and answers where? The woodman's axe and the corroding elements of decay have done their work; but one remains, a monument of the past and fostering care of the late Neil McIlwain. It stands in front of the family residence on South Avenue.

On the borders of the slough referred to, a narrow path led through a dense thicket of bushes, impervious to vision on each side: whilst yet within its gloomy depths, we were suddenly started by a wailing cry, the sound of which, to my inexperienced mind, indicated the presence of some wild animal; not so with my mother. Her maternal instincts told her the nature of the cry. She forthwith determined to investigate matters, plunging into the *chaparral.* I followed her hasty footsteps with fear and trembling. There, within its deep recesses, we found the Morgan family, who had just arrived from their far-off native land (Wales), seeking a more congenial home in the Western world.

In the open air this little family were gathered in their lonely camp, the great round harvest moon sailing through the heavens, looking down in silent majesty upon the scene. The monotonous hum of insects, the melancholy cry of the loon sporting in the waters of the Allegheny, the dismal hoot of the owl, and doleful sound of the katydid, added to the general loneliness of the place. It was a scene well calculated to arouse the sympathetic feelings of our nature. I saw by my mother's dewy cheek and glistening eye, that her generous heart was touched. She at once tendered to them a shelter under her own roof, until one more suitable to their wants could be provided. The night having now advanced, and there being no practicable way of removing them at the time, it had to be abandoned until the following morning. After a further examination of the surroundings, with a view to their comfort, and perfect understanding in regard to removal in the morning, we took our leave, and hastened home to put matters in shape to meet the contemplated addition to the family.

Early on the following morning, in accordance with the previous understanding, they were again visited. After getting things in order, they were conducted to the quarters prepared for them.

You may well imagine the condition of this family, when I tell you that all their worldly possessions were transported from the city of New York to Allegheny on a hand-cart drawn by the husband, the wife carrying one of the children. All those weary miles were traversed with a trust in their heavenly Father well worthy the consideration and imitation of us all. ·

Some time during the year 1818, Mr. Morgan obtained employment as a stone-mason, on the Western Penitentiary, then in course of erection. His ability as an expert mechanic was considered of the highest order. The population at this early period being sparse, and dwellings scarce, in order to secure a home for his family, he determined to erect a rude shanty out of the material obtained from the numerous drift-piles lodged on the head of Smoky Island and adjacent tow heads. On the neutral or disputed territory known as Smoky or Killbuck Island, — the title to which has so long occupied the attention of our courts, the question of ownership having been recently settled by a decree of the Supreme Court, — he erected his humble dwelling. Here he lived in comparative peace and contentment in the midst of his happy family until the occurrence of the distressing calamity I am now about to relate.

If my memory serves me right, it was in the autumn of 1820. Their nearest neighbors, Mr. Jacob Cupps and wife, invited them to spend a social evening with them, the distance intervening being about one hundred and fifty yards. Prior to leaving home, they carefully put their four children in bed, and made such other arrangements as the necessity of the case required. The respective ages of the children were about seven, five, three, and one years. There was but one mode of exit, the door of which was securely fastened on the outside, thus unfortunately defeating the main object they had in view, — the safety of their little ones. If it had not been for the latter circumstance, the destruction of life might not have been so general.

During their absence, a fire occurred in their home. The theory of the cause that led to it was never satisfactorily explained: it remains a mystery to this day. The first knowledge they had of the disaster, which rendered them childless, was the reflection of the light of the burning building. On making the woful discovery, they and the Cupps family rushed in frantic haste, hoping to save their little ones, but alas! too late: the devouring elements had done their work. They were the first on the ground: up to this time, there had been no alarm given. Silent had been the work of destruction. Many of the neighbors knew nothing of what had occurred until the following morning.

In a part of the house not yet thoroughly enveloped in the flames, the cradle of the babe was known to be. Tearing off some of the slabs used in its construction, the father penetrated the burning building, and rescued the babe, so horribly burned, that death in a very short time put an end to its life and sufferings. He was badly burned himself, barely escaping with life.

As the burning building fell, a clear sheet of flame shot upwards, rendering surrounding objects clear and distinct; and then all was total darkness, except when a flickering gleam was emitted from the smouldering *débris* that marked the spot of the conflagration. Under these cruel circumstances the neighbors found these unfortunate parents, mourning over the ashes of their lost ones. Notwithstanding this sad bereavement, their Christian fortitude never forsook them: relying upon the Divine promise to bless them that mourn, they lifted up their crushed and suffering souls to Heaven, and with lips all alive and tremulous with the love of a parent's heart, came forth the touching declaration of Job, "The Lord gave, and the Lord hath taken away: blessed be the name of the Lord!"

Owing to the severe injuries received, Mr. Morgan was compelled to cease work on the Penitentiary. Subsequently he obtained a lease of twenty acres of land for the term of seven years, belonging to our estate, on very favorable terms; the conditions being the payment of taxes, and make such improvements as he might deem necessary for his own convenience. It was then an open common : it is now bounded by Beaver and Pennsylvania Avenues, Fulton and Fayette Streets, Fifth Ward, this city, and is densely populated. From the proceeds realized from the operations under this lease, he was enabled to purchase a farm of one hundred acres in Brighton township, Beaver County, to which he removed. To the indomitable energy and business management of Mrs. Morgan, may be attributed in a great measure the prosperous condition of affairs. Every thing connected with the operation of the farm, and support of the family, was left entirely to her judgment ; and well did she perform the duties of the trust. In early life they espoused the cause of religion, and were connected with the regular Baptist church. After their advent in Allegheny, they joined the Methodist-Episcopal church, and have always proved themselves humble and devoted Christians.

He died some years ago, surrounded by his family, full of years, and hopes of a blessed immortality.

He leaves behind, a wife and seven children (four sons and three daughters) to mourn his loss. Two of his daughters are widows, their husbands having lost their lives in defence of the Union in the late war.

ALLEGHENY, Jan. 15, 1879.

RIOT AT THE TEMPERANCE ARK, ALLEGHENY, MAY 16, 1843.

FRANK JOHNSTON and his celebrated brass band, having performed successfully for several evenings before a Pittsburg audience, were invited by some of the leading "Washingtonians" of Allegheny to give a series of concerts in the "Ark." With their accustomed generosity, they readily complied. These concerts were to inure to the benefit of the temperance cause. On Tuesday evening they gave their first concert; and on this occasion a large crowd of men and boys gathered about the doors and windows, and by their riotous conduct did all in their power to mar the entertainment of the evening, and convert the "harmony of sweet sounds" into terrible discords. Notwithstanding these outside demonstrations, the music went on, failing, however, by its soothing influence to calm the savages without.

Although the authorities did every thing in their power to suppress the tumult, yet the ringleaders of the atrocious outrage upon these peaceful and unoffending colored citizens were permitted to escape the penalty of a broken law.

After the close of the entertainment, and while the members of the band were on their way to their lodgings, they were set upon by the mob, and ruthlessly assaulted with such missiles as the assailants could lay their hands on, together with rotten eggs previously provided for the occasion.

Frank Johnston, the leader, was slightly wounded, and three or four of his band seriously hurt about the head, so much so that they were confined to their rooms for several days on account of the injuries received.

It was a happy thing for all, especially for the ringleaders of the mob, that there were no lives taken ; for they hurled their missiles with murderous recklessness, if not with murderous intent. And when the fact is taken into consideration, that this gentlemanly band gave no provocation for the assault, but on the contrary were devoting their time and talents for the promotion of a good cause, the outrage appears all the more aggravating, and it was regarded by all law-abiding citizens with indignation.

Frank Johnston was then considered one of the best cornet-players in the United States : he and his company having made the tour of Europe, performed before crowned heads, and having given concerts in all the principal cities of the South and South-West, were highly appreciated, wherever they performed, for their gentlemanly manners, and artistic delineation of character of the Southern negro ; and the first insult received was on the occasion of their visit to Allegheny.

Active measures were immediately adopted to bring the authors of the outrage to justice. There were two arrests made, who proved, during the trial of the case, that they were culpable only in being present among the rioters, apparently taking no active part in the assault.

In consideration of this fact, a verdict of not guilty was rendered, and that the defendants pay the costs of prosecution. In view of the latter, a motion was made for a new trial, which never came up for argument.

By invitation of the citizens, Mr. Johnston and his company gave another concert at the " Ark " on the following Saturday evening ; and the performance on that occasion passed off without disturbance or interruption.

THE COTTON MILL RIOTS IN THE CITY OF ALLE GHENY, MONDAY, JULY 31, 1848.

DURING this period, the political party in power in the State was fast losing its ascendency; their opponents having already elected their candidate, William F. Johnston, governor. To regain and maintain its lost prestige required a bold effort for a continuance of political power. With this view, the enactment of a stringent ten-hour law, with fines and penalties for its violation, was made a party measure.

It was an easy matter to demonstrate that utter ruin would result to the cotton-mills in Allegheny, by running ten hours a day, against thirteen hours a day in the Eastern States. So, by common consent, all the mills closed operations, and discharged their employees, on the first day of July, when the ten-hour Act became a law.

It soon became apparent that a majority of the operatives were anxious and willing to return to work under the former *régime;* and with the view of determining the question, it was thought advisable that on a certain day all the cotton-mills should resume operations at twelve hours a day as before.

Unfortunately, at this period, the iron-mill hands were on a strike; so that at the appointed time, of the five mills, but one, the Penn, started up.

The engines were promptly started in the morning, and by noon about one-half of the machinery was working. Trouble, however, was anticipated. Sheriff Forsyth was early on the ground. A large and highly excited crowd gathered around the premises, composed of both sexes, and demanded the discharge of the employees then at work, and the closing of the mill. This unreasonable demand being refused, the mob, with angry shouts and threats, forced an entrance, breaking doors and windows, driving from the building all who were at work, compelling the engineer to shut off steam, injuring the machinery, and causing much damage generally.

The appeal of the sheriff to the rioters was met with sullen indifference ; and there being no response to his call upon the *Posse Comitatus*, he was powerless to quell the disturbance, leaving the mob in entire possession of the premises. It is proper to state, that no employee of the Penn was engaged in these riotous proceedings.

Perhaps no single element in bringing about this unfortunate state of affairs was more conspicuous than the course adopted by the organ of the then political party in power, published in the city of Pittsburg.

From day to day before the riot, its editorial columns teemed with appeals to the lowest passions of our human nature, and afterwards defended the gross outrage, holding up for public odium and contumely the honored names of some of our best merchants and manufacturers of both cities, whose only offence consisted in being interested in those extensive establishments that had proved of vast public benefit.

The destruction of property occasioned by turbulent acts of this sort, is of secondary consequence when compared with the gross outrage on society, the disturbance of peace and good order, the interference with the liberty of action, and danger to life.

The best interests of all are indentified with the growing industries of our country ; and those who seek to array labor against capital, as antagonists, make a fatal mistake. They are, and ought to be, natural allies, bound by a common community of interest to afford mutual assistance and protection.

The violence of a mob is not confined, as a general thing, to those against whom it is directed : others are in as much danger from violence as those who are its intended victims.

Thirteen of the principal characters engaged in this riot were placed under arrest, and bound over to appear at court for trial. The question to be determined at these trials, was not only the conviction of the guilty, but to ascertain if property paying heavy taxes was entitled to the protection of law.

Much interest was manifested in the result of these trials: many members of the Pittsburg bar had volunteered in the defence. It became evident that the prosecuting attorney would need assistance: and Edwin M. Stanton (himself a Democrat) was appealed to, and nobly responded, by assuming the lead in the prosecution; and by the justice of the cause he represented, and with the power of his great talents and eloquence, won the victory, which resulted in the conviction of eight of the thirteen accused. Seven of these forfeited their bail, and "fled to other fields and pastures new;" while the remaining one was sentenced by Judge Patton to hard labor in the Western Penitentiary for a term of years. Gov. Johnston, on the petition of the mill-owners, pardoned him before the expiration of his sentence.

A special Act of the Legislature, applicable to the county of Philadelphia, made the county liable for all damage done to property therein by the act of a mob; and, at the session of the Legislature subsequent to the cotton-mill riots, the provisions of the Act were extended to Allegheny County. It is therefore but fair to conclude, that, but for these cotton-mill riots, the county of Allegheny would not now be groaning under the Supreme Court verdict for the millions of damages awarded for property destroyed by the great railroad riots at Pittsburg within the last few years, and illustrative of the scriptural declaration, that "They who sow the wind may reap the whirlwind."

The cotton-mills in operation at the time were the —

Anchor, established in 1828 by Blackstock, Bell, & Co., in the First Ward, on Robinson Street, between Federal and Balkam Streets, extending along the latter to Lacock Street.

Eagle King, Pennock & Co., bounded by Sandusky, Robinson, and Isabella Streets, Fourth Ward, established in 1832 by Arbuckle & Avery.

Hope, Pollard McCormick, on the corner of Lacock and Hope Streets, Fourth Ward.

· Penn,[1] Kennedy, Childs, & Co., fronting on River Avenue, between Federal and Sandusky Streets, extending back to Isabella Court, Fourth Ward, established in 1846.

Banner, I. K. Moorhead & Co., on the corner of Main and Sycamore Streets, extending back to Carpenter's Alley, Fourth Ward, established in 1836 by Voeghtly & Bro.

Franklin, E. Hyde & Sons, on West Canal Street, between Robinson and Lacock Streets, First Ward, established in 1858 by E. Hyde.

It was estimated, at the time of the occurrence, that these six mills operated over thirty-five thousand spindles, six hundred and fifty looms, and one hundred seventy-five cards, manufacturing annually over eleven thousand bales of cotton into sheeting, ticking, cotton-yarn, and cordage, to the value of over eight hundred thousand dollars, and afforded employment to at least one thousand hands.

On the 7th of July, 1850, from the same cause which led to the troubles at the Penn mill, a disturbance took place among the female employees of the Eagle and Hope mills. This occurred during Mayor Fleming's first term, who, by his characteristic prompt and energetic measures, quelled the tumult before any serious damage had been accomplished.

NOTE. — Railroad riot occurred 21 and 22 July, 1877.

[1] The first slate roof in Allegheny County was put on this mill by Thomas Arnold, in 1845, the year of the great Pittsburg fire.

GAS EXPLOSION AT THE METHODIST PROTESTANT CHURCH, ALLEGHENY.

On the thirteenth day of August, 1845, at six o'clock P.M., a terrible explosion of gas occurred in the gas-room connected with this church, situate on the East Common (now Union Avenue), near the corner of Ohio Street. This was anterior to the formation of the present gas-company. The late Rev. Charles Avery [1] had procured a patent gas-apparatus from Cincinnati, for the use of the church, which had been in successful operation for over a year. The gasometer having commenced leaking, some of the leading members of the church were called together, to assist the workmen in raising the gasometer out of the pit, in order to repair the damage. Having accomplished this, they were about to leave the building, when Mr. Karns discovered that he had left behind his walking-cane. Mr. Charles Brown proposed to go back to the gas-room, and get it for him : if it had not been for the latter circumstance, he would probably not have been killed.

The sexton, — Mr. Herron, — Messrs. Russell and Eyester, were still in the gas-room, securing the gasometer: the others were standing outside.

By this time it had become quite dark ; and Mr. Brown, supposing that all the gas had escaped from the building, entered it with a lighted candle, when the gas exploded, blowing the building to atoms.

---

[1] The well-known philanthropist, the late Rev. Charles Avery, contributed largely to the building of this church, and subsequently erected the parsonage solely at his own cost. At his death he bequeathed to the church the sum of five thousand dollars, the interest of which was to be applied to the payment of the current expenses during the maintenance of the same.

Messrs. Eyester, Russell, and Herron were so terribly burned, that death ended their sufferings the same evening. Mr. Brown lingered in extreme torture for about ten days, when a merciful death put an end to his sufferings.

Messrs. Karns and Williams, although severely burned, recovered.

STEAM BOILER EXPLOSION, OF THE COTTON BATTING FACTORY OF JAMES AND ANDREW FIFE.

PRECISELY at eleven o'clock A.M., on the twenty-sixth day of March, 1849, the steam-boiler of the Cotton-Batting Factory, owned and operated by James and Andrew Fife, exploded, completely wrecking the building, setting it on fire, and entirely. consuming it, with all its effects, together with other buildings in the immediate neighborhood.

The melancholy feature of this disaster was the loss of life. James Fife and his daughter ——, Miss Elizabeth Staley, and William Bell, were the prominent victims: there were three others who died afterwards from injuries received on this occasion.

William Bell, nephew of the Fifes, had his head completely severed from his body by a portion of the boiler. Mr. Fife and his daughter, and Miss Staley, were caught among the falling timbers and machinery, buried beneath the *débris;* and before assistance could reach them, the fire had done its work, and a merciful death ended their life and sufferings.

It is related by an eye-witness of the shocking calamity, that Miss Staley having been caught, and firmly held between portions of the machinery, a brave effort was made to save her: the attempt, however, proved abortive. Failing to move the machinery under which she was held, and the flames rapidly surrounding them, to save their own lives, they were reluctantly compelled to abandon her to her awful fate. She heroically urged them to desist, and said her only hope was in death.

Mary Staley (now Mrs. Showers), then ten years of age, a sister of the one above mentioned, was rescued from the ruins, uninjured physically, but mentally demoralized from the effects of her perilous situation.

Another of the young girls employed in the factory, whilst fleeing to a place of safety, was caught by some of the falling timbers, but was rescued before the flames reached her.

The factory was located on the rear of the lot, now No. 89 Ohio Street, between East Common and Sandusky Street. The front on Ohio Street was occupied by frame-dwellings, in which the families of the Fifes resided.

There were two buildings connected with this factory : the one on the west side of the lot was occupied by the Fife Brothers for the manufacture of cotton-batting. They subsequently erected a three-story building on the east side, adjoining the former, and had it rented out for the manufacture of hat-bodies, picture and looking-glass frames. The steam-power for this was supplied from the boilers in the basement of the cotton-batting factory. This was also destroyed, together with its entire effects. There were employed in both these factories some twenty men and women.

When the boiler exploded, a portion of it passed through the rear end of the building No. 97, north-west corner of East Common (now Union Avenue) and Ohio Street, and landed on the East Common ; another portion was carried towards Sandusky Street. The main body of the boiler was deposited on the porch of house No. 37 East Common.

The frame-dwelling occupied by the Fifes ; the ancient log house built and occupied by the late Hugh McGonnigle (who was among the first settlers in Allegheny), situate on the north-west corner of Ohio Street and East Common, — were also entirely consumed. Nos. 37 and 38 East Common, although considerably damaged, would have shared the same fate, had the wind not changed to a northerly point, and driven the flames towards Ohio Street.

Jonathan Rush, who was subsequently elected mayor of the city, was engaged at the time in the hat-body department, and received some slight injuries.

The house on the west side of the factory, now No. 87, was

so much shattered by the force of the explosion, that it had to be strengthened with iron rods, etc.

The factory was never rebuilt. The disaster having determined the ruin of the firm financially, the survivor was unable to re-establish the business.

EAGLE COTTON—MILL DISASTER.

On Monday morning, in the month of October, in the year 1833 or 1834, the boilers of the Eagle Cotton-Mill exploded, causing a partial destruction of the building and the death of thirteen of the employees.

A dense fog was prevailing at the time, rendering surrounding objects dimly visible through its murky veil.

The employees had not all arrived : half an hour later, the mortality would doubtless have been much greater.

The first bell had sent forth its warning note : many were on their way, anticipating the second ringing, for all to be promptly at their position when the engine would start putting the machinery in motion. Just before the time for commencing operations, the engineer, Alexander Morrow, discovered that the packing in the cylinder required adjusting. Supposing it would occupy but a few moments of time to remedy it, he neglected to open the furnace-doors, and shift the weight on the safety-valve ; and, returning to his post at the throttle-valve, he started the engine. On the first revolution, the boilers exploded, creating a scene of desolation and ruin fearful to behold. In addition to the number killed outright, there were several more or less injured, who finally recovered.

Alexander Morrow, the engineer, was frightfully scalded : he lingered in terrible torment for a few hours, when a merciful death terminated his distress.

James Fleming, a promising youth, brother to the well-known firm of Fleming Brothers, an employee of the mill, was among those instantly killed.

An excited multitude soon assembled on the ground, and with willing hands and anxious hearts commenced the work of removing the wreck, in order to reach those who were caught between the timbers and machinery, or buried beneath the chaotic mass. Guided by the groans of the unfortunate victims, every effort was made to reach and save them from the horrors of impending death.

A Frenchman, commonly known as "French Louis," a machinist, was just entering the door of the engine-room at the time of the explosion: a portion of the boiler struck him between the mouth and eyes, carrying away the entire top of his head.

Another Frenchman, familiarly known as "French Jimmy," generally employed about the machinery, was also severely injured, but ultimately recovered.

A FIRE.

DURING the year of 1856, a disastrous fire broke out in the extensive Wagon Works of Phelps, Carr, & Co., extending to the Plow Works of Hall & Spear, both of which were entirely consumed, together with their principal contents, and all the buildings on the two squares bounded by Beaver Avenue, Locust, Walnut, and Market Streets, except the three-story brick building situate on the south-west corner of Beaver Avenue and Locust Street, and the one-story frame-dwelling on the north-east corner of Walnut and Market Streets, both of which were considerably damaged.

This fire was evidently the work of an incendiary, and was the third effort made to fire the same, — the two first proving unsuccessful. General suspicion was aroused, and pointed to one person, who, strange to relate, was never made to suffer the penalty of his crime. There was about $10,000 insurance on the Wagon Works; but owing to these suspicions, and the insolvency of some of the insurance companies, very little was realized. The Plow Works were fully insured.

The Wagon Works were rebuilt by Phelps, Parke, & Co. in 1857, who operated the same until 1874, when they were succeeded by the Pittsburg Wagon Works Company. The works were again destroyed by fire on the evening of the 16th of August, 1878. There was no insurance. This also was said to be the work of an incendiary. During the progress of the fire, a fatal accident occurred, resulting in the death of John Hurber of No. 3 Long Alley, Third Ward. A large amount of government work, together with other unfinished work, machinery, tools, etc., was entirely consumed.

The first and second stories of the brick building on the corner of Beaver Avenue and Locust Street (occupied by D. Hamilton as a drug-store and dwelling), and the third story (by Davage Lodge of Masons), and contents of each, were much damaged by water, — the former to the amount of $500, upon which there was no insurance, and the latter to the amount of $300, covered by the Armenia.

The fire, crossing Locust Street, partially destroyed the buildings owned by William F. Trimble, Mrs. Watson, S. Wadsworth, and the Patterson heirs, all of which were fully insured by the Humboldt, Allegheny, Pennsylvania, and People's, except the building owned by the Widow Watson.

FIREMEN'S RIOT, 1849.

On Monday, July 16, 1849, the great firemen's riot, and consequent loss of property, took place. Those who lost their property have abundant reason to remember the event, and regret the impotency of the city authorities to deal with lawlessness.

The deep mutterings of discontent on the part of the firemen, caused by the refusal of councils to increase the annual appropriation for the department, produced considerable alarm among the citizens. The matter was officially brought to the notice of councils by the firemen in the form of a memorial, setting forth the causes which led to the dissatisfaction. The language, unfortunately, was of a threatening nature: it declared, that, if their demands were not affirmatively acted upon, they would stand aloof with their apparatus in case of fires. Notwithstanding this dictatorial and disrespectful language, councils treated the question in a prudent and proper manner, by the appointment of a committee to confer with the men, and report a basis for the settlement of the difficulty. This, however, did not appear to meet with favor. The unhappy state of affairs continued, with no hope of its peaceful adjudication, until it culminated in the disaster of the 16th (which some averred was specially gotten up for the occasion). The insubordination exhibited by the firemen on that day, effectually sealed the fate of the independent fire-department of Allegheny. It is but justice to say, that many of the members of the department, although they acquiesced in the demand for an increase of the annual appropriation, condemned the language employed, and the course pursued, by their colleagues. By a resolution of council specially convened, the mayor was instructed and authorized to take possession of the entire fire-apparatus of the city, and to call a public meeting of the citizens without delay, to consider the condition of affairs, and report a plan to councils to meet the extraordinary emergency.

In pursuance of the call of Mayor Rush, the citizens in general meeting assembled in the Fourth-ward schoolhouse, when the following suggestions were recommended to councils for adoption : to wit, —

To re-organize the entire fire-department, and to appoint a superintendent for the same ; to appropriate $500 for the prosecution of the leading spirits engaged in the riot, and to distribute the four engines and apparatus as follows : —

The "Wm. Penn" in the First Ward.

The "Washington" in the Second Ward.

The "Uncle Sam" in the Third Ward.

The "President" in the Fourth Ward.

A resolution of thanks is justly due to the indefatigable firemen of our sister city, who, notwithstanding the threats of the rioters, nobly exerted themselves in staying the spread of the flames. They were early on the ground ; but alas! vandal-like, the rioters cut and otherwise mutilated their hose, rendering them entirely useless, thus carrying out the nefarious orders of the chief conspirators, — to prevent at all hazard the saving of property.

There can be no good reason assigned to justify an act so treacherous on the part of the firemen in betraying the confidence of the citizens in their efficiency and integrity. The refusal of the councils to accede to their demands for material aid, was not in itself a sufficient cause to warrant them in withholding their own aid, much less, by threats and overt acts, intimidate others who felt disposed to do all in their power to save their neighbor's property. To discuss the policy of party at this late day, would be productive of no good, as many of the actors on that occasion have long since passed away. We would, however, hazard the opinion, that, if a different course had been adopted by the firemen, they would have covered themselves with imperishable renown instead of lasting disgrace.

The fire commenced on the south side of Gay Alley, between Arch Street and the Diamond, in a carpenter-shop occupied by Henry Charles.

The origin of the fire was never satisfactorily accounted for : it was alleged that the proprietor, who was an inveterate smoker, had carelessly dropped a match among the shavings after lighting his cigar, and immediately left the building on business.

Soon the whole shop was enveloped in a mass of flames. A light wind from the south prevailing at the time, the fire crossed the alley to the Dewdrop property, from which it rapidly spread to buildings on Arch and Ohio Streets and the Diamond, crossing Arch, and setting fire to the First Presbyterian Church, accomplishing its entire ruin, together with other valuable property on the same square.

At this unfortunate period, the fire-apparatus of the city was not in very efficient order. The Wm. Penn and Washington, located in the old Town-house on the south-west Diamond Square ; and the President, on the corner of Lacock and Anderson Streets; and the Uncle Sam, on Union Avenue,— at no time were considered equal to extinguishing large fires. They were worthless now, owing to the complications existing between the councils and the firemen. On the first alarm, the firemen hastened to their respective engine-houses, in order to prevent the citizens from taking out the engines, and carefully guarded the doors, and whilst the destructive element spread, and enveloped their neighbors' property, and in a most determined and malignant manner threatened with personal violence all who would attempt to interfere.

As an instance of the riotous conduct of the firemen, and sympathy of many of the citizens therewith, the following is related : The La Fayette from the borough of Manchester was brought early on the ground : not being aware of the condition of affairs, the company commenced unreeling their hose, and getting their engine in position to go into operation, with a view to save the church if possible, and check the spread of the flames to surrounding buildings.

This could have been easily accomplished if they had been

permitted to do so, as the fire had only slightly taken effect on the heavy cornice under the roof. Threats, however, of personal violence, and destruction of their apparatus, caused a delay; and in the mean time the progress of the flames rendered the saving of the church impossible.

This company possessed the means and the will to render efficient aid if they had been let alone; or if the men had received the least encouragement from the citizens, they would have run the risk of personal violence and the destruction of their engine. Failing in this, they heroically formed a bucket-brigade, with a determination to assist in this way in staying the further progress of the fire.

It was fortunate for the citizens of Allegheny, that the day was calm : otherwise it would have been impossible to tell where the destruction would have ceased.

The appeal of the venerable pastor of the church (Rev. E. P. Swift) to the firemen, with a view to saving the church,[1] backed by the liberal offer of his year's salary as an inducement, was received by them with sullen indifference ; but, whenever danger threatened property belonging to sympathizers, it was promptly met, and the danger avoided.

The loss was estimated at $60,000, on which there was a small amount of insurance, say $5,000, the principal part of which was on the church.

---

[1] The church was rebuilt, and opened for public worship May 12, A.D. 1850.

THE GREAT FIRE.

ON the Fourth July, 1874, at twelve o'clock M., a disastrous fire broke out in the Second Ward, in a large frame carpenter-shop, Nos. 255 and 257 Federal Street, occupied by Messrs. Cresswell and Burgoyne.

For some days before the fire occurred, the weather had been dry, with high winds prevailing from a north-westerly point: notwithstanding this fact, the heat was oppressive. The origin of the fire was evidently caused by the too careless use of fire-crackers, igniting the dry *débris* in and around the shop. In a very short time the devouring element spread with startling rapidity throughout the doomed district. The day being intensely warm, the hot rays of the sun, together with the heat arising from the burning buildings, rendered the situation of the firemen almost intolerable, and their efforts to save embarrassing. Not a cloud obscured the brightness of the noonday sun. The gale continued to augment, carrying with it the flames and burning cinders, until a large portion of the ward lying west of Federal Street, south of Sampson Street, east of Arch, and north of Benton Alley, was a tempest of fire.

The panic among the citizens now became serious, and apprehensions were entertained that the whole northern section of the city would become involved in the ruin.

In addition to the general consternation, a report of a deficiency of a supply of water in the reservoirs, the result of the disabled condition of the forcing-engines, created grave fears that the gallant efforts of the firemen would prove unequal to the emergency: consequently particular attention was directed to the saving of buildings on the verge of the fire, with a view to confine the damage to as small a space as possible.

In view of this alarming state of affairs, orders were issued to shut off the water in the lower districts of the city, in order that the fast-failing supply might be concentrated in the neighborhood of the burning district : it was owing to this wise measure, together with the efficient aid and gallant efforts of the fire-department of our sister city, that the progress of the conflagration was checked.

The imminent danger stimulated every house-holder to be watchful, and to adopt prompt measures to extinguish incipient flames communicated by floating sparks, etc. Toward evening a happy sense of relief was evinced by expressions of joy and hope, as it became apparent that the heroic firemen would win the battle. Although exhausted by their mighty efforts, they still maintained their positions until success crowned their labors. The indomitable spirit and efficiency manifested by them on that occasion elicited the highest praise and earnest commendation of the citizens generally.

At three o'clock P.M. the fire crossed Federal Street, destroying and damaging buildings from No. 248 to 274 inclusive, besides several others on White-oak Alley, Hemlock and Pearl Streets. Ere night came, it was under complete subjection ; but its work had been accomplished, and nothing remained of that thickly populated district but a mass of smouldering ruins.

The total amount of loss was estimated at $244,742 ; total amount of insurance on the same, $111,815.04 ; number of buildings consumed and damaged, 199.

THE GREAT RAIN STORM AND LOCAL FLOOD OF THE 26TH JULY, 1874.

THE citizens of Allegheny have abundant reason to remember the month of July, 1874. They had scarcely recovered from the shock of the calamitous fire of the Fourth, ere they were again called upon to witness a scene far more appalling, because it not only involved the loss of property, but a terrible destruction of life.

Appalling disasters, like appalling crimes, are too rare to discipline the heart to ponder over the shocking details with ordinary emotions.

Our most enlarged benefactions are insufficient to mitigate the terrible sorrows of those whose family and property have been destroyed as thoroughly as if they had never been. It was altogether a sad and melancholy scene, — one that, if spread on canvas, would surely fix the eye for a long time, but in the reality creates an indelible impression upon the memory. The shocking details which go to make up the picture of this terrible calamity are utterly indescribable. They pass before us as a weird vision, and make us feel the poverty of words and the weakness of eloquence.

The weather in the afternoon was somewhat showery, unportentous of any unusual disturbance.

The rain ceased about seven o'clock, and the rays of a gorgeous sunset lit up the western horizon with the glory of departing day.

The people attended religious services in their respective

churches as usual; whilst many promenaded the public parks and avenues, seeking pleasure or recreation, discussing the events of the day, and prospects of the morrow, which, alas! to many never came.

Thus fell the shades of night. The weary retired to rest, and silence brooded over the deserted streets. What a wonderful change was effected in a few short hours! About eight o'clock vivid flashes of lightning in the north and south, accompanied by loud peals of thunder, heralded the coming torrent. Soon the gathering storm-clouds came together with terrible force, opening their flood-gates of destruction over the doomed districts, extending from the valleys of Butcher's, Spring Garden, and Wood's Runs on the north, to McLaughlin's, Painter's, Saw-mill, and Beck's Runs on the south, covering an area of about sixteen miles from north to south, and five miles from east to west.

The storm appeared to be the result of a combination of, or rather a collision between, separate forces approaching from opposite directions; coming together over the doomed districts, covering the heads of the streams above mentioned, whose valleys were filled with the pluvial down-pour, until each became a mighty river, carrying death and destruction as it rushed onward towards its natural outlet.

Never, within the recollection of its oldest inhabitant, has Allegheny been visited by a rain-storm so disastrous in its consequences. Down from the neighboring hillsides came the rushing waters, to add their instalments to the overflow on the plain below, gathering strength and motion by the concentration of the numerous rivulets, forming gullies, down which the roaring waters swept with irresistible power, leaving the surface as if it had been riven by an earthquake.

Every obstacle opposing the mighty flow went down before it. Substantial brick buildings melted away as if they were constructed of quicksand: wooden structures arose from their foundations, were carried along on the bosom of the fast-accumulating waters, and broken up when hurled against other buildings which vainly opposed their onward course. Nothing in its path escaped destruction, — houses, bridges, trestle-work, trees, etc., all going down before it, presenting to the eye a scene of ruin and dismay the like of which it is to be hoped we shall never witness again

The destruction of property, although immense, is nothing when compared with the loss of human life. Many who retired to rest on that fatal night, in the doomed districts, were pallid corpses when the morning light broke upon the terrible scene.

Little children, lisping their appropriate nursery-rhymes, had no thought that the full significance of their prayer would be realized ere morning came. Their delicate bodies were recovered from the chaotic mass, so horribly disfigured and covered with foul and loathsome impurities as to be scarcely recognizable. It was a scene well calculated to arouse the sympathies of our nature : strong men wept ; and feeble women wailed, and were borne fainting away. Whole families, in some instances, were lost, their dwellings falling in ruins upon them.

Language fails to do justice to the terrible scenes presented to our gaze on the following morning. Those who escaped the disaster of the night hastened to the scene of ruin, in search of the bodies of the lost ones.

Willing hands were soon at work, removing the *débris ;* while others waited with anxious hearts, hoping their missing ones had escaped. As corpse after corpse was recovered from the ruins, and identified, the spectators stood awe-struck.

As the storm-clouds burst, and the descending rain fell upon the range of hills north of the city, the waters sought their natural outlets through the valleys of Butcher, Spring-garden, and Wood's Runs, expanding the streams flowing through them into terrible elements of destruction, against which man's efforts were impotent. In the Butcher's-run Valley, some distance from its intersection with Spring-garden Valley, the accumulating water first appeared, gathering strength and volume from the flow from the hillsides, and swept on its headlong course, making a clean sweep of every thing in its path, until it met the equally impetuous outpouring of the flood of Spring Garden.

In the upper portion of the latter, the damage was less than in the former: nevertheless, the marks of the flood were as clearly defined. This valley, for over a mile, presented a most melancholy appearance. Buildings of every description were carried away, and huddled together in confused masses, forming a picture of desolation and ruin which beggars description.

At the intersection of Madison Avenue and East Street, the water, relieved from its comparatively narrow limits, spread with startling rapidity upon the improved thoroughfares, rushed through them, gaining strength, causing a terrible loss of life and property. On East Street the water flowed a short distance, causing considerable damage: thence it took an easterly course, until it met the impetuous flow which had taken Madison Avenue for its channel. The large sewer under the latter, constructed with a view to receive the ordinary flow of the stream, was rent asunder by the pent-up waters, leaving a yawning chasm twenty feet in depth. For nearly a mile, the thoroughfares were gashed and hollowed out from twelve to fifteen feet deep. The buildings on both sides were flooded, and the weaker ones wrecked: others, lifted from their foundations, held together until Vista Street was reached; the terrified occupants imprisoned in the upper stories, escaped a death which otherwise seemed inevitable.

Concord Street crosses the run at a grade of about eighteen feet above the natural bed of the stream: the turbulent waters rushed through the channel, under the bridge, until obstructed by floating wrecks, and a dam was formed. For a short time it withstood the pressure, but finally gave way, the waters making a clean breach through it, of at least forty feet in width. O'Hara Street, which is the next parallel to Concord, descends by an easy grade to its junction with Springgarden Avenue, on both of which were neat and substantial brick and frame dwellings, owned and occupied by persons in comfortable, and some of them in affluent, circumstances. As the flood, checked for a moment at Concord Street, burst its way through other channels, it precipitated itself upon the large culvert beneath O'Hara and adjacent streets, tearing them asunder with the power of an earthquake, upheaving the surface, and demolishing solid buildings.   Here the great destruction of life took place.

The weary had retired to rest, with feelings of confidence that the crisis had been reached and passed. But alas! how soon they realized their fatal mistake! Ere slumber had locked their senses in forgetfulness, with the pent-up waters above bursting their barriers, came the awful noise of the impetuous flood, as it sought its way into the sewers constructed to receive the ordinary flow of the streams through the valleys of Butcher's Run and Spring Garden.

These sewers were deemed of sufficient capacity to meet all ordinary contingencies : in this case, however, they proved an element of destruction, rather than a means of safety. The increasing flood rendered the capacity of the sewers inadequate to its free discharge : resisting the mighty pressure for a short time, their confines finally burst, creating a vortex, through which the vehement waters whirled and tossed in their mad career.

The sudden upheaval of the sewers was alike destructive to life and property. Substantial buildings were lifted from their foundations as if caught in the embrace of an earthquake, over which the mighty avalanche of waters passed, carrying death and destruction to many : even whole families were swept away, to be seen no more in life.

Merciful slumber had rendered many of the victims oblivious of their surroundings ere the advent of the dark angel. Some were found stretched upon their beds, their bodies stained with foul and loathsome impurities, which otherwise had the appearance of voluntary repose. To such, the sudden darkness, the lightning blaze, the boom of the distant thunder, and the roar of the rapidly accumulating waters, gave no warning of the awful calamity that was approaching.

In the valley of Wood's Run, the disaster was marked with the same features of death, destruction of property, and narrow escapes.

At the intersection of Wood's-run and McClure Avenues, the full force of the flood was felt : from this point to the river, its flow was impetuous and destructive. This locality was not so thickly settled; and the damage, though great, was not to be compared with the losses in the Butcher's-run and Spring-garden districts: the loss of life, however, was proportionably as serious.

The same tragedy was enacted, the same scenes of desperate effort and calm despair took place, each one indulging in his own private griefs, to the exclusion of all thought of the heavier calamity which had fallen upon others.

On the south side, from the Monongahela Bridge to where Saw-mill Run empties into the Ohio, although considerable damage and discomfort were caused by the scour and *débris* from the hillsides flooding the basements of buildings between the hill and Carson Street, there is no record of the loss of a single life. But in the Saw-mill Run Valley, the terrible nature and devastating effects of the flood became more apparent as the eye took in the scenes of sudden desolation. For a long distance up this valley, the evidence of its irresistible power was everywhere visible. Every opposing object was swept away in a moment. Dwellings, out-houses, bridges, and trestle-work, all went down before its mighty power, tossed and hurled about like leaves on the surging waters.

The new and substantial iron bridge over the stream near the Gas Works, and the one at Carson Street, were torn from their foundations, and carried into the river.

On Beck's Run, the storm was equally severe, and has also left its sad record of mortality, and destruction of property. The distance of this valley from the Monongahela River to the base of the hills is about two miles. The hills at the head and on each side are precipitous, and cut up with gullies, through which its small streams flow.

These, arising among the range of hills covered by the storm, at once became raging torrents, hurling, with the power of an avalanche, every thing movable in their course to the valley below. Here the vast accumulation of timber, etc., formed a temporary dam, above which the turbulent waters rose with frightful rapidity. For a brief period, the obstruction withstood the mighty pressure, then broke away, carrying every thing before it in its mad career to the river.

At Butcher's, Spring-garden, and Wood's Runs .	70
At Chartiers Creek, including McLaughlin's and Painter's Runs	13
At Saw-mill Run	32
At Beck's Run	9
Total	124

As an evidence of the impetuosity of the current in the Saw-mill Run Valley, an instance is related of a very valuable lead-horse, attached to a team belonging to "Taylor's" Salt Works, being carried along amidst floating *débris* into the river, and, by the force of the out-flow, carried across the river, and landed, without injury, on the northern bank, immediately below the end of Chartiers Street.

REMINISCENCES OF THE OLD THIRD-STREET THEATRE.

THE onward march of improvement, and ceaseless desire for change, will soon obliterate the few remaining old landmarks of the city of smoke. In the following brief memoir, the author has endeavored to elaborate events of a period when the genius of Ross, Baldwin, Forward, Biddle, Wilkins, Dallas, Craig, Shaler, Breckenridge, Lowrie, and Walker enlivened the halls of justice with the power of their eloquence; the faithful ministers of grace, Taylor, Heron, Bruce, Black, Swift, Stockton, Shinn, Kerr, Fathers McGuire and O'Brien, heralded forth from the sacred desk the glad tidings of salvation to a sinful people; and Mowry, Agnew, Lewis, Gazzam, Stevenson, Brunot, Irwin, Holmes, Speer, and Armstrong occupied the front rank of the medical profession.

The first theatre built in Pittsburg was located on the east side of Third Street, near the corner of Smithfield Street, on the westerly half of lot marked No. 310 in the general plan of the city, which was conveyed by John Penn, and John Penn, jun., to Robert Smith by deed dated Sept. 30, 1790, and from Smith to Samuel Peoples by deed dated 26th March, 1813, who conveyed the same to Henry Holdship, Feb. 6, 1828, who, by deed dated Sept. 25, 1833, conveyed the same to John McGill and George Davies, who conveyed the same to Zantzinger McDonald by deed dated Feb. 23, 1835, who conveyed the same to Thomas Hanna by deed dated March 25, 1836, who, by deed dated Aug. 5, 1836, conveyed to William Stewart, Jan. 5, 1837, and by the latter conveyed the same, by deed bearing date

March 27, 1837, to James Wood, and on the second day of March, 1868, the heirs of James Wood conveyed the premises to the Dollar Bank, the present owner.

The Pittsburg Gymnasium was erected about the year 1842 or 1843, by Samuel Barrett, on the site of the old theatre. It was quite a favorite institution, and was conducted on scientific principles by the projector and his successor, the late John McClelland.

The gymnasium, like its time-honored predecessor, had to bow down before the advancing tide of improvement. Although their glories have departed, their old-time votaries still remember them with pride and pleasure.

The theatre was erected between the years 1817 and 1820, by Charles Weidner, architect and builder, and was a substantial frame structure, sixty feet front, two stories in height, with a projection over the entrance, supported by plain columns, ticket-office on the right, and the passage-way to the pit and gallery on the left. The rear of the lot, twenty-five feet, was occupied by a one-story building of sufficient height for the proper working of the stage-machinery. The interior was tastefully fitted up with dress-circle, pit, gallery, and pro-scenium boxes (the latter for special patrons of the drama), with the usual orchestra accommodation in front of the foot-lights. The painting under the proscenium arch, which extended to the full height of the building, was a fine specimen of art, representing the several phases of the drama, — tragedy, comedy, pantomime, etc., — under which appeared the Latin motto, *Veluti in speculum.*

The author's first recollection of its occupancy was by the first Thespian Society, in 1823 and 1824. Prominent among the members, and playing the leading characters, were George Beale, Richard Biddle, Magnus M. Murray, Matthew Magee, Morgan Neville, Charles Shaler, James B. Butler, Duncan Walker, Alexander Breckenridge, Sidney Mountain, Alexander Johnston, jun., William Wilkins, Benjamin Evans, R. B. Barker, T. B. Dallas, J. S. Craft.

The object and aim of these gentlemen was to create a fund for the relief of the suffering poor. Many hearts were made glad by these truly philanthropic efforts, so quietly executed that the recipients were entirely ignorant of the source from whence it came. At the close and disbandment of the society, Messrs. Pelby and Jones became the lessees. Edwin Forrest was a member of this company, and made his first appearance in genteel comedy ; also the beautiful and accomplished Miss Riddle, in the *rôle* of leading lady.

Messrs. Collins and Jones succeeded the above, with Mrs. Entwistle playing the character of leading lady. Then followed the Drakes, Samuel and Alexander, who were succeeded by the renowned Sol Smith. Poor Sol's efforts proved unsuccessful in a financial point of view. His creditors not appreciating the situation of affairs, he was compelled to beat an inglorious retreat.

The gentlemanly N. M. Ludlow next assumed the management, with a very strong company, himself one of the ablest genteel comedians of that day, and quite a favorite with the patrons of the drama : he introduced the amiable, beautiful, and accomplished *artiste*, Mrs. Ball, who subsequently became the wife of one of our most esteemed citizens, at which time she retired from the stage.

Mr. Fuller succeeded Mr. Ludlow with a very respectable stock-company, under whose management considerable changes and improvements were effected in scenery, decorations, etc. Many new scenes were added, and the whole appearance changed for the better. The latter, after a brief but unsuccessful season, sold out to the Thespian Society, composed of the following amateurs : Richard Agnew, J. R. McClintock, William Mountain, W. W. Peters, Charles Dennison, William C. Chaplin, John C. Mowry, H. N. Barker, S. Brunot, M. B. Miltenberger, B. J. Wallace, J. J. Marks, Alfred Marks, Alfred Cochran, Lewis Peters, George Holmes, Thomas Collins, Peter Freeby, John E. Parke, and William Goff. The latter was a member of Mr. Fuller's company, and remained in Pittsburg with a view of making it his home. As a musical director, his talent and services were highly appreciated. His harp, however, has long since been "hung upon the willows;" and in the dreams of the past, his pupils now living hear its strings sounding their old-time melodies.

The above amateurs purchased from Mr. Fuller his entire scenery, etc., at a cost of seven hundred dollars, and opened with the play of "Who wants a Guinea?" with marked success, except the unfortunate rendition of the character of the irascible Sir Jonathan Oldskirt, by Mr. Freeby, who was inflexible in sticking to the "text," and who, upon completing a passionate peroration, turned to the audience, exclaiming as he retired, in the words of the parenthesis, "(Exit Sir Jonathan Oldskirt in a rage.)" This new rendition of the character proved too much for an appreciative audience, as well as for poor Freeby, who finally retired on this vociferous though doubtful evidence of the popular applause. It was his first and last appearance behind the foot-lights.

Shortly after the opening, Mrs. Tatnall, and her young and beautiful pupil, Miss Carpenter, arrived in the city on a professional tour to the South, and were delayed here on account of bad roads, and the suspension of navigation by ice. At their request, they were engaged to perform in conjunction with the company during their stay in the city. Mrs. Tatnall was celebrated as a melo-dramatic *artiste.* Her talent as a vocalist was of sufficient culture to insure a popular reception to the rollicking play of "Tom and Jerry; or, High Life in London," infusing into it a spirit of "fun, fashion, and frolic," which was promptly and gallantly sustained by her amateur assistants.

During the season the following pieces were performed viz., "Who wants a Guinea?" "Tekeli; or, The Siege of Montgats," "Tom and Jerry; or, High Life in London," "Heir-at-Law," "Who's the Dupe?" "Floating Beacon," "Spoiled Child," "Adopted Child," "Day after the Wedding," "American Captive," "Four Gentlemen," and "The Devil upon Two Sticks."

Many of the members of the company were students of the Western University, and the whole thing was suddenly brought to a full stop by the faculty taking the matter in hand.

For over six months the amateurs worshipped at the shrine of Thespis, until parental remonstrance, long-neglected studies, and determined opposition of teachers, recalled them to duty: then Old Drury closed forever, its amateur players bearing with them such fruits as their conduct and purpose merit.

From personal regard for the members of the company, Magnus M. Murray, who was then chief magistrate of the city, cheerfully assumed the censorship and direction; and to his counsel they were eminently indebted. He was beloved for his cheerful and friendly disposition; prompt in reproving wrong, he was equally so in awarding praise where it was due; in short, he proved himself efficient, and was acknowledged by his *protégés in loco parentis.* Financially the venture proved a failure. The debt incurred by the purchase of the scenery was for a long period an incubus on the members, until finally liquidated. Had the ticket-agent and door-keepers proved faithful, the debts could have been paid without difficulty. The net proceeds were intended for charitable purposes. The only case in which the receipts exceeded the expenditures, was on the occasion of the play of "Tom and Jerry; or, High Life in London," for the benefit of the Greeks after the fall of Missolonghi, on which occasion the amount realized was transmitted to the treasurer of that fund by our preceptor, Magnus M. Murray. With this company closed forever the old Third-street Theatre, the premises having been purchased by the late Henry Holdship, who immediately demolished the building, and confiscated the property of the society.

The entire lot extending from Third to Fourth Street is now occupied by the "Dollar Bank." It was incorporated by Act of the State Legislature approved April 27, A.D. 1855, as the "Pittsburg Dollar Savings Institution." The name, however, was subsequently changed to the present one.

This magnificent building was erected in 1870, and occupied in the following year. To the genius and indefatigable exertions of the late Charles A. Colton, treasurer, is justly due the credit of its success and prosperous condition. Its principal front, on Fourth Street, is a fine specimen of elaborate and comprehensive architecture: the interior is tastefully arranged with all the appliances necessary for banking operations. The Third-street front is approached by a paved court sixty by sixty feet, in the centre of which is erected a large water-basin and fountain, surmounted by a life-size statue of the mythical god of the sea, wielding the trident, the emblem of his power.

THE FIRST BANK ROBBERY IN PITTSBURG.

As early as the year 1815, there were only three banks in Pittsburg ; viz., the Bank of Pennsylvania, located on the north side of Second Avenue, between Chancery Lane and Ferry Street ; Bank of Pittsburg, south-west corner of Market and Third Streets ; Farmers and Mechanics' Bank, north side of Third, between Wood and Market Streets, — the aggregate capital amounting to less than two million dollars, which was considered abundantly adequate to the business of that period. When contrasted with the rapid growth and prosperity of the city and vicinity of to-day, the immense banking capital now involved, and deemed necessary to carry on its trade and commerce, is simply amazing ; and the fact had scarcely entered into the minds of its most sanguine citizen of that early day. Among the incidents connected with the history of these banks, it may not be considered uninteresting to relate briefly the bold but unsuccessful attempt to rob the Bank of Pennsylvania by Plymart and Emmons, two of the most daring and expert robbers of their day. The cause of the failure was subsequently told by Plymart himself on his arrest for the successful robbery of the Farmers and Mechanics' Bank. It was frustrated by the simple device of placing over the keyhole a slip of paper, the least disturbance of which would render detection inevitable.

It must be remembered that this was long before the era of combination-locks and the modern improvements ; and the expert robber of that day experienced comparatively little difficulty in accomplishing his nefarious purposes, compared with the present time. To insure success, it was necessary to make two visits to the interior of a bank, the first to take the impression of the lock, the second to abstract the treasure. Plymart successfully accomplished the first ; but, with all his experience and ingenuity, he was completely baffled by the simple device of the slip of paper over the keyhole. By this expedient the safety of the bank was insured. The subsequent bold and successful robbery of the Farmers and Mechanics' Bank by these parties was a matter of more notoriety, and created intense excitement at the time. Relying upon the safety of its granite vaults and ponderous locks, the officers had failed to adopt those simple expedients so embarrassing to the professional burglar ; and thus Plymart was able on his first visit to procure a correct impression of the lock, from which Emmons (who was an expert mechanic) fashioned a key that enabled them to penetrate the vault, and abstract the entire moneyed capital of the bank. They were pursued by the officers of the bank, and Plymart was arrested. The money, however, was only partially recovered. In consequence thereof, the bank was compelled to close its doors, and go into liquidation. Among the articles stolen, was the gold medal, commemorating the battle of the Cowpens, awarded to Gen. Morgan, by a grateful country, for his meritorious services during the Revolutionary war, and special gallantry at the battle of the Cowpens, South Carolina. The medal was recovered from Plymart, who was brought to bay on the borders of Lake Erie, at or near Cleveland, O., by an offer of some immunity to be granted in conveying him to the place of trial. This offer was made in order to prevent him from casting it into the lake, which he threatened to do.

On their return to Pittsburg, Plymart proposed to the authorities of the bank (no legal process having been issued), to make a clean breast of it, by telling where the treasure was concealed, upon the assurance that he would not be prosecuted. With this view, the matter was arranged. In company with Plymart, and under his direction, the officers of the bank proceeded to a point on the north bank of the Ohio River, a few miles below Beaver. Before, however, pointing out the spot where the treasure was concealed, he wished it to be understood, that, as far as he was concerned, they would find the amount intact. What his confederate, Emmons, had done in the mean time, he could not say, — as they had separated at the time, — and was unwilling to be held responsible therefor. With this additional understanding, he directed operations, the result of which proved his faithfulness in this particular, and the recovery of a large portion of the money stolen. Matters having thus been satisfactorily adjusted, he was permitted to depart. If my memory serves me right, he was subsequently arrested on a similar charge, tried, convicted, and sentenced to the State Prison, and was pardoned out before the expiration of the time of sentence. What ultimately became of him and his partner Emmons, I am unable to say. Shortly before the event of the robbery, an incident occurred, in reference to this medal, that made an impression on my memory which the lapse of over sixty years has failed to obliterate. My grandfather, Robert Magee, had occasion to send me to the bank for change for a note. Morgan Neville, then an officer, — whether cashier or teller, I cannot now determine, — in handing me the change, in a joke, included the medal. I confess I failed to see it in that light at the time : before leaving, however, and still pondering on the novelty of the thing, without arriving at a satisfactory conclusion, I forthwith determined to return it, and in lieu thereof insist upon receiving change of a more comprehensive kind.

PAPER FOR THE SOCIETY OF OLD RESIDENTS.

"THE Society of Old Residents" is the one for which this paper was prepared : —

MR. PRESIDENT, AND MEMBERS OF THE ASSOCIATION.

The committee to whom was referred the subject-matter of the late base attempt to assassinate the chief magistrate of the nation, have instructed me to submit for your consideration the following preamble and resolutions, expressive of the sense of this association.

Since the last meeting of the association, an event has occurred, painful and startling in its nature. Again has a chief magistrate of the nation become the victim of the assassin's bullet.

Shocking events, like shocking crimes, are too rare to discipline the heart to ponder over the distressing details with ordinary emotion.

The memory of the tragical death of the good and faithful "Lincoln" is still green in our hearts; and we are again called upon to mourn a similar attempt to destroy the life of our present honored chief magistrate, James A. Garfield.

Although the consequence of the act has not proved immediate in its effects, yet the nature of the wound received is of such as to create grave doubts of a favorable termination. Alternate hope and fear still agitate the national heart ; and if he is again permitted, by a wise and merciful Providence, to assume the duties of every-day life, his physical powers and thorough temperate habits may be considered essential factors in bringing about a result so desirable and important to his friends and the nation at large.

Our most enlarged sympathies are insufficient to mitigate the terrible sufferings of the victim, or soothe the anguish of the family and friends. The cruel event passes before us as a mighty vision, making us feel the poverty of language, and weakness of eloquence, when startling realities and sudden calamities which have overtaken us, are to be described.

In all the relations of life, whether in Church or State, President Garfield has proved himself a citizen of rare ability, religiously discharging the duties and trusts committed to his care. Wise in his counsel, firm in his friendship, as a Christian, husband, parent, and friend, he possesses the best of all records, — an untarnished reputation and an honored name.

Be it therefore

Resolved, That the members of this association, individually and collectively, express our utter detestation of an act so atrocious, and that we extend to our suffering President and family the assurance of our heartfelt sympathy in their sad affliction, and sincerely trust that Providence will restore him to health, family, and friends.

Resolved, That the foregoing preamble and resolutions be engrossed upon our minutes, and a copy of the same be transmitted to the President and family, through the Hon. James G. Blaine, Secretary of State, with the hope that they may prove acceptable memorials of our profound sympathy.

SANITARY FAIR.

No. 50 Stockton Avenue, Allegheny,
April 5, 1881.

Hon. John E. Parke.

Dear Sir, — I hope my delay in answering your request for a copy of the final report of the Executive Committee of the Sanitary Fair, has not caused you any serious inconvenience in the purpose for which you desired it, and that I may be excused. I now send you a copy.

In the early part of March, 1864, the Pittsburg and Allegheny branch of the Sanitary Commission, having exhausted its funds for the relief of the sick and wounded soldiers, decided to hold a Sanitary Fair. A committee was appointed to take the work in hand. There being no suitable buildings in the city, it was decided to erect such as were required; and, after examination of the various sites proposed, it was found that the public square in Allegheny was the only convenient place which would afford room enough for their erection.

A scarcity of materials in the city was the next obstacle encountered; and, withal, there was no money on hand to begin the proposed extensive operations.

A Sanitary Fair was just closing its work at Cleveland; and Messrs. C. W. Batchelor, James Park, jr., and John W. Chalfaut, were appointed a sub-committee to proceed to Cleveland, with authority to purchase such of the temporary buildings there erected as should be deemed suitable for our purpose, and the lumber necessary for the additional buildings, and arrange for their transportation to Allegheny. The purchase was made, the committee giving their individual note for about ten thousand dollars, at short time, for the payment; and on the 29th of March, the Executive Committee issued an address to the public, which appointed June 1st as the day upon which the Fair should be opened.

The Cleveland buildings were too small, and too few, for our requirements; and the following are the dimensions of those which were erected in the Allegheny Public Square : —

Mechanics' Hall	192 feet long,	by 51 feet wide.
Audience Hall	186 " " " 93 " "
Monitor Building	150 " " " 50 " "
Floral Hall	160 " " " 80 " "
Bazaar	180 " " " 93 " "
Dining-Hall	180 " " " 51 " "

Covering an aggregate of 73,200 square feet of space.

In addition to this, the entire upper floor of the new City Hall, which had been generously granted for the purpose by the Allegheny councils, was occupied by the "Art Gallery" and the "Old Curiosity Shop;" and there were extensive buildings for the exhibition of fine live-stock.

For a description of the opening on the 1st of June, and of the details in regard to the contents of the Fair-buildings, I must refer you to the files of the city papers of that date.

As will be seen from the final report, the total receipts of the Sanitary Fair amounted to $363,370.09.

Net receipts paid over to the Pittsburg Sanitary Committee, by the Executive Committee of the Fair, $319,217.98.

Happily, the Executive Committee, before the opening of the Fair, anticipating the possible closing of the war before all the funds to be raised should be used, made a proviso whereby the remainder could be applied to some other benevolent purpose in Allegheny County. This remainder proved to be even larger than was anticipated, and it now constitutes the endowment fund of the medical and surgical branch of the Western Pennsylvania Hospital. It amounts to two hundred thousand dollars, and the interest is used in ministrations for the relief of human suffering.

Presuming that I have furnished the information for which you asked me, but quite willing to respond further, if in my power, to any wishes you may indicate to me,

I am very respectfully and truly yours,

FELIX R. BRUNOT.

To the Contributors and Promoters of the Pittsburg Sanitary Fair.

The Executive Committee of the Pittsburg Sanitary Fair present the following summary of the result of your effort in behalf of the sick and wounded soldiers of the Union Army : —

Cash received by N. Holmes, treasurer, from all sources .	$361,516 17
Goods and cash handed over to Thomas Bakewell, Esq., president of the Pittsburg Sanitary Committee, which did not pass through the hands of the treasurer . . .	2,053 92
Total receipts from all sources . . .	$363,570 09

Net amount paid to Thomas Bakewell, Esq., president of the
Pittsburg Sanitary Committee $319,217 98
Monument Fund 3,000 00
Paid N. Holmes, treasurer, sums received for lumber, gas-
fixtures, etc. 8,272 32
Expenses of the Fair 33,079 79
                                                       ————————
        Total $363,570 09

[COPY.]

Received of Felix R. Brunot, chairman of the Executive Committee of
the Pittsburg Sanitary Fair, $319,217.98, as per several receipts given, of
which this is a duplicate engrossment.

                                   THOS. BAKEWELL,
                              President of Pittsburg Sanitary Committee.
PITTSBURG, April 8, 1865.

[COPY.]

The undersigned committee, appointed to audit the accounts of the
Pittsburg Sanitary Fair, hereby certify that the vouchers in the hands of
the secretary and treasurer exactly correspond with the disbursements as
exhibited in the condensed statement, and they cordially commend the neat
and accurate manner in which the accounts appear to have been kept.

                              GEO. T. VANDOREN, *Chairman.*
                              I. R. McCUNE,
                              WM. ROSEBURGH,
                              JOHN MAGOFFIN,
                                                       Committee.
PITTSBURG, March 27, 1865.

Pittsburg may be justly proud of the result of the Fair; for relatively to
the population involved, and the restricted area from which the revenues
of the Fair were derived, it places her far in the lead of all the patriotic
cities of the Union which have made similar efforts.

Taking the census of 1860 as the basis for calculation, and including
the population of Pittsburg, Allegheny City, Manchester, Lawrenceville,
Birmingham, and the other boroughs, the *net proceeds* show an average of
three dollars and forty-seven cents for every man, woman, and child.

The annexed table is given as interesting matter of record : —

	Net proceeds of Fairs.	Average to Population.
St. Louis	$554,591 00	$3 44
New York	1,184,000 00	1 47
Brooklyn	400,000 00	1 50
Philadelphia	1,035,378 96	1 83
Cleveland	78,551 33	1 81
Cincinnati	235,405 35	1 46
Pittsburg	322,217 98	3 47

The total money contributions amounted to	$202,156 00
Of this sum, Venango County sent . .	18,555 70
Lawrence County	8,144 16
All other counties of Western Pennsylvania	13,761 14
Places outside the limits of Western Pennsylvania	4,719 00

The only considerable contribution from any one locality outside of Western Pennsylvania, was that of Chicago, which, in cash and goods, was about six thousand dollars.

Among the many trades and professions contributing in kind, it may not be considered invidious to mention the newspaper press. The reporters rendered invaluable aid in time and labor; and the proprietors, besides making generous donations, spared no pains in contributing to the successful result.

In regard to the expenses of the Fair, it is deemed proper to state distinctly, that no officer of the Fair, member of the Executive Committee, or of any other committee, received any salary, pay, or allowance whatever. Dr. William D. McGowan and Mr. B. F. Brown, the efficient acting secretary and assistant, were entitled to salary for four months of active labor. They received only a sum sufficient to cover their expenses, thus placing themselves among the most liberal contributors.

In closing our official duty, in connection with the Pittsburg Sanitary Fair, the members of the Executive Committee desire to express their obligations to the many generous hearts and busy hands which have co-operated with them, and especially to the ladies, without whom there could have been no such magnificent result. For ourselves, and in behalf of the thousands of our country's defenders, who have reaped, and are continuing to reap, the benefits of their generous labors, we offer to them all our grateful thanks.

> FELIX R. BRUNOT, *Chairman.*
> JAS. PARK, JR.,
> JNO. W. CHALFAUT,
> B. F. JONES,
> I. I. BENNETT,
> JAS. O'CONNOR,
> CHAS. W. BATCHELOR,
> M. W. WATSON,
> JOHN WATT,
> W. S. HAVEN,
> JNO. H. SHOENBERGER,
> THOS. M. HOWE,
>
> *Executive Committee.*

FERRIES.

THE following is a paper in full read by Hon. John E. Parke before the Old Residenters' Association on the subject of "Ancient and Modern Ferries on the Ohio, Monongahela, and Allegheny Rivers:" —

MR. PRESIDENT, — From my own recollections, and information derived from others whose age and experience qualify them to impart the same, I have carefully prepared the following statement of facts in relation to the ancient and modern ferries that have from time to time been established over the Ohio, Monongahela, and Allegheny Rivers in the immediate vicinity of Pittsburg and Allegheny; and it is offered here for the purpose of inviting criticism, in order that the errors, if any, in the memoirs, may be corrected.

About the beginning of the present century, a ferry, operated by hand, was established by West Elliott, on the Ohio River, from the mouth of Ferry Lane, North Side, from which the lane derived the name, to a point on the South Side, immediately opposite.

At this point, the great buffalo trails from the South-East to the feeding-grounds on the North-western plains connect, over which the various Indian tribes roamed to and fro in their periodical visits, in order to concoct and perfect their nefarious schemes to crush out their indomitable Anglo-Saxon foe. This undertaking, not proving profitable, was, after a short experience, abandoned.

In 1832 Mr. Nolan established a ferry at the points above referred to, operated by a wire rope, and buoys to support the same. It proving detrimental to the free navigation of the river, and dangerous to those operating it, it was also subsequently abandoned.

Capt. Valentine Shorts succeeded Mr. Nolan, and operated the ferry by horse-power for a number of years quite successfully. In the mean time Capt. Stoops established a steam-ferry above from the mouth of Chartiers Street to a point on the South Side above the mouth of Saw-mill Run. Capt. Stoops subsequently sold his entire interest to Messrs. Lea & Holmes, they to William McKee, who applied for and obtained a charter from the Legislature to operate the same, one of the provisions of which was that the said William McKee and his successors were not to interfere with the running of the ferry below, except in the legitimate competition for the travel across the river. Johnston Brothers succeeded William McKee. Then Capt. William M. Claney became the purchaser, and established the first side-wheeler. Capt. Claney disposed of his interest to Messrs. Krepps Brothers & Force; this firm was subsequently dissolved, Capt. Jerry Force purchasing the interest of his partners, who, after operating the ferry for a short period, sold out to Capt. William J. Kountz, the present owner.

The foregoing are by no means the first ferries established on the North Side, although they are the first established over the Ohio River at the points designated.

As early as 1786, Col. William Butler was granted, by Act of the State Legislature (*vide* Colonial Record., vol. xv. p. 42), the right to establish a ferry on the Allegheny River, from a point on the Pittsburg side to a point opposite, to where the line of Bank Lane would strike the Allegheny at what is now the mouth of School Street.

The nature of the ground at this point was deemed altogether unsuitable for a landing; and representation having been made to the authorities to that effect, on consideration thereof, it was ordered and decreed by the Supreme Executive Council, that the " said grantee be authorized and empowered to establish a landing, and erect a ferry-house, upon such other part of the 'Reserve Tract opposite Pittsburg' as will best promote the convenience of the public and the intentions of the Legislature as set forth in the Act granting the same. He is also permitted to occupy such land as has been improved and hitherto cultivated by James Boggs, deceased, for which privilege he shall exercise a supervisory care, so as to prevent the undue destruction of the timber of the Reserve Tract above referred to."

In pursuance of the authority given, the ferry was established at the mouth of St. Clair (now Sixth Street) to the mouth of Federal Street directly opposite.

Col. Butler, it seems, disposed of his interest to Robert Knox and John Morrison ; the former conducting affairs on the Pittsburg side, and the latter on the Allegheny side. They were succeeded by Robert Stewart and Mr. Battrocks. Mr. Cassily succeeded the latter. Under Messrs. Stewart & Cassily the ferry was carried on until the completion of the Allegheny Bridge in 1820.

There was also an ancient ferry established from a point a short distance below the railroad viaduct, Allegheny, to the mouth of Hand Street (now Ninth), Pittsburg. It was carried on by Mr. Yerkins, under the management of David Haney, an old and experienced water-man, and continued in operation until about the year 1830, when it was abandoned. In 1834 Mr. George A. Kurtz established a wire-rope ferry from the mouth of Hancock Street (now Eighth Street), Pittsburg, to a point about midway between Sandusky and Anderson Streets, Allegheny. The amount of travel not justifying its continuance, it was abandoned the following year.

Contemporary with the establishment of the ferries on the Allegheny, there was one established on the Monongahela opposite the "Point" to the mouth of Liberty Street, by Ephraim Jones, in 1779, who operated the same by hand until his death, after which his son Thomas carried it on for a number of years by the same process ; then by horse, and subsequently by steam power. After the death of the latter, his heirs carried on the business until after the close of the late war, about 1864, when they sold out to a chartered joint company under the name and title of the "Jones Ferry Company." The South-side landing was then changed to a point a short distance above the mouth of Saw-mill Run.

Upon the completion of the "Point Bridge," and in pursuance of the negotiations entered into by the rival companies, and in order to do away with competition for the travel, the entire franchises of the "Jones Ferry Company" became vested in the "Point Bridge Company," and the ferry abandoned.

Subsequent to the establishment of the Point Ferry, Jacob Beltzhoover commenced one from the mouth of Wood Street to a point opposite, called the Upper Ferry, under the management of William Graham, who kept a public house of entertainment on the north-western corner of Wood and Water Streets. This ferry was in operation until the completion of the Monongahela Bridge in 1818, which monopolized the travel. This, together with the difficulties presented by the sand-bar, which, in low water at this point, occupied about one-half of the entire width of the river, and which had to be overcome by boats on each side, connected by a roadway across the bar, caused it to be abandoned.

Of the above enumerated ferries, only three were chartered; viz., one on the Allegheny, one on the Monongahela, and one on the Ohio.

The perils encountered during storms, floods, floating ice, and driftwood by this early mode of transit were of a very serious character; and many who had the temerity to brave the dangers had abundant reasons to regret it ere they reached the desired haven. Some of the incidents connected with these occasions are so deeply impressed upon my memory, that the lapse of over sixty years has failed to obliterate them.

During the fall of 1817 the stone foundations of the piers of the Allegheny Bridge were finished to a sufficient height to be covered by an ordinary stage of water, and left so until the following spring, in order to avoid any damage that might occur to the work by floating *débris* and breaking up of the ice in the floods during the winter and spring.

Early in the month of December of the year above referred to, the river was frozen over with a coating of ice about two and one-half inches thick. At this time, in company with my elder sister, on a visit to our friends in Pittsburg, we took passage on the ferry-boat crowded with passengers and horses, it being the intention of the ferry-man to open a passage through the ice to the other shore. When about midway over, the ice parted from the shores, and commenced breaking up, making a clear breach over the low sides of the boat, creating a fearful panic among the passengers and horses.

The massing of the ice in and around the boat rendered our situation perilous, and efforts to reach either shore unavailing; and all attempts on the part of our friends to aid us proved a failure. Passing the " Point," the rapid current of the Allegheny carried us to within a short distance of the southern shore of the Ohio, which enabled us to make a landing just above the mouth of Saw-mill Run. To the experience and presence of mind displayed by the ferry-man, David Haney, and his comrade, may be attributed the happy termination of an adventure which might have, under other circumstances, proved fatal to all on board.

During the summer of 1833, returning from a visit to the South Side, I met my military friend, Major Andrew McFarland, arrayed in all the pomp and circumstance of his official character as brigade inspector, *en route* to inspect the troops belonging to his brigade. Arriving at the Jones-ferry landing, we boarded the hook-boat, Johnny Welsh acting in the capacity of engineer, pilot, and chief commander. All aboard being announced, we started for the opposite shore, full of passengers and a large load of hay. The day was clear and calm, unportentous of any elementary disturbance. About midway of the stream, a sudden violent wind-storm arose, which rendered the boat unmanageable, and demoralizing to our brave commander, who, usually calm and self-possessed, on this occasion entirely lost his presence of mind. Johnny was a peculiar character, mentally weak, but honest and faithful in the discharge of his duties, peaceful in his habits and disposition. Those who knew him best gave him full credit for his integrity and goodness of heart.

The roaring wind, tumultuous waves of the otherwise placid Monongahela, and struggling horses, created a scene of terror and dismay not easily described. In the emergency, Major McFarland seized the tiller, in order, if possible, to control the movements of the vessel. In his laudable effort to accomplish it, he had the misfortune to lose his military hat. Finding it out of the question to reach either shore, he directed the course of the vessel up the river until it caught on one of the piers of the bridge. Here we remained until the storm abated, when we commenced working our way to the landing at Liberty Street, where we arrived without serious damages.

Upon leaving the boat, the major, after giving vent to a deep sigh, remarked in his peculiar manner, "that a load of hay was an awful thing in a high wind."

BRIDGES.

THE ALLEGHENY BRIDGE.

THE building of this bridge was commenced in 1818. It was constructed on the arch principle, from the mouth of St. Clair Street, Pittsburg, to the mouth of Federal Street, Allegheny. It was opened for travel, Feb. 20, 1820.

The first charter obtained was granted by the Legislature, March 20, 1810 : this was suffered to lapse. On application, a new charter was granted, Feb. 17, 1816, and approved by the governor, May 31, 1816.

July 8, 1816, the company was organized with the following officers : —

WILLIAM ROBINSON, Jun., *President.*

DIRECTORS.

JAMES ADAMS.	JOHN DARRAGH.
JAMES ANDERSON.	HUGH DAVIS.
ABNER BARKER.	EBENEZER DENNY.
ROBERT CAMPBELL.	WILLIAM HAYS.
THOMAS CROMWELL.	GEORGE POE, Jun.

A. ZEIGLER.

Cost of construction, $80,000.

May 7, 1857, a supplement to the charter was obtained, authorizing the demolition of the old wooden structure and the erection of the present one. It was completed and opened to the public in 1860. The two centre spans are each three hundred and fifty feet in length, with shorter spans at each end, the whole intended to form a graceful arch from bank to bank. It is the first iron suspension bridge erected over a navigable stream in the United States, and is admitted by experts to be the most important work in the country. As long as it endures, it will be a monument to the genius and engineering skill of its contractor, the late John A. Roebling.

It cost $250,000.

The State of Pennsylvania owned $40,000 of stock in the first structure, which was disposed of in 1843, the par value being $25 per share: at the sale the stock realized over $30 per share.

PITTSBURG AND ALLEGHENY BRIDGE.

This bridge, erected from the mouth of Hand Street (now Ninth Street), Pittsburg, to the mouth of Cedar Street (now Anderson Street), Allegheny, was contracted for in January, 1837, to be completed Oct. 1, 1838. (Act of incorporation was passed by the Legislature at the session of 1836, and approved by the governor, June 26, 1836.) It was completed and opened for travel in 1839. It is constructed on the arch principle, the whole forming one graceful arch from bank to bank.

On the roof a promenade was constructed, which in pleasant weather was quite a fashionable resort, until it became prostituted to base purposes, and had to be abandoned. The entire structure was thoroughly examined and repaired, at a cost of over $30,000, by contractor Daniel McCain.

The original contractors for constructing the bridge were, —

WILLIAM LA BARRON, *Wood-work.*
PAGAN & ALLSTON, *Stone-work.*
SYLVANUS LOTHROP, *Architect.*

The first officers elected under the charter were, —

JOHN TASSEY, *President.*

DIRECTORS.

WILLIAM LARIMER, Jun.	CHARLES AVERY.
RICHARD GRAY.	ROBERT GALWAY.
SYLVANUS LOTHROP.	F. G. BAILY.
WILLIAM ROBINSON.	GEORGE OGDEN.
MALCOM LEECH.	JOHN GRIER.

ALEXANDER BRECKENRIDGE, *Treasurer.*

WILLIAM FITZSIMONS, *Secretary.*

NOTE. — The promenade above referred to was at one time the objective point of a ludicrous practical joke perpetrated on the citizens of both cities. About the year 1852, handbills were prominently posted over the cities, to the effect that a man would, on a certain day, fly from the roof of the Hand-street Bridge, and pass over the Suspension Bridge to the south side. Long before the hour had arrived for the performance, the shore on each side of the river, and the Suspension Bridge, were densely crowded, and every available water-craft was brought into requisition to view the novel sight of a man flying. Promptly at the hour indicated, the practical jokers made their appearance on the roof of the bridge, bearing a mysterious-looking green bag. Then the roar of the multitude commenced, and ended as the bag was opened, giving flight to a large gray goose. Thus ended the farce; and not one in all that vast crowd was willing to admit the next day that he was there, although there must have been at least twenty thousand people present.

MECHANIC-STREET BRIDGE.

This bridge was charted in 1836, and erected the following year, from the mouth of Mechanic Street, now Sixteenth Street, Pittsburg, to the mouth of Chestnut Street, Allegheny, and opened for public travel in 1837. It was destroyed by fire, Jan. 26, 1851, and rebuilt the same year. Total loss, $75,000, on which there was an insurance of $20,000.

The first officers elected under the charter: —

F. LORENZ, *President.*

MANAGERS.

JOHN SHOENBERGER.   SAMUEL McKELVY.
WILLIAM WADE.   JOHN KEOWN.
N. VOIGHTLY.   SYLVANUS LOTHROP.
            JACOB PAINTER.

G. E. WARNER, *Treasurer.*
WALTER H. LOWRIE, *Secretary.*

CONTRACTORS.

J. K. MOORHEAD, E. OLES, *Wood-work.*
WILLIAM PAGAN & CO., *Stone-work.*

THE SHARPSBURG BRIDGE.

The Sharpsburg Bridge was erected in 1856; destroyed by fire in 1864, and rebuilt the following year. In 1870 it was again destroyed by fire, and rebuilt in 1871.

THE UNION BRIDGE.

The Union Bridge, erected from the Point, Pittsburg, to the mouth of Grant Avenue, Allegheny, is constructed of wood, on the arch principle, and is considered one of the finest structures of the kind erected in this vicinity. Its erection was commenced in 1874, and it was completed and opened for travel in the following year. Cost, $300,000.

THE POINT BRIDGE.

The Point Bridge, over the Monongahela, from the junction of Water Street and Duquesne Way, Pittsburg, to Carson Street, S. S., is a magnificent structure composed of iron, built at a sufficient elevation so as not to interfere with the free navigation of the river. It was built in 1876, and cost $500,000.

MONONGAHELA BRIDGE.

This bridge has an eventful history. It was chartered by the Legislature in 1810, and a re-issue of charter was made in 1816. In pursuance of the provisions of the charter, the bridge was erected on the arch principle. It was completed and opened for public travel from the mouth of Smithford Street, Pittsburg, to Carson Street, S. S., Dec. 31, 1818. In January, 1831, the first pier on the Pittsburg side gave way, and precipitated the first span into the river : it was promptly repaired, and re-opened for travel Sept. 18, 1831. Cost, $61,000.

It was completely destroyed in the great fire of the 10th of April, 1845, and was replaced by a wire suspension bridge, under the direction of Mr. John A. Roebling, the builder of the great East-river Bridge, connecting the cities of New York and Brooklyn. This Pittsburg work was Mr. Roebling's first road-bridge. In the course of time it became very shaky and loose, and its continuous swaying and creaking convinced every one that it was becoming unsafe for travel. In the summer of 1880 it was decided to build a new one in its place. After a good deal of discussion as to the kind of bridge that should be built, Mr. G. Lindenthal, the well-known engineer, was invited to prepare plans for a bridge that would not be subject to undulations, and would be capable of enduring the constantly increasing traffic without limitation of load or speed. His plans were accepted, and in 1881 the work was commenced.

The new structure being elevated twenty feet above the old, the work was carried on and completed in August, 1883, without interfering with travel. The bridge is of the kind known as the Pauli truss. It rests on seven stone piers, and has two cast-iron towers 160 feet high, very massive and elaborately ornamented. The full length of the bridge is 1,221 feet. The two main spans are each 360 feet: the north approach is 320 feet from Water Street to the first large span, and from the toll-house to the span 208 feet. On the south end the distance from the toll-house to the first large span is 290 feet, and from Carson Street 515 feet. From the roadway of the centre span to the river at low water it is a distance of 61.08 feet, and from the under side of the floor 57.08 feet. The old bridge left only 36.03 feet clear between the water and its lower side.

The roadway at present is 22 feet 10 inches wide in the clear, and the two sidewalks are each 10 feet in the clear. The full width of the bridge on the deck-span approaches is 43 feet 6 inches, and on the channel-spans, which are through spans, 48 feet. The bridge can be widened out, should it ever prove necessary, to 64 feet. The use of steel instead of iron wherever possible, was based on the grounds of economy as much as any thing, especially in the trusses, $21,600 being saved by taking that course. The flooring of the roadway and sidewalk is preserved wood; viz., gumwood and white pine, submitted to the zinc tannin process. The ornamental cast-iron towers are roofed with wrought-iron.

The masonry of the piers and approaches consists of a gray, hard, durable sandstone, free from admixture of clay or iron oxide particles. The dimensions of the stones used are from 24 to 16 inches in thickness, 7 to 4 feet in length, and from 3 to 1¾ feet in width, with beds and joints dressed regularly and true. The quantities of material used in the construction of the bridge were as follows: For foundations — lumber, 594,000 feet, board-measure; piles, 10,800 lineal feet; concrete, 1,280 cubic yards; iron, 322 tons; stone-masonry, 10,500 cubic yards. For superstructure — iron, 1,070 tons; steel, 740 tons; cast-iron of towers, pedestals, etc., 196 tons; preserved lumber for floor, 358,000 feet, board-measure; steel rails, 134 tons. For approaches — filling, 10,000 cubic yards; sidewalk pavements, 1,400 square yards; street pavements, 2,200 square yards. The total cost of the bridge is $458,000.

NOTE.—The last bridge was completed after the death of Judge Parke, and the above description was copied by the editor from one of the city papers.

FLOODS.

HEIGHT of the periodical floods in the Ohio, Monongahela, and Allegheny Rivers, above low-water mark, at Pittsburg, Penn., since the occurrence of the Pumpkin Flood in 1810.

		FEET.			FEET.
1806.	April 10	33.9	1869.	March 31 .	19.6
1810.	November 10 . . .	32	1870.	January 19 .	18
1813.	January	29	1871.	" 15 .	19
1816.	February	33	1872.	April 11 .	20.6
1832.	" 10	35	1873.	December 14 .	25.6
1840.	" 1	26.9	1874.	January 8 . .	22.4
1847.	" 1	26	1875.	August 3	25
1851.	September 20 . . .	30.9	"	December 28 .	21.6
1852.	April 19	31.9	1876.	September 19	26
1858.	. . . .	26	1877.	January 17 .	25
1860.	April 12	29.7	1878.	December 11	24.6
1861.	September 29 . . .	30.9½	.1879.	March 19 . .	20
1862.	January 20	28.7	1880.	February 14 .	22
"	April 22	25.4	1881.	" 11	25
1863.	January 16	16	"	June 10 . . .	28
1864.	" 17	18.6	1882.	January 28 .	22
1865.	March 4	24.6	"	February 22 .	22
"	" 18	31.4	1883.	" 5	26
"	April 1	21.6	"	" 8	28
"	May 12	21.6	"	" 11	21
1866.	February 25	14.7	"	" 17	21
1867.	" 15	22	1884.	" 1	21
"	March 13	22.6	"	7 *	34.6
1868.	" 18	22			
"	April 15	20.6			

* Some marks indicate eight inches more.

INSTITUTIONS.

TRADESMEN'S INDUSTRIAL INSTITUTE.

IT was in November, 1874, that the project of establishing in Pittsburg a permanent exposition of the arts, sciences, and industries of Western Pennsylvania began to assume palpable shape. For some time previous, there had been desultory discussions in offices, stores, and other public places, when the necessity for such an enterprise had been generally admitted, and when the germ of the idea that was afterwards to bear rich fruit was gradually evolved. Many of the most prominent citizens of Pittsburg and Allegheny interested themselves actively in the matter ; and the result was a public meeting, held in the Chamber of Commerce in the month above mentioned. A number of gentlemen, representing a large amount of wealth and influence, were present. Thomas S. Mitchell acted as chairman, and J. Vanote as secretary. The following named persons were elected directors : Messrs. Thomas S. Mitchell, David M. Brush, J. Vanote, James B. Lyon, Henry Lloyd, A. J. Nellis, Joshua Rhodes, R. E. Breed, and William G. Johnston. A charter had been previously prepared and framed under that section of the Wallace Act which provides for corporations without profits. The charter was approved at this meeting, and subsequently confirmed in open court. It was recorded in the recorder's office of Allegheny County.

Under this charter, Henry Lloyd was chosen president, J. Vanote secretary, and Fred A. Parke general manager. In the mean time, there had been some changes in the number and *personnel* of the directors of the board. Messrs. A. J. Nellis, Thomas S. Mitchell, Columbus Coleman, J. Vanote, James M. Johnston, James B. Lyon, Joshua Rhodes, W. G. Johnston, A. M. Brown, Henry Lloyd, R. E. Breed, J. H. Walter, and R. M. Gilleland finally constituted it.

Some half a dozen public-spirited gentlemen having pledged themselves to contribute fifty thousand dollars, the attention of the board was next directed to the matter of securing a site for the proposed institute. Several pieces of property were suggested as being suitable for the purpose. For various reasons, all these locations were rejected. Then it was that Mr. F. A. Parke, who had all along taken the deepest and most active interest in the project, suggested the neutral or disputed territory known as Smoky or Killbuck Island. The matter was, mainly through the instrumentality of Mr. Parke, brought to the notice of the city authorities of Allegheny, which ultimately resulted in a lease of the ground from the city of Allegheny to the Tradesmen's Industrial Institute for and during the term of fifteen years free of rent.

This site having been adopted, the board proceeded vigorously to prepare for the erection of suitable buildings. Mr. E. M. Butz, architect, of Allegheny, was chosen to prepare suitable plans and specifications. The contract was awarded to Messrs. Frazier Brothers at $49,750. Mr. Lloyd at this juncture resigned from the board of directors, and Mr. A. J. Nellis was elected president. The supervision of the building and other matters connected with the Institute was given in charge of an executive committee, consisting of Thomas S. Mitchell, chairman, J. Vanote, secretary, A. J. Nellis, Columbus Coleman, and James Johnston.

The building was finished in due course of time, and active preparation made for holding an exposition.

Exhibits were made by most of the prominent merchants and manufacturers of both cities, and by many from surrounding points.

Public interest, however, did not seem to keep pace with the hopes of its friends. Complications and financial embarrassment unfortunately having arisen after the first year's exhibition, it was found impossible to obtain the necessary material aid to place the enterprise on a permanent basis.

Owing to a want of proper harmony between the members of executive committee themselves, the superintendent resigned. This was followed by the temporary appointment of John E. Parke, who also resigned for similar cause. Then followed the appointment of Charles McKnight as general manager. Why the board of managers permitted this state of things to continue was a matter of surprise to the friends of the enterprise, and unsatisfactory to exhibiters and visitors.

Mr. William G. Johnston, aided by a few indomitable spirits, however, with laudable zeal, determined that the public disgrace of a failure should not rest upon the twin cities if it could possibly be avoided.

On the 7th of March, 1877, in pursuance of public notice, a meeting of the citizens was held, to take into consideration the future of the enterprise, resulting in its complete re-organization under the name and style of the Pittsburg Exposition Society, with the following officers : to wit, William G. Johnston, president ; S. S. Marvin, vice-president ; J. J. Donnell, treasurer ; W. C. Smyth, manager ; and F. A. Parke, secretary.

It was determined to hold an exposition commencing Tuesday, Sept. 4, proximo, and closing Saturday, Oct. 6 ; and steps were at once taken towards securing and preparing the building in Allegheny for that purpose. Articles of agreement were entered into with the owners of the building, the same having been sold to satisfy heirs, etc. ; and satisfactory arrangements having been made with all parties in interest, the board of managers proceeded at once to put the buildings and grounds in complete order. A new roof was put on the main building; and every thing accomplished with a view to the comfort and convenience of exhibiters and visitors. The grounds were tastefully laid out with flower-beds, gravel-walks, arbors, ornaments, etc., mainly under the immediate supervision of Mr. F. A. Parke.

The exhibition opened at the appointed time, and both the exhibits and the number of visitors were beyond the expectation of the most sanguine friend of the enterprise. In his published report, the president, W. G. Johnston, speaks with praise of the efforts of Mr. Smyth. He says of Mr. J. J. Donnell, treasurer, and Mr. J. B. Stevenson, cashier, "The earnest and intelligent labors of these gentlemen, performed with a due regard to system and order, have not hitherto been the subject of public notice ; and I fear I should greatly misrepresent their wishes should I attempt to bring them any notoriety. It is nevertheless due to them to say that the members of the board appreciate the services so ably and faithfully rendered by them." The following paragraph is quoted from the same official document : "We may here also take occasion to say, that whilst the origin of the society is mainly due to the persistent and laborious efforts of our secretary, Mr. F. A. Parke, very much also of the success which attended the late exhibition was the result of the interest he continually manifested in it. Through his exertions, mainly, the funds were obtained which were required prior to the opening of the exposition; and he was indefatigable in awakening an interest on the part of man- ufacturers in this enterprise, and in securing exhibits."

In the progress of events, there were various changes in the board of managers and executive staff. Mr. F. A. Parke was appointed general manager, and subsequently resigned to the regret of the patrons generally; Mr. Ezra P. Young assuming the *rôle* of general manager, and J. C. Patterson, secretary.

In view of the fact that the State Agricultural Society had determined to hold their annual exhibition in 1882 in Alle- gheny County, an arrangement was made with the Society to hold a joint exhibition in that year. With this object in view, the board of managers proceeded at once to the erection of new additional buildings adjoining the main building on the west, to be utilized as power-hall and agricultural machinery department.

Upon the completion of the new buildings, a new and pow- erful high-pressure engine of one hundred horse-power was placed in position for the use of exhibiters of machinery.

The exposition was continued from year to year with varied success until 1883, when, unfortunately, on the night of the 2d of October, the buildings with their entire contents were totally destroyed by fire.

The loss to the public by the disaster can hardly be esti- mated, while the intrinsic value of the material destroyed can be put down in round numbers at about three million dollars. There were many valuable relics that nothing can replace.

It was without doubt one of the largest and most destructive conflagrations that ever visited the city of Allegheny.

The officers of the exposition at the time of the fire were D. W. C. Carroll, president; Joseph T. Spear, vice-president; E. P. Young, superintendent; J. C. Patterson, secretary; and E. P. Haynes, press agent.

There was a total amount of insurance on buildings and machinery of forty thousand dollars.

WESTERN THEOLOGICAL SEMINARY.

THE history of this institution since its advent in Allegheny is somewhat peculiar, and is deserving of a more than passing notice, especially in relation to the occupancy of the common ground.

The General Assembly of the Presbyterian Church in the United States, having declared their intention of establishing, at some point in the West, a theological seminary, similar to the one at Princeton, N.J., certain citizens, land-owners in the town of Allegheny, sensible of the great advantages that would result from the location of such an institution in their midst, called a public meeting in the said town of Allegheny, Nov. 11, 1825, for the consideration of the project.

After a free interchange of opinions on the subject, a certain written instrument was drawn up and executed by the citizens there assembled, granting and transferring to the General Assembly of the Presbyterian Church all their right, title, interest and claim, to the free and entire use to a certain portion of the common ground belonging to the said town of Allegheny, bounded and described as follows: to wit, —

"Commencing at the distance of forty feet from the south line of the commons, and five perches from the west line; thence northerly parallel with said west line forty-five perches nine and one-half feet to a post; thence easterly parallel with the south line of said commons sixty-four perches to a post; thence southerly parallel with the west line of commons forty-five perches nine and one-half feet to a post, forty feet from the south line of the same; thence westerly parallel with said south line sixty-four perches to the place of beginning, containing an area of eighteen acres and thirty-seven perches, hereby granting unto the said General Assembly of the Presbyterian Church in the United States, all our right of common for the sole use and benefit of the said Western Theological Seminary, provided that the same shall be located on the ground indicated, and commenced within four years from the date of this grant, hereby warranting and defending the premises demised unto the General Assembly aforesaid, on the conditions therein stated, against us the grantors, our heirs and assigns, forever." In view of the above declaration, the Legislature, by the Act of the seventeenth day of April, A.D. 1827, and 29th March, 1844, conveyed all the right, title, and claim of the Commonwealth in the soil of the eighteen acres and thirty-seven perches, and vested the same in James Brown, John Hannen, and Hugh Davis, in trust for the free use, occupation, and benefit of the Western Theological Seminary, to be erected and established under the auspices of the General Assembly of the Presbyterian Church in the United States.

By means of the foregoing grant, and a generous subscription on the part of the citizens, the trustees of the seminary were induced — and, it appeared, with some hesitation — to pass over other advantageous offers made by citizens of other places, and establish the institution in the town of Allegheny.

Before commencing operations, a committee was employed to procure the written consent or release of all then known to possess an in-lot in whole or in part within the town, whether resident or otherwise. On the ground thus donated, and with the assurance that the assent of all who had an interest in the public ground had been obtained, the authorities of the seminary commenced, in 1825, the excavation for their building, on the crest of the elevation known as "Hogback." The building was completed in 1831, at a cost of over twenty-five thousand dollars.

Two years were spent in making these expenditures, during which time no mutterings of discontent were heard, nor were the trustees apprised that there were any serious objections to the occupancy of the eighteen acres and thirty-seven perches of the commons for the   poses desi ned.

By the Act of the Legislature approved March 12, A.D. 1783, appropriating certain lands for the liquidation of depreciated certificates, a certain tract of three thousand acres was reserved for the use of the commonwealth, opposite Fort Pitt. By a subsequent Act, approved the eleventh day of September, A.D. 1787, the Supreme Executive Council was empowered to have laid out and surveyed a town with a competent number of lots for the accommodation thereof, and to cause to be laid out and surveyed the residue of the said three thousand acres in out-lots which should not be less than one acre, nor more than ten acres, each. They were also directed to set apart within the town, for the use of the State, so much land as they might deem necessary for a court-house, jail, market-house, etc. ; and without the town, one hundred acres for a common pasture.

In pursuance of the Act, the town of Allegheny was laid out, and the lots sold at public auction in the city of Philadelphia : every purchaser of an in-lot got an out-lot in connection with it. The patent deeds describe the commons as belonging to the town.

By this Act, it is clearly defined, that, whilst the State retained the right of soil, it guaranteed the right of surface to the purchasers of the in-lots for a common pasture for cattle, etc., and they could not be legally divested of their inherent right of surface without their consent. In order to test the question, an action was brought in the District Court of Allegheny County by Samuel Carr *vs.* Mary Wallace (the real defendants being the Western Theological Seminary), to test the plaintiff's right founded upon his claim as an owner of an in-lot in the town. After a patient trial of the case, and upon the charge of the learned judge who presided, the jury rendered a verdict in favor of the defendant. To this charge, plaintiff's counsel excepted, and carried the case to the Supreme Court on a writ of error.

There is no principle better settled, none founded on more solid considerations of equity and public utility, than that which declares that if any one knowingly suffers another to purchase, and lay out money on, land under a mistaken notion of title, without making known his claim, he shall not afterwards be permitted to exercise his legal right in the premises. " To be silent when in conscience he should have spoken, he shall be debarred from speaking when conscience and public policy require him to be silent."

The judgment rendered by the court below was therefore affirmed.

In the matter of the suit brought by the Trustees of the Seminary *vs.* Samuel S. Shields, George R. Kiddle, and others, at the November term, 1843, of the District Court of Allegheny County, tried Nov. 11, 1844, for trespass, damages to the amount of twenty thousand dollars were claimed.

The syllabus of the case upon which the suit was based, may be thus briefly stated. The trustees of the seminary had commenced the excavation for a building on the plain at the base of the hill on a portion of the common ground, over which no right had been exercised by the plaintiffs, other than claiming it as being included in the grant of the 18 acres and 37 perches. The defendants resisted the occupancy of the ground, and succeeded in filling up the excavation. This action was instituted by the trustees to recover damages as above stated.

The charge of the court was rendered by the late Judge Hepburn, before whom the case was tried: it was clear, comprehensive, and exhaustive in every particular, upon which the jury rendered their verdict in favor of the plaintiffs. To the charge of the court, defendant's counsel took exceptions, and at their instance it was written and filed.

In 1844 the Western Theological Seminary was chartered.

In view of the complications surrounding the question of title, etc., a compromise was effected between the city of Allegheny and the trustees of the seminary on the 20th of December, 1850, whereby the latter relinquished to the former, by deed dated Dec. 3, 1849, all their right, title, interest, and claim to all the property embraced in the original grant, except about one acre on the corner of Ridge and Irwin Avenues, which was reserved: in consideration thereof, the city of Allegheny executed to the trustees a perpetual loan of $35,000, bearing interest at the rate of six per cent, payable semi-annually.

On the 24th of January, 1854, the buildings were entirely

consumed by fire, with a large portion of the valuable library; upon each there was an insurance of $5,000.

In 1854 there were two professors' houses erected on the ground reserved, at a cost of $5,000 each; and on the 10th of January, 1856, the new seminary building was completed, at a cost of $22,000. During this year, there were also two additional professors' houses erected, costing $5,000 each.

Beatty Hall was erected in 1859, at a cost of $15,000. In 1868 it was remodelled, at an expense of $3,586. In 1872 the library was erected, costing $25,000. Subsequently, to wit, in 1878, Beatty Hall was taken down, and Memorial Hall, a building much better adapted to the purposes designed, was erected on the site; estimated cost, $25,000.

The above buildings were erected on the north side of Ridge, between Irwin and Grant Avenues, and not on the public ground, as by some supposed.

OCCUPANCY OF THE COMMONS BY THE WESTERN UNIVERSITY AND THE WESTERN PENITENTIARY.

In the case of the Trustees of the Western University of Pennsylvania *vs.* Robinson, and others, tried in the Court of Common Pleas of Allegheny County, Sept. term, 1824, the same legal questions were involved: the parties, however, were entirely different. The Act of the 18th of February, 1819, vested in the trustees of the university the title to forty acres of the commons lying between the town and the out-lots, subject, however, to the right of pasture, granted by the Act of the 11th of September, 1787, to the inhabitants of said town.

This was an action of ejectment, brought for forty acres of the common ground. The plaintiff, relying solely upon the grant conferred by the Act of the 18th of February, 1819, made but little effort, if any, to obtain the assent or release of those having the right of pasture, etc.

In view of the manner in which the trustees of the university undertook to locate their grant, the lot-holders, deeming it highly injurious to their rights as commoners, resolved to resist the university claim, and thus determine the constitutionality of the law: upon this, the trustees of the university brought suit, as above stated.

The learned judge, before whom it was tried, charged the jury in favor of the defendants, for whom a verdict and judgment were rendered.

To this charge, the plaintiff's counsel excepted, and the case was carried to the Supreme Court, who, on a careful review of the case, affirmed the judgment of the court below, thus determining that the rights of the commoners are unextinguished and unextinguishable unless by their own consent.

The Act of the third day of March, 1818, provides for the erection of a State prison, on the principle of solitary confinement of the convicts, "the same as now is, or may hereafter be, established by law; shall be erected on the public land surrounding the town of Allegheny; appropriating sixty thousand dollars for that purpose; and that the select and common councils of the city of Pittsburg, at their first stated meeting in April next, shall, in joint meeting, appoint five competent persons as commissioners, who shall select a suitable site for a penitentiary of not less than ten acres of the public ground aforesaid, which is hereby appropriated and set apart for that purpose." In pursuance of the Act above quoted, the ground was selected, and the foundations commenced.

Although, as is stated elsewhere, the State possesses the right of soil, subject, however, to the right of common, it also possesses the inherent power to appropriate to itself for public purposes any private property, awarding just compensation, on the principle that "no man's property shall be taken or applied to public use without his consent, and just and equitable compensation being made," etc. Now, in this case, it was understood that the commoners were of the opinion that the location and erection of the prison, on the site selected, was for their interest, without further compensation; and in this aspect of the case, the buildings were erected at a large public expense; and by their silent acquiescence, they are bound as much as if they had executed a release. It appears there were ten acres selected, six acres of which were

within the walls, leaving four acres outside of the west wall ·
this was fenced in and appropriated for a burial-ground, and
pasture-lot, for the use of the prison. The enclosing of the
four acres without the wall, the citizens objected to, as not
coming within the meaning of the intention of the grant.
Meetings of the citizens were frequently called, and council
importuned in relation thereto, in order, if possible, to remedy
the same. Committees were appointed by council to confer
with the inspectors, to induce them to amicably remove the
cause of offence, without avail. At length the virtue of forbear-
ance ceased; and on the 9th of May, 1838, the borough council, by resolution, instructed the street-commissioner to remove
the nuisance within thirty days, dispose of the materials to the
best advantage, liquidate the expense of the same, and the
balance, if any remain, pay over to the prison inspectors. The
proceedings, it appears, were quietly acquiesced in by the
inspectors.

By the Act of the 18th of March, 1840, this ground was
revested in the commoners. By the language of the Act,
the commoners are highly complimented for their liberality in
granting to the State their right of common in the public
ground, for the uses of the State prison; and, further, that the
said grant embraced a larger area than now, appears to have
been necessary for the purpose: and part thereof never having been used for the object of the grant, it was therefore
ordered and decreed, that so much of the public ground on the
west side of the prison-walls, as is now, or may not hereafter
become, necessary for the use of said prison, be reverted and
restored to its original condition, as a part of the common
ground.

PITTSBURG AND ALLEGHENY ORPHAN ASYLUM.

THE nucleus around which this noble and home-like institution was erected, originated at a meeting held by a few charitable ladies of the city of Allegheny, at the house of Professor Halsey, for the purpose of forming a sewing-society.

At a subsequent meeting, at the home of Rev. Joseph Stockton, it was decided, after a free interchange of opinions, to form an asylum for orphan children, and to appoint a committee to draught a constitution for the government of the same. In order to carry out more fully this benevolent object, a meeting was held in the First Presbyterian Church of Pittsburg on the 17th of April, 1832, at which a preliminary organization was effected, William Robinson, jun., presiding, Ross Wilkins acting as secretary.

After a brief address by the presiding officer, the committee on constitution, etc., made their report, which was adopted, and a full board of managers and officers elected.

Application having been made to the Legislature, an Act was passed, incorporating "The Orphan Asylum of Pittsburg and Allegheny," approved March 20, 1834.

Under this Act, the following managers were appointed: viz., —

ELIZABETH F. DENNY.	ANNA HALSEY.
MARY ROBINSON.	MARY B. HOLMES.
ELIZABETH TIERNAN.	MARY WILKINS.
MARIAN YOUNG.	MARGARET GEORGE.
MARGARET BRUCE.	HANNAH HIGBY.
ELIZABETH P. HALSEY.	MARY A. S. BAIRD.
SUSAN K. WADE.	ISABELLA SIMPSON.

Under the provisions of the Act, every woman contributing, and paying into the treasury, the annual sum of one dollar, was entitled to all the rights and privileges of membership, so long as the contribution should be continued, and upon the payment of fifty dollars entitled to the privileges of life-membership. The grounds and improvements were exempted from taxation so long as the same should be occupied for the object designed. The Act also limited the income to eight thousand dollars annually. A supplementary Act was passed and approved the twelfth day of March, 1866, extending the annual income to twenty-five thousand dollars.

A commencement was made with three inmates in a small house rented for the purpose, situated on the bank of the Ohio river, under the care of Mrs. McKee as matron, and her daughter as teacher. The maintenance was assured by the annual subscriptions and donations, collected from time to time by the active members going from house to house throughout the two cities, together with the aid afforded by the active operations of the sewing-society.

In order to raise a fund for the purchase of a suitable site and the erection of buildings, a fair was projected, and held in September, 1833, and also one in the year following: the results from both were highly encouraging.

Through the active and forcible manner in which the ministers of some of the churches presented the objects and aims of the institution to their several congregations, collections were taken up, and encouraging amounts realized. Concerts were given by amateur musical societies of both cities, and the proceeds appropriated in aid of this benevolent enterprise. Contribution-boxes were also placed in all the steam and canal boats trading with the cities, and in the public hotels. During this period the managers experienced many trials and diffculties, and the strictest economy had to be observed in the management.

In the year 1835 the late Mrs. N. W. Campbell was elected secretary. It was during this year that the subject of purchasing suitable grounds, and the erection of the necessary buildings, was freely discussed: a considerable difference of opinions existed in regard to locality, some advocating Pittsburg, others

Allegheny, as the most suitable and convenient. The matter, however, was finally settled Aug. 16, 1836, by the offer of the late William Robinson of the fee-simple title of a lot of ground in the Second Ward, Allegheny, situated on the corner of Taylor Avenue and Webster Street.

At this time a building committee was appointed, consisting of Mrs. Robinson, Mrs. Denny, Mrs. Wade, and Mrs. Montgomery. The plans and specifications were gratuitously drawn up by the late John Chislett.

In view of the high rate of labor and building material, operations were suspended until the following spring.

By the efforts of the late Mrs. Mary Robinson, through the aid of the late Hon. Cornelius Darragh, a bill was passed by the Legislature at the session of 1838, appropriating the sum of ten thousand dollars to the institution, payable in annual instalments of one thousand dollars. In the spring of this year, ground was broken, and the building commenced, and was so far finished before the close of the year as to be occupied by a family of thirty children. During the year the sewing-society held fairs in one of the lower rooms of the building : the object was to raise means to purchase an adjoining lot for the purpose of a play-ground for the children committed to their care; and by their continued efforts, the lot was purchased, at a cost of two thousand dollars, and deeded to the institution.

The community now became thoroughly awakened, and seemed greatly interested in the cause; liberal donations and legacies were received from time to time ; and upon the return of each Thanksgiving Day, the cause of this much-needed institution was not forgotten by the benevolent.

Notwithstanding the means derived from all these sources to meet the wants of the increasing family, the arduous and thankless duty of collecting the annual subscriptions had still to be continued by the managers.

In order to relieve the managers of this onerous duty, a number of benevolent gentlemen contributed each the annual sum of ten dollars, amounting to over one thousand dollars. This amount was only realized for a few years, when it ceased altogether : still, the cause has been greatly favored by the following legacies and donations of those friendly to the enterprise, which have been safely invested, and the interest utilized for the current expenses of the institution : viz., —

LEGACIES.

Charles Brown's estate	$112,917 40
James McAuley's estate, farm and stock in Mercer County, Penn., value . . .	2,950 00
Mary O'Hara's estate, five lots in the city of Pittsburg, value	2,500 00
Samuel Hall's estate	1,000 00
Michael Allen's estate	1,719 00
Thomas Holmes's estate	500 00
Isabella McDonald's estate	500 00
Mrs. Mowry's estate	1,000 00
J. R. Weldin's estate	300 00
James Frazier's estate	500 00
Thomas Hartford's estate, contingent on the death of his widow, who died in February, 1874	39,000 00
Mr. Plummer's estate	250 00
Mrs. James Park's estate	1,000 00
James Crawford's estate (by Thomas Holmes)	1,000 00
Thomas Bakewell's estate	1,000 00
Thomas S. Clarke's estate	5,000 00
Mrs. Albree's estate	500 00
Miss Rose McCabe's estate	300 00

DONATIONS.

Elizabeth F. Denny, 100 shares Pennsylvania Railroad stock, value	5,000 00
M. J. Semple	1,000 00
Messrs. McKnight, Hogg, and Childs, " Fortification Fund "	778 90
Mrs. James Anderson, 27 shares Allegheny Bridge stock, value	675 00
John Reddick, quit-claim deed for lot on Ridge, Grant, and Lincoln Avenues, 150 and 250 feet, new site	
State Pennsylvania, by Act of the Legislature, approved April 14, A.D. 1838	10,000 00
William Robinson, jun., lot of ground, corner of Webster Street and Taylor Avenue, valued at	2,000 00
Allegheny Sewing-Society, lot of ground adjoining the one donated by William Robinson, jun., valued at	2,000 00

John Irwin . . .	2,000 00
William Thaw . .	3,000 00
A. and W. K. Nimick	3,000 00
William Holmes & Co.	2,103 00
J. M. Pennock	1,390 00
William Holmes	1,000 00
Charles Knap	1,000 00
Nathaniel Holmes	1,000 00
M. J. Semple	1,000 00
James Park, jun.	1,000 00
Economy Society	1,000 00
Mary B. Jackson	1,000 00
Isaac Jones	750 00
Thomas S. Clarke	750 00
Reuben Miller, jun.	600 00
James McAuley	500 00
John Bissell	500 00
William M. Lyon	500 00
James Caldwell . .	500 00
Others in less sums, aggregating, in 1868	9,051 00

In view of the contingency involved in the donation of $15,000, and legacy of $52,000, of the late Charles Brown, and the location on Taylor Avenue and Webster Street not proving altogether healthy, the managers resolved to commence the erection of new buildings on the corner of Ridge and Grant Avenues, on the property deeded to them by John Reddick. In 1866 it was completed and made ready for occupancy.

On the twentieth day of March, 1872, a further supplement to the Act of incorporation was enacted, changing the corporate title to the "Protestant Orphan Asylum of Pittsburg and Allegheny;" and in accordance with the supplementary Act, the following ladies were constituted a board of managers : viz., —

MRS. ELIZABETH F. DENNY,
 " MARY WILKINS
 " MARY J. HAYS,
 " H. B. LOGAN,
 " MARY H. BRUNOT,
 " J. E. CHILDS,
 " H. W. HEATH,
 " LETITIA B. HOLMES,
 " J. F. JENNINGS,

MRS. A. C. KAY,
 " WILLIAM VANKIRK,
 " LOIS J. CAMPBELL,
 " JAMES VERNER,
 " E. FAWCETT,
MISS M. H. SMITH,
 " H. S. LOTHROP,
 " E. P. ALBREE,

And such other ladies as the board may from time to time elect to fill vacancies, so that the said board shall always consist of seventeen members, ten of which shall constitute a quorum.

Nearly fifty years, from its inception to the present year, 1880, have passed away; and all who have aided in the noble and unselfish enterprise, certainly deserve the earnest commendation of the public for their labor of love and earnest work in the completion of an edifice that is an ornament to the city, and a monument to the memory of the friends of the orphan.

The revenue of the institution is steadily on the increase, and enjoys, as in the past, the confidence and esteem of every good and philanthropic citizen.

The number of orphan children cared for and trained up in the paths of rectitude have reached over two thousand, many of whom have been furnished with comfortable homes and profitable situations, who might have otherwise become inmates of reformatories and prisons.

The liberal donations and legacies received from time to time, would not in themselves have been adequate to complete the extensive improvements designed on the new location, if it had not been for the untiring zeal and indomitable energy of the late William Holmes, who by his timely advice, and liberal contributions of himself and friends, assured the early completion of the new buildings.

The late Thomas F. Dale, M.D., for many years before his death, with commendable zeal, added largely to the success of the institution, by contributing gratuitously his valuable services.

On the twelfth day of August, 1862, the much-esteemed and ever faithful secretary, Mrs. N. W. Campbell, died. From the earliest inception of the institution to the day of her death, she was its firm friend, and took an active and intelligent interest in all its movements. Her influence, energy, moral and intellectual powers, were freely and consistently exerted in its behalf. From 1835 to the day of her death she occupied the responsible position of secretary, and well did she perform the duties of the trust committed to her care. She was correct in her judgment, and an affectionate parent and friend: she leaves behind the proud record of a blameless life and a spotless name.

She has finished her work ; she has gone to her reward ; she died as she lived, a devout and humble Christian.

> " Oh for the death of those
> Who slumber in the Lord!
> Oh, be like theirs my last repose,
> Like theirs my last reward ! "

Mrs. Campbell, during her early womanhood, wrote an admirable little work, entitled, "Why I am a Christian," in which she treats her subject in a plain and logical manner, creditable alike to her Christian character and literary attainments.

Socially and religiously, good women in their lives exert an influence silent but powerful and all-pervading. The flower may wither and decay, but the fragrance is wafted onward. It is said by an eminent writer, that "the hand that rocks the cradle rules the world ;" and while we commemorate the virtues of men, both great and good, let us not forget how dear and hallowed is the name of woman. How seldom do we award the meed of praise to that gentle, thoughtful, and loving hand, so potent in forming the fabric of society, and shaping the destiny of man!

LIST OF MANAGERS, 1880.

PRESIDENT.

Mrs. Elizabeth D. McKnight   *Western Avenue, Allegheny.*

VICE-PRESIDENT.

Mrs. Annie A. Speer   .   .   . *12 Stockton Avenue, Allegheny.*

TREASURER.

Mrs. H. B. Logan   .   .   . *Lincoln Avenue, Allegheny.*

SECRETARY.

Mrs. Lois J. Campbell   *Parnassus, Penn.*

MANAGERS.

Mrs. Mary J. Hays.
" J. E. Childs.
" Letitia Holmes.
" Elizabeth Van Kirk.
" Dalzell.
" Mary A. Brunot.
" Anna C. Kay.
" Mary N. Murray.

Mrs. E. G. King.
" J. E. Hanna.
Miss H. B. Lothrop.
" Jane Holmes.
" Garrison.
" Amelia Greer.
" Eliza Forsythe.

COMMITTEES.

PURCHASING COMMITTEE.

Miss Jane Holmes.   Mrs. Letitia Holmes.

RECEIVING AND INDENTURE COMMITTEE FOR PITTSBURG.

Miss Holmes . . . . *No. 109 Penn Avenue.*
" Amelia Greer . . . . . . *No. 29 Fifth Street.*
Mrs. Mary N. Murray   *No. 102 Penn Avenue.*

RECEIVING AND INDENTURE COMMITTEE FOR ALLEGHENY.

Mrs. R. S. Hays . . . . . . *No. 6 Stockton Avenue.*
Miss S. Garrison . . . . . . *No. 218 Ridge Avenue.*
" H. B. Lothrop . . . . . . *Western Avenue.*

OFFICERS.

Mrs. Weineman, *Matron.*
Miss E. Hervey, *Assistant Matron.*
" M. Wallace, *Principal Teacher.*
Mrs. Snowden, *Primary Teacher.*
Miss McMarlen, *Hospital Nurse.*
Physician, Dr. O. L. Miller, *Montgomery Avenue.*
Consulting Physician, Dr. R. B. Mowry, *Allegheny.*

In 1874 the soldiers' orphans under the care of the State having decreased in number, it was deemed best by the authorities to remove all those who were then inmates, and place them in the schools provided by the State for their maintenance and education, many of whom were inmates of the Pittsburg and Allegheny Protestant Orphans' Asylum for a number of years, and the managers regretted the necessity of the removal. The first ones were received in January, 1865, and at one time there were one hundred and fifty on the roll ; six have died; eight have remained until their discharge, at the age of sixteen ; the whole number received being two hundred and thirty. The amount realized for each has averaged $102.50; and the whole amount received from the State, during the time they were domiciled in the institution, from 1865 to 1874, reached the sum of $78,927.45.

PITTSBURG AND ALLEGHENY HOME FOR THE FRIENDLESS.

THIS institution is located in the Fourth Ward, between Washington Street and Church Avenue. It was organized Feb. 26, 1861, by a few charitable ladies connected with the "Pittsburg and Allegheny Relief Society," who formed an association for the establishment of a home for destitute children who were excluded from admission into the "Orphan Asylum," and also to provide a temporary "home" for destitute women of reputable character. The latter feature they have ceased to carry out, and have concentrated their energies on the care of their more youthful charges.

From year to year, the managers have labored with becoming zeal and untiring energy, surmounting all the difficulties incident to an undertaking of this kind, and have now the proud satisfaction of knowing that their labors of love have not proved fruitless.

The institution is supported by aid derived from voluntary contribution, and revenue arising from an endowment fund established through the benefactions of the following charitable friends : viz., —

Morrison Underwood $5,000 00
Charles Brewer 3,000 00
James McAuley,[1] 50 shares People's National Bank
    stock, par value 5,000 00

[1] Twenty shares of this stock to be sold, and the proceeds to be used in the construction of the contemplated buildings, the dividends arising from thirty shares for the support of the inmates.

Richard Glyde	1,000 00
James Caldwell	1,000 00
Samuel Gordon	800 00
Miss Helen Wilson	1,000 00
Lippincott & Bakewell	500 00

These liberal donations, with several others of less amount, have been safely invested, and, with the accrued interest on the same, make the endowment fund about eighteen thousand dollars.

The value of the buildings and grounds is estimated at forty thousand dollars, and has a frontage of about one hundred and fifty feet on Washington Street, extending in depth southerly to Church Avenue about three hundred and ten feet, comprising what was formerly the homesteads of Henry Forsyth and Samuel Baily, both deceased. It is eligibly located, having a capacity for the accommodation of from one hundred and twenty-five to one hundred and thirty children. It is clear of debt, and the managers have abundant cause to be proud of the good resulting from their truly philanthropic work; and it is to be hoped that the noble undertaking, with its bright record of care for the unfortunate little ones, will stimulate the philanthropists to renewed efforts, in placing the institution upon a more substantial basis.

Leaving out of view the Christian and humanitarian aspect of the case, would not a more generous support and encouragement be a wise and economical measure? Many of these unfortunates, who have been brought within the happy influence of the " Home," are now respected members of society, who otherwise might be the occupants of a criminal's cell or a pauper's grave.

There are no trusts committed to our care so important and responsible as the proper training of the young: it requires more wisdom, sagacity, and grace than all the pretentious and various worldly schemes which occupy the time and intellect of our Christian people.

In 1871 the following subscriptions were effected, in order to consummate the purchase of the adjoining property, belonging to Henry Forsyth: viz., —

Mrs. E. F. Denny	$1,000 00	D. M. Smith	$500 00
Alexander Nimick	1,000 00	James Laughlin . . .	500 00
John Holmes .	1,000 00	Spang, Chalfaut, & Co.	500 00
Richard Hays .	1,000 00	Mrs. William A. Reed .	500 00
William Holmes	1,000 00	Hostetter & Smith .	250 00
William Thaw .	1,000 00	J. K. Moorhead . .	200 00
Charles Clark .	1,000 00	James Irwin . . .	100 00
A. Carnegie . .	1,000 00	William B. Holmes	100 00
Lyon Shorb & Co. .	1,000 00	Jane Holmes .	100 00
Estate F. G. Bailey	892 50	James Park, jun.	100 00
John Jackson	500 00	William M. Hersh	100 00
Mrs. E. Mowry .	500 00	Robert Beer	100 00
James P. Hanna	500 00	Joseph Horne	100 00
John Moorhead .	500 00	Thomas M. Howe	100 00
George Black . .	500 00	Thompson Bell	100 00
Isaac Jones . .	500 00	William P. Weyman	100 00
William Morrison	500 00	Rees, Graff, & Co.	100 00
Charles Arbuthnot .	500 00	William Walker	50 00
C. G. Hussey .	50 00	Samuel McKee .	50 00
Jacob Painter	100 00		
A. D. Smith .	500 00	Total	$18,192 50

The nineteenth annual report, from June 1, 1879, to June 1, 1880, verified by the following statement of Mrs. Belle D. Foster, treasurer, of the receipts and expenditures during the period, will exhibit the condition of the treasury: viz., —

DR.

To balance in treasury, including amount received from former treasurer	$940 04
To amount received for boarding . .	1,691 82
" " " from collections .	2,880 10
" " " " donations .	565 10
" " " " ground-rent . .	93 50
" " " " dividend bank-stock	300 00
" " " " guardians of the poor .	156 00
" " " " fees and fines .	29 75
" " " " proceeds of fair . .	760 81
" " " " interest on endowment fund	150 00
" " " " endowment fund to meet contingencies .	646 83
	$8,213 95

CR.

By amount paid salaries	$1,607	42
" " " milk	1,071	60
" " " bread	1,101	70
" " " groceries .	546	31
" " " repairs	588	11
" " " drugs and medicines	53	83
" " " gas and coal .	237	23
" " " shoes and mending	259	92
" " " dry-goods	430	88
" " " marketing	729	16
" " " insurance	188	56
" " " stationery	27	84
" " " miscellaneous	101	82
Balance in treasury	1,269	57
Total.	$8,213	95

OFFICERS AND MANAGERS.

OFFICERS.

Mrs. ROBERT MCKNIGHT, *President.*
 "   H. P. SCHWARTZ, *Vice-President.*
 "   BELLE D. FOSTER, *Treasurer.*
 "   GEORGE A. KELLY, *Secretary.*

MANAGERS.

Mrs. C. J. AGNEW.
 "   E. M. BYERS.
 "   E. E. BREADING.
 "   CHARLES COLE.
 "   DR. DALE.
 "   J. E. B. DALZELL.
 "   WILLIAM H. EWING.
 "   G. FOLLANSBEE.
 "   RICHARD HAYS.
 "   ALBERT HORNE.

Mrs. REV. JOSEPH KING.
 "   JAMES LAUGHLIN.
 "   JAMES B. MCFADDEN.
 "   HENRY PHIPPS.
 "   WILLIAM B. RHOADES.
 "   C. B. SHEA.
Miss MARY NIMICK.
 "   MARY MCKEE.
 "   LYDIA HAYS.
 "   MARY SCHWARTZ.

HOME FOR THE CARE AND MAINTENANCE OF THE POOR OF THE CITY OF ALLEGHENY.

IN pursuance of the provisions of a special Act of the Legislature approved April 9, 1844, John Morrison, Henry Hannen, Robert S. Cassatt, Thomas Barnett, L. O. Reynolds, E. W. Stephens, Thomas Farly, Thomas H. Stewart, and William Tate were appointed commissioners to select and purchase a site within ten miles of the city, for the purpose of erecting suitable buildings for the care and employment of the indigent of the city. On the 20th of September, 1844, the commissioners concluded to purchase the farm of John Sample, consisting of 166 acres, situated in the valley of Girty's Run in Shaler township; the distance from the Diamond Squares being a little over two miles. The contract for the erection of the building was awarded to Messrs. Moore & Walker: it was completed, and made ready for the reception of inmates, late in the winter of 1845. Cost of the farm, $12,000. Contract for the buildings, $4,500.

This location not proving suitable for the object contemplated, a subsequent Act was passed by the Legislature, approved April 12, 1867, authorizing the sale of the 166 acres in convenient sized building-lots, the proceeds of the sale to be appropriated to the purchase of another more suitable location, and the erection thereon of buildings better adapted for the object sought. In the following June, the farm was laid out in lots; and the first public sale was held on the 4th of September, 1867, and the second and last on the 11th August, 1875.

The total amount realized from these sales was $292,396.72, which was appropriated to the purchase of a new site, and erection of the necessary buildings.

On the tenth day of March, 1871, the present location at Claremont in O'Hara township, containing ninety-six (96) acres, was purchased from James T. Beatty at $600 per acre, payable, twenty-five per cent in cash, and the balance in city bonds having twenty years to run.

Peter Beard, Thomas Barnett, and Thomas H. Stewart, the first Board of Directors, were elected Jan. 14, 1845. As will be observed, the board consisted of three members elected triennially, until the passage of the Act of Assembly approved April 16, 1870, in which the number was changed, to consist of one member from each ward of the city, to be chosen for a term of two years, by the citizens at the general city election. It was ordered that the persons elected meet for organization on the first Monday of February ensuing the election, and hold their regular monthly sessions at their office in Municipal Hall on the first Friday of each month.

The work of laying the foundations of the new buildings at Claremont was commenced in June, 1871, and was entirely completed in December, 1873. It was, however, occupied July 29, 1873, although but partially finished. The building, when completed, together with the amount paid for the land, cost in round numbers $230,000. The main structure is 286 feet in front, by 46 feet in depth, with a corridor 10 feet wide, extending the whole length of the building. The east and west wings each extend back from the main building 150 feet in depth by 50 feet wide, the whole being three stories high. The steward's department is connected with the centre of the main building, and is 52 feet in depth by 35 feet wide, and is supplied with corridors in each story 12 feet wide, and provided with separate stairways leading to each. In this department, there are twelve commodious rooms, each 16 by 20 feet. In the main building, in the department assigned to females, there are three sitting-rooms, each 15 by 20 feet; thirty-nine dormitories, 8 feet by 15 feet. The wing connected with this department has also thirty-one family-rooms, each 15 by 21 feet; twelve large dormitories with all the necessary modern improvements, such as wash-rooms, bath-rooms, water-closets, ventilators, etc. The other wing, which is assigned to the males, is substantially the same, except the sitting-rooms, which are larger. The two rooms occupied by the medical director are 15 feet by 18 feet, adjoining each other, and reached from the outside of the main building by a hall.

The attic over the front building is finished throughout, and lighted by the ordinary dormer-windows. In the central building, there is a dining-room with two pantries, and a hall leading into the culinary department between them.

The chapel is situated over the dining-room, the laundry and bake-house in the rear of the kitchen. The department for the insane is situated over the laundry and bake-house, in the rear of the chapel, and is approached by a hall seven feet wide. All these apartments are spacious, and finished in the most approved manner. The insane-department contains twenty-six rooms, with separate water-closets, bath-rooms, and dining-rooms for each sex, and elevators leading from the kitchen to each. The entire building is heated with steam by direct and indirect radiation: it is also supplied with pure water forced from the Allegheny River to an elevation in the rear of the buildings. It is also lighted throughout with gas made on the ground. The heights of the several stories, commencing with the first floor, are respectively 13, 12, and 11 feet, and each floor is reached by seven separate stairways, affording an excellent mode of egress in case of fires.

This large, well-planned, and magnificent structure is located on an elevated plateau on the north bank of the Allegheny River, about two hundred feet from the Western Pennsylvania Railroad, overlooking the river, and commanding a beautiful view of the surrounding country. It is generally conceded that there are but few, if any, of this class of institutions that equal the Allegheny Home, in point of beauty of location, design, and appointments. It is intended to accommodate from six to eight hundred inmates.

The total expenditure in 1879 for maintenance was net $35,696.01. Out of this sum, $8,671.96 were expended for outside relief.

A LIST OF DIRECTORS AND OFFICERS OF THE ALLEGHENY POOR-BOARD,

FROM ITS FIRST ORGANIZATION IN 1844 TO 1880, CAREFULLY COMPILED FROM THE MINUTES OF THE BOARD, AND ARRANGED IN THE ORDER OF SUCCESSION.

DIRECTORS ELECTED BY GENERAL TICKET.

THOMAS H. STEWART.	JAMES L. GRAHAM.	JAMES SLOSS.
PETER BEARD.	THOMAS FARLY.	J. V. HOAG.
THOMAS BARNETT.	D. BOISOL.	JOHN N. BARR.
HENRY HANNEN, M.D.	ANDREW DAVIDSON.	GEORGE GERST.
JACOB GEYER.	JAMES P. FLEMING.	E. GLEASON.
WILLIAM B. COPELAND.	J. G. COFFIN.	WILLIAM MURDOCK.
ROBERT DAVIS.	ROBERT ASHWORTH.	JOHN BROWN, JUN.
A. CAMERON.		

In pursuance of the provisions of a supplementary Act, approved April 16, 1870, the number of directors was changed from three members to one member from each ward, to be chosen annually.

First Ward.—THOMAS SCANDRETT, J. F. NEELY, THOMAS PATTERSON, JOSEPH WASHINGTON.

Second Ward.—JOHN BROWN, JUN., GEORGE BOTHWELL, ABRAHAM DICKSON, JAMES E. STRICKLER.

Third Ward.—GEORGE GERST, WILLIAM WALKER.

Fourth Ward.—JOHN DEAN, LEONARD WALTER, SEN., JOSEPH LAUTNER.

Fifth Ward.—GEORGE PARKINS, ISAAC A. REED, W. W. SPEER, JAMES R. REED, J. B. JOHNSTON, M.D.

Sixth Ward.—JOHN SPEER, JAMES LOWRIE, HENRY FAULKNER, WILLIAM F. TRIMBLE.

Seventh Ward.—MARTIN LEY, VALENTINE BAKER.

Eighth Ward.—ERNEST EGGERS, JOHN H. MORRISON, DAVID F. JACKSON, ALONZO M. YOUNG.

Ninth Ward. — E. N. Riggs, M.D., Cyrus Hutchison, George Wittmer, David H. McCarthy.

Tenth Ward. — T. F. Grubbs, John Q. Workman, Charles B. Welte.

Eleventh Ward. — Thomas B. Kerr, Henry H. Phillips.

Twelfth Ward. — Henry Snaman, Peter Meinninger.

Thirteenth Ward. — This ward elects no member. It is represented by the chairman of the farm committee of councils, as provided for by law.

PRESIDENTS OF THE BOARD.

Jacob Geyer.	George Gerst.	A. Dickson.
A. Davidson.	J. H. Morrison.	H. H. Phillips.
James Sloss.	J. F. Neely.	

SECRETARIES OF THE BOARD.

Wm. B. Copeland.	James P. Fleming.	E. N. Riggs, M.D.
Henry Hannen, M.D.	Robert Ashworth.	A. Dickson.
A. Cameron.	John Dean.	J. B. Johnston, M.D.
James L. Graham.		

STEWARDS.

A. Montgomery.	Andrew Barclay.	D. T. Johnston.
William Martin.	John S. Gould.	T. F. Grubbs.
John Silliman.		

AGENT OF OUT-DOOR RELIEF.

John H. Stewart.

CLERKS.

Charles Kelly.	M. McGonnigle.	R. D. McGonnigle.

CHAPLAINS.

Rev. Mr. Cleveland.	Rev. A. Williams.	Rev. William Collier.

MEDICAL DIRECTORS.

Dr. R. B. Mowry.	Dr. James Scroggs	Dr. John Hamilton.
Dr. T. H. Elliott.	Dr. A. Perchment.	Dr. B. B. Smith.
Dr. James B. Herron.	Dr. H. F. Campbell.	Dr. R. H. Gilliford.
Dr. M. M. Knox.	Dr. W. V. Marcus.	Dr. C. H. Voight.

INSANE-DEPARTMENT.

SUPERINTENDENTS.

J. B. Graham.	R. Crane.	R. Whittaker.	R. B. Crawford.

MATRONS.

Mrs. E. J. KARNS.   Mrs. M. J. KELLOGG.

SOLICITORS.

STEPHEN GEYER and WILLIAM B. RODGERS.

TREASURER.

DAVID MACFERRON.

CHAIRMEN OF FARM COMMITTEE OF COUNCILS.

Hon. HUGH McNEIL.   ROBERT WILSON.   JOHN A. BECK.
PETER WALTER, JUN.   JOHN SEILING.

These gentlemen, as members of common council by virtue of their appointment as chairmen of the farm committee. are also members of the board.

PENNSYLVANIA REFORM SCHOOL.

THE necessity for the removal of this institution (its re-organization and the causes which led to it), from its location in the Ninth Ward of the city of Allegheny, to its present location in Washington County, Penn., may be better comprehended in the following brief history of the project, from its incipiency to its final consummation, in purchase of a farm in Cecil township, Washington County, and the adoption of what is termed the family system.

The steadily increasing number of the inmates rendered it absolutely necessary that some provision should be speedily adopted for their accommodation.

The building was originally intended to accommodate less than two hundred children, yet the number had increased to over three hundred.

As early as 1870 the attention of the Board of Managers was particularly directed to the matter, and it was from that time forward the subject of frequent and anxious discussion.

The original plan of the building did not admit of extension; and it was obvious, that, even with expensive alterations, it would be insufficient for the males, while a new building would have to be erected for the accommodation of the females.

A careful estimation of the cost of the necessary alterations and the construction of new building exceeded the sum of two hundred thousand dollars.

During the time of the consideration of the subject, the location of the institution was included in the corporate limits of the city of Allegheny.

The constantly increasing population, and consequent erec-

tion of dwellings, rolling-mills, and other factories in close proximity to the institution, rendered it an unsuitable site for a
reformatory.

In this new view of the question, the Board of Managers
hesitated to ask for a large appropriation from the State, for the
erection of new buildings, notwithstanding the crowded condition of the institution was seriously retarding its usefulness.

General attention in the mean time having been directed to
the subject, the public sentiment clearly sanctioned the removal
of the institution to a county site.

Successive grand juries recommended it because of the
unsuitable nature of its location and buildings, the extensive
alterations and additions that would be necessary to adapt them
to the requirement of the institution, and its unfavorable position in the midst of a thronged neighborhood and close proximity to rolling-mills, etc.

The public press also pointed triumphantly to the success
attending county schools in other States, especially to the Ohio
State Reform School, as conclusive evidence of the superiority
of the family over the congregate system, and the advantage of
a farm-life for the class of children usually received in reformatories.

The counties also urged it as an effective means of lessening
expenses; and philanthropists, and friends of the institution generally, advocated it as in all respects calculated to promote the
moral welfare and physical health of the inmates, and render
more effective the efforts for their reformation.

There was no definite action taken by the Board of Managers,
until a special committee of the Senate visited the institution,
who, in their report to the Legislature, recommended its
removal to a farm site.

It was not till then, with the approval of the Board of Public
Charities, and in pursuance of an Act of the Legislature, the
first tangible steps were taken, which resulted in the purchase
of the farm of five hundred and two acres in Cecil township,
Washington County, and subsequent erection of new buildings
suitable for the farm and family organization.

In the re-organization of the institution on the plan familiarly known as the family system, which has been so eminently popular and successful in Ohio and other States, the Board of Managers believe they recognized, and acted in accordance with, natural laws.

The family is a divine institution, and is so arranged by the Creator, that every human being is influenced more for good by it than by any other thing in social life. This influence is indefinable, and pervades the whole social organization : it appeals to our self-respect, and stimulates our hopes by opening to our view fair prospects in life. The nearer we approach to the home and family circle, the greater will be the influence for good felt in the hearts and lives of each individual member of society.

Impressed with these views, the Board of Managers determined, in the erection of the new buildings, to ignore stone walls, bolts and bars, and all other prison appliances, and establish, in the true meaning of the term, a school for the proper training and education of wayward and neglected children, so that the pupils can go out into the world fully educated for its duties and responsibilities, with no brand attached to their names, and be received with as much trust and confidence as any of those who go out from the public schools.

In accordance with this view, the inmates are divided into families of fifty each, occupying separate buildings, and governed by separate officers. In its local management, each family is distinct from the others, but, nevertheless, are united in government under one central head.

Each family building has a separate dormitory, schoolroom, dining-room, wash-room, and playground.

The government in all respects is parental, or such as would be adopted in any well-disciplined home : coercion is not to be resorted to until all moral means have failed.

This system evidently affords the best facilities for classification and individualization. Children as well as adults are seldom reformed in masses : reformation is mostly effected by well-directed effort acting upon the individual heart.

In carrying out the division of the inmates into families, the policy adopted does not depend so much upon age or character as upon adaptation ; although the very small children are placed in a family by themselves. Special qualifications of officers in charge of the families are considered, as well as the peculiar habits and disposition of the child. Those that are more difficult to manage are placed in small families in charge of officers, who, by tact and executive ability, are enabled to exert the most effective influence. Care, however, is taken to limit this class of children in any one family. To associate together the incorrigible and vicious, and designate them as a dishonored class, give power to evil influence, and afford facilities for combination in concocting wickedness, rendering reformation almost hopeless.

In order to afford a better opportunity for determining character and disposition, children, when first admitted to the institution, are placed in one of the families occupying the main building, under the more direct observation of the superintendent, there to remain until a sufficient knowledge is obtained of them ; and from thence they are placed in the family where the association and discipline are adapted to exert the best influence.

By this means, the individual is never lost sight of in the crowd : his case is separately and carefully considered, and measures adopted to remedy defects in his character or previous training.

To check the young in the commencement of their criminal course, is the primary object of the institution. The necessity of an institution of this character grows out of the fact that the ordinary checks of society, including our well-adjusted system of education, have been found inadequate for the purpose.

The youthful offender must be removed from the community and the sphere where he moves, only to corrupt and be corrupted, and placed where he will be subject to a new life and training, and his future demoralization carefully guarded against, where reliance on self is more externally sustained, and less dependent on its own self-determining power.

Remove from the schoolroom and out of the neighborhood the presiding genius of evil, the radiating point of demoralization, remove from the community these ulcers, and having lost their centre, the cause of irritation taken away, soon the surrounding parts will begin to feel a healthy action.

To these outcasts of society, the doors of the institution open, and rescue him from a prison, and associations with others probably worse than himself, and save him from utter hopelessness and ruin, introducing him to new scenes, unfolding to him a new life, and inspiring him with higher notions and more exalted aspirations.

By a few years' detention in the institution of the youthful offender, even if his reformation proves incomplete, society will doubtless be the gainer. Removed from temptations, and his proneness to do evil curbed, his small villanies stopped, and higher crime prevented, even if he should relapse after release, still something is gained. ·

In a financial point of view, it is infinitely better to keep all such in a reformatory during their natural lives, than leave them unrestrained to prey upon the community. It is less expensive to thus control them than to suffer them to run at large. To follow them in their career of crime, and take note of the amount of property they destroy, would afford abundant proof of this.

The worst of this class may be rescued. A Magdalen was reformed, and a thief on the cross saved. According to the records, fully three-fourths of the children committed to the institution since its opening have become respectable and useful members of society. Although the work is arduous, and requires constant and unremitting care, it is, nevertheless, a grand and noble charity. The price of a human being may be inferred by what it costs to reclaim him. Brought into the world in corruption, nurtured in crime, associated with vice, with a hardened conscience and benighted mind, in this institution he is brought to realize the comforts of a quiet home, wholesome food, healthful and invigorating exercise, and harmless amusement; while to his ill-directed mind is unfolded the beneficial working of the Golden Rule, " Do to others as you would have them do unto you ;" and induced to look upon God as his Father, and heaven as his ultimate home.

Here he is instructed in the elementary principles of science, and such habits sought to be induced as will tend to make him an honest and useful member of society. When sufficiently educated, and character established for good, he is placed out of the institution in a position where he may acquire a knowledge of some good trade or employment.

Even then the guardianship of the institution does not forsake him : it follows him, and spreads over him the wings of its protection, counsels, and care, until he is able to maintain the struggles of the new life he has commenced.   If he falls, it still cares for him, and receives him back into the ark of his safety, and again essays to restore him to an honest life.

These children are scattered over the entire continent, from the Atlantic to the Pacific : they are found engaged in various reputable employments, some of them are happy heads of families, who train up their little ones as they were trained in the Reform School.

By patient and persevering industry, some have become successful in acquiring a moderate share of this world's goods; while others, pressed down by anxious cares, have not been so fortunate, yet in all their trials they still retain their integrity.

It is gratifying to observe the marked change that has been effected in a few short weeks in the appearance, habits, and sometimes even in the character, of the child committed to the care of the institution ; and it is difficult to recognize in the bright-eyed child, clothed in the neat uniform of the school, the demoralized little wretch brought from the streets and slums of the cities, by the police, whose general ragged appearance bore ample testimony of neglect, and inclination to vagrancy and crime.   Relieved of his rags, and clad in clean clothes, he rises from wretchedness and shame, which even to his clouded perceptions were a grievous burden, and feels and realizes the current of a new life.

The mild and firm discipline of a few weeks has brought a wonderful change, under a judicious continuance of which the child may become corrigible, and make a good and useful citizen.

It must be borne in mind, that the Reform School is not simply a charitable institution, notwithstanding the absence of stone walls, bolts and bars, and the inauguration of a mild paternal discipline, to soften the asperities of confinement, by impressing upon the mind of the children that it is a home rather than a prison; the fact remains, that it is correctional a penal institution, as much connected with the administration of criminal law as any of our prisons. The Commonwealth, therefore, recognizes the Reform School as one of her penal institutions, and makes provision for its support as an imperative public necessity on the grounds that it is better to be taxed for the virtue of the child than to pay for the vices of the man.

The institution is in no sense sectarian. All religious denominations are recognized by its managers as having an equal right, through their teachers and ministers, to impart religious instruction to the inmates. The object of the managers has always been to invite the services of ministers of all denominations, thus rendering the pulpit free to all of whatever creed.

The invariable practice is to permit ministers of any religious belief to visit the inmates at any time during health or sickness, to administer *private* religious instruction without the presence or interference of the officers of the institution; and no restraint is permitted to be placed upon either minister or child, which could in the least interfere with *free* and *private* communication between them.

In cases of sickness, the parent, guardian, or friends are immediately summoned, who, in serious cases, remain in the institution, assisting in the care of the patient.

PITTSBURG ALMSHOUSE.

THE history of this institution may be briefly stated thus: Prior to the death of the late Col. James O'Hara, which occurred in 1819, the overseers of the poor of the city of Pittsburg were in negotiation with him for the purchase of out-lot No. 256, containing ten acres, situated on the north side of Ohio Lane, in the Reserve Tract opposite Pittsburg, for the purpose of erecting thereon suitable buildings for the maintenance of the poor of said city. The sale was consummated by his executors; the deed, bearing date Feb. 10, 1821, recorded in Allegheny County, in vol. xxviii. p. 145; consideration, $750. This lot was patented, *inter alia*, to John Park in 1789, and conveyed by him to James O'Hara in 1796.

During 1821 and 1822 the overseers erected a large, two-story frame-building about three hundred feet from the line of Ohio Lane, midway from east to west, of sufficient dimensions to meet the present as well as the future wants. On the westerly part of the lot, the cemetery was located.

The buildings were finished in the latter part of 1822, and the inmates removed from their then location on the west side of Virgin Alley, near the corner of Wood Street, Pittsburg, to the new quarters prepared for them. Here the poor were maintained and cared for until the latter part of 1848, when they were again removed to a new home provided for them on the south side of the Monongahela River, in Mifflin township; the poor-authorities having purchased fifty acres with improvements in 1850, and subsequently one hundred acres adjoining, upon which they erected extensive and costly brick buildings, the corner-stone of which was laid in the latter part of 1850, and completed Jan. 9, 1852, and occupied immediately.

The institution was chartered by Act of the General Assembly, approved in 1847, under the name of the "Guardians for the Relief and Employment of the Poor of the City of Pittsburg," and the board organized in February of the following year. Immediately after the removal, the land in Allegheny was laid out in building-lots, and sold, and the old buildings demolished.

The remains of the dead were disinterred, and removed to Mount Union Cemetery. Many of the graves were found empty, clearly indicating that the bodies had been removed, doubtless for scientific purposes.

FIFTH WARD PUBLIC SCHOOLS.

By the Act of the Legislature approved March 12, 1867, the borough of Manchester was annexed to the city of Allegheny.

By an ordinance of the city councils passed subsequently, to wit, on the 9th of May, enlarging what was then the boundaries of the borough, so as to embrace the portions of the First and Second Wards lying between Fulton Street and Allegheny Avenue, the whole was divided into two wards. A line running north and south through the centre of Allegheny Avenue, and east and west through the centre of Locust Street to the Ohio River, marked the division between them. All the territory lying south of this line was designated the Fifth Ward; and all north, the Sixth Ward.

In consequence of this division, the greater portion of the school property belonging to the Manchester district fell into the Sixth Ward.

The number of children of school age in the Fifth Ward at the time was nearly six hundred; whilst the only accommodation for this large number was the two-story brick building, 35 by 63 feet, situate on the corner of Chartiers and Fayette Streets.

This building, by no means prepossessing in appearance, contained but four rooms, poorly furnished, and partitioned with unpainted boards, presented a striking contrast to the one afterwards erected in the ward.

There were but two legally authorized school directors residing within the limits of the ward at the time of its organization, — N. McClinton, a member of the Manchester board, and Samuel I. Kay of the Second Ward board.

In accordance with the instructions of the State Superintendent, these gentlemen met on the fourth day of October, 1867, and appointed four additional members, viz., Joseph Walton, Byron Painter, Alexander Patterson, and C. B. Shea; thus constituting a full board for the transaction of business.

On the second day of November following, the first complete organization was effected. No effort was made towards the purchase of real estate and the erection of suitable buildings until after the election of school directors, and organization of the board, Jan. 20, 1868.

The earliest measure adopted by the newly elected board was the appointment of Messrs. Robert Lea, Joseph Walton, and John E. Parke, a committee to confer with a similar committee from the First, Second, and Sixth Wards, in regard to an equitable adjustment of the school property.

As a result of this conference, the Fifth Ward retained the building on the corner of Chartiers and Fayette Streets at a valuation of $4,000, and received from the First Ward, $5,000, in three annual instalments of $1,666.66 each; from the Second Ward, $5,200, in four annual instalments of $1,300 each; and from the Sixth Ward, $7,000, payable in three annual instalments of $2,333.33 each, all the above payments without interest.

As a step towards securing better school accommodations, which were felt to be imperatively demanded, a site was purchased in March, 1868, on the corner of Fulton and Page Streets, containing an area of 132 feet on Fulton, and 224½ feet on Page.

Plans and specifications having been adopted, Messrs. Trimble and McIntyre were awarded the contract. On the first day of May, 1868, ground was broken; and on the first Monday of September in the following year, the entire structure was completed, and ready for occupancy.

The building, a substantial brick, with all the modern appliances then in vogue, is 134 feet in front on Page Street, by 68 feet on Fulton Street, three stories in height, and is divided into eighteen rooms, having on the third story a large and commodious auditorium 35 by 68 feet, with a gallery on each side.

Nearly all the schoolrooms are provided with ample cloak-rooms.

The building is heated by low-pressure steam, and lighted throughout with gas ; the surroundings paved with brick, and neatly enclosed on the Fulton and Page Streets fronts by an iron fence.

The cost of the building is $47,786.39; improvements, $19,-460.01 ; eleven lots of ground, $10,400; in all, $77,646.40.

During the construction of the new building, the large increase of the number of applicants for admission made it necessary to make other arrangements for the accommodation of the pupils than that afforded by the building on the corner of Chartiers and Fayette Streets. Union Hall, on the corner of Beaver Avenue and Sheffield Street, was, therefore, leased and occupied as a grammar school.

On the evening of the 2d of September, 1869, the new school-house was formally dedicated, being complete in all its arrangements, and lighted up throughout with gas, for the inspection of the citizens. Its appearance seemed to meet the approval of every one present. After all parts of the building had been visited, a meeting was organized in the auditorium, by calling the late Rev. J. B. Clarke to officiate as chairman. The report of the board was then read, and a number of congratulatory addresses delivered, after which a vote of thanks was unanimously tendered to the board of directors for their zeal and success in providing a school-building so ample in dimensions, and so well adapted to its educational wants. Schools were opened on the 6th of September following, with a total enrolment of six hundred and twelve pupils. On the evening of the 21st of December, a disastrous fire occurred, which, for a time, threatened to lay the entire structure in ashes. The second and third stories were entirely destroyed, nothing remaining except the bare walls. The first story suffered considerably from the water used in extinguishing the flames.

The estimated loss, thirty thousand dollars, was fully covered by insurance. The fire was evidently the result of a want of proper care in the construction of the smoke-flues: it originated near the roof, where the flue was carried over a window. Prompt measures were at once adopted to repair the damage. The contract was awarded to Messrs. William Boyd & Son.

In the mean time, the grammar and medium schools occupied the building on the corner of Fayette and Chartiers Streets; the high school, Union Hall; while the little folks conned over their primary lessons in the building on Market Street, near Greenwood, formerly used as the M. E. Church. In August, 1870, the building was again completed, and in the following month re-occupied.

On the morning following the fire, large crowds assembled to view the ruins. It was deemed unsafe to permit persons within or near the building; and every effort was made by the directors to induce the people to keep away, but without effect. A storm of wind and rain occurring at the time, a rush was made towards the ruins in order to avoid the storm as much as possible. At this moment the part of the front wall between the towers was blown over, seriously injuring two children of Mr. Jekel of the Fifth Ward, one of whom subsequently died from the effects of the injury received.

An incident connected with the burning of the building is related by one of the directors, which, had it not been for the timely warning given, might have resulted in a loss of life. In the evening, shortly after the fire had commenced, it was deemed absolutely necessary to keep the outside doors closed, in order to shut off the draught: otherwise the fierce wind rushed with terrible fury through the halls and stairways, adding additional fierceness to the mad flames.

A number of youths had assembled in the vestibule of the bell-tower: the director referred to, remonstrated with them, and quietly asked them to leave. They at first felt disposed to disobey; but when told of the danger from the falling of the bell, which might occur at any moment, they acquiesced, and had scarcely left, when down it came, carrying every thing in its course to the basement.

The Act of the Legislature approved March 12, A.D. 1867, consolidating the borough of Manchester with the city of Allegheny, and the ordinance passed by councils of the said city,

May 9, A.D. 1867, made no provision for the adjudication of the school property when the school district in said borough and in the old wards of the city were divided in arranging the several wards of said city after the passage of said Act and ordinance aforesaid.

In view of which, the Legislature, upon application, passed an Act approved March 18, A.D. 1869, setting forth the manner of making a division: to wit, "If the school directors in the several wards cannot agree in arriving at an equitable division of the school property, in that case application shall be made to the Court of Common Pleas of Allegheny County, who shall determine whether any such new ward has its proper and equitable proportion of the school property belonging to the old ward or wards out of which such new ward was created under the Act of Assembly and ordinance of the city "

By the Act of the General Assembly of the Commonwealth, approved March 6, A.D. 1868 (*vide* P. Laws, p. 278), the school directors of the ward were empowered to borrow the sum of $30,000, payable within ten years from the passage of the Act, at a rate of interest not exceeding 8 per cent. This amount not proving adequate to the object contemplated, a supplementary Act was passed, approved Feb. 10, A.D. 1869 (*vide* P. Laws, p. 134), authorizing the directors to borrow the additional sum of $30,000, payable within twenty years from the passage of the Act, at a rate of interest not exceeding 8 per cent. In 1872 the bonded indebtedness had reached its highest point, the amount outstanding at the time being $58,240.40. Since then it has been steadily decreased; the amount outstanding on the 1st of February, 1881, being $16,700.

In 1873, June 17, the school property situate on the corner of Chartiers and Fayette Streets was disposed of to Messrs. Wilson for $5,000, payable in six annual instalments, with interest added at the rate of 8 per cent.

HISTORY OF THE ALLEGHENY
OBSERVATORY

HISTORY OF THE ALLEGHENY OBSERVATORY.

S. P. LANGLEY, DIRECTOR.

(Prepared at the Request of Mr. Parke.)

THIS institution was founded in 1860 by the subscriptions of citizens, induced to promote the undertaking by the exertions of Mr. L. Bradley, to whom the inception of public interest in the plan was due. A building was erected, and a large equatorial telescope procured, when pecuniary difficulties arose to hinder immediate farther progress. In 1866 the donation of a large sum by William Thaw, Esq., of Pittsburg, with aid from others, freed the Observatory from debt, and furnished means for a partial endowment, whose income should supply its more urgent future current needs. At the same time the original contributors were induced, at the solicitation of Dr. G. Woods, to convey their title in the property to the trustees of the Western University of Pennsylvania, conditionally upon this property being restricted to the uses of the Observatory, and on the appointment and maintenance of an observer. In consequence of this change, the trustees, in 1867, invited Professor S. P. Langley to assume the office of director; but it was not until 1869 that the equipment was in such a state of forwardness as to permit systematic observation, such as has since been uninterruptedly maintained. It is proper to state, that the considerable means for this equipment, procured by Professor Langley, were also due chiefly to the generous donor whose name has just been mentioned.

The Observatory is situated on the high ground just north of the most populous part of the city of Allegheny, about four hundred and fifty feet above the Ohio River, and eleven hundred and fifty feet above sea-level. The original building was seventy-two feet in length, and consisted of a principal story and basement, the façade looking toward the south, and being divided into a central dome with two wings. Additions have been made from time to time; and the newer part, which adjoins the eastern wing, extends in a northerly direction, eighty-eight feet. The material is brick, excepting the "dark room," or physical laboratory, for investigations in light and heat, which is of wood. The revolving dome (having an internal diameter of twenty feet) is of wood and iron.

Beneath the dome is the principal instrument, the equatorial, of thirteen inches aperture (with an excellent objective by Clarke, the mounting being by Fitz of New York), with hour-circle, reading to seconds of time, declination circle reading to ten seconds of arc, and clock-movement controlled by Bond's system. The instrument has also a position filar micrometer, polarizing solar eye-piece, star-spectroscope with two prisms of Huggins's pattern, a large and a small grating spectroscope, and accessories for attaching a reflecting telescope (employing no lenses whatever) for special heat researches, — for attaching an optically plane mirror to the polar axis (thus forming a Fahrenheit heliostat), and for converting the inverted telescope into a great equatorially mounted spectroscope.

In the western wing is the transit-room, containing an instrument of four-inch aperture by Simms, a standard barometer by Green, the sidereal clock by Frodsham, and the principal mean-time clock by Howard. Both clocks, as well as the observer at the meridian instrument, or the equatorial, can be placed in electric connection with the rest of the building, and also with the lines of telegraph connecting the Observatory with the city, so that beats of the clocks can at a few moments' notice be transmitted to any part of the country, — those of the sidereal clock for the determination of longitude, and those of the mean-time clock for supplying time to near or distant cities, and to railroads.

In the small hall connecting this room with the dome is a

stand for the galvanometer when this is used in connection with thermo-electric apparatus, attached to the equatorial in differential measurements of the heat from different parts of the sun. From this hall, access is also had to the self-registering and other thermometers. In the east wing is the room containing the chronograph, various pieces of electric apparatus, a third clock, and chronometers. It is occupied by the assistant in charge of the time-service.

The north wing contains the private study of the director, the library (which has also been used as a workroom and study for one of the assistants), and, in an extension (constructed in 1881, at the cost of Mr. William Thaw, with the exception of five hundred dollars contributed by Dr. C. G. Hussy), a sleeping-room, a small workshop, an alcove fitted up with a cabinet of shelves and drawers for instruments, and the "dark room," or physical laboratory. The latter is provided with two stone tables, on which are mounted galvanometers of great delicacy, and three stone piers in line with each other, on which are placed various instruments for researches in solar physics, which do not form part of the equipment proper of the Observatory. The principal of these, the spectro-bolometer (constructed from designs of the director for the study of invisible radiations), stands in the centre of the room, and receives sunlight through an aperture in the north wall from the mirror of a large Foucault siderostat.

This last important instrument is placed upon a pier of masonry outside the building, but connected with it by a platform, and protected from the weather by a "rolling house." It carries a twelve-inch optically plane silvered glass mirror, by Clarke, and was made by Hilger of London. It is in constant use.

The equatorial is mainly used in the study of the sun's surface, of which daily drawings on a scale of eight inches to the solar diameter have been made for several years; but for lack of hands, these are at present (April, 1884) discontinued. Besides these drawings, others on a much larger scale have been made, on favorable occasions, by the aid of the polarizing eye-piece. The larger part have never been published, but some of them have furnished valuable information in regard to the minute structure of the solar photosphere.

Researches upon the relative thermal, luminous, and actinic intensities of different parts of the sun's disk, have been carried on with thermopiles and special optical devices ; and these are now being greatly extended by the use of the new bolometric and spectroscopic apparatus.

In 1879 the director, finding himself unable to proceed farther in certain investigations without the aid of a more delicate heat-measuring apparatus than any then constructed, devised and perfected an instrument called the *bolometer*, for the measurement of feeble radiation. With this apparatus, an entirely new field of observation has been opened. By its aid, the first accurate determination of the wave-lengths of points in the extreme infra-red spectrum has been made, and the quantitative distribution of energy throughout the spectrum has been measured. The nature of atmospheric absorption, both for the solar and terrestrial envelope, has been partly elucidated, and definite measurements of the effect of certain atmospheric constituents have been made.

The library of the Observatory now contains about fifteen hundred volumes ; but this is still very insufficient, as this number must take the place, to this Observatory, of all the great public libraries, belonging to cities elsewhere, to which other observatories have access.

A mention of the Observatory's work would be incomplete without some account of its system of time-distribution introduced by its present director in 1869. Previous to that date, time had been sent in occasional instances from American observatories for public use, but in a temporary or casual manner. The Allegheny system, inaugurated in that year, is believed to be the parent of the present ones used in this country, in that it was, so far as is known, the first regular and systematic system of time-distribution to railroads and cities adopting it as an official standard. Two especially constructed lines of telegraph connect with the municipal offices in Pittsburg and Allegheny, with the telegraph-lines of the Western Union Telegraph Company, and with the private lines of the railroads.

A turret-clock in the city-hall of Pittsburg has been provided with electric mechanism, which enables it to be regulated from the Observatory, so that its movement may be made synchronous with that of the principal mean-time standard there, which is itself corrected by nightly observations.

The electric mechanism of the distant turret-clock causes a stroke upon a heavy bell above the summit of the tower to be given with exact precision at the first second of every third hour, so that it is audible throughout the city. The mechanism of the same turret-clock is arranged so that the pendulums of clocks in any distant police, fire-alarm, or other municipal offices, can be controlled by it, and compelled to move synchronously with its own; and at the same time it can, if desired, automatically report its own time upon the electric recording-apparatus at the Observatory. The automatic signals of the Observatory clock are rendered audible in these offices, and in the still more distant stations along the lines of the railways, by simple pieces of telegraphic apparatus known as "sounders," which are placed beside their own regulating-clocks, and enable them to give these latter an astronomical precision. The private lines of the railroads carry these beats over the country from New York upon the east to Chicago upon the west, and from Erie upon the northern lakes to Baltimore in the south. Over forty associated railroad companies are thus not only in permanent electric connection with the Observatory, but, their managers having adopted its time as the official standard, their employees are instructed to make regular comparisons with it; and for this purpose, during a certain time every day the ordinary transmission of time ceases, while the wires are engaged in transmitting the beats of the Observatory clock.

To enumerate all the different railroads thus adopting the Observatory time, would be too long; but to give an idea of the early extent and use which has been made of it, it may be mentioned that in 1872 these were grouped into three systems, — the Southern, including originally seven railroad companies, and extending 1,150 miles; the Eastern, including seventeen associated companies, 2,000 miles; and the Northern, including eighteen companies, 1,563 miles. This aggregate of 4,713 English miles did not even at that time represent the whole use of the Observatory by railroad companies, since only those which have officially instructed their employees to adopt its time as their standard were included in this estimate.

Over the network of railroad lines uniting the Atlantic, through the Middle States, with the Western lakes, all trains are moved, and all business carried on, by time primarily derived from a single clock, whose beats, by the repeating instruments of the telegraph lines, are virtually made audible at least once a day over a considerable part of the country. The advantages of so simple and accessible means of regulating the traffic through a large portion of the continent, are obvious; and as it is not only of important advantage in other respects to the companies employing it, but by diminishing the chances of accident in travelling to contribute largely to the public safety, the Observatory has seen with pleasure the use made of it in this interesting application of the processes of an exact science to the general welfare, the more as it is in no way incompatible with the steady pursuit of other and purely scientific duties.

For the benefit of any future writer of the history of the subject, it may be stated, that in 1870 the Observatory had already in extended operation the system of time-distribution above described; that about 1873 the director at Cambridge, after conference with the writer, introduced substantially the same provisions for connecting Harvard College Observatory with the New-England roads; and that about the same time the Washington Observatory, which had previously sent signals in a limited and desultory manner, commenced to do so in emulation of the new system.

More recently, observatories all over the country have introduced like connections, in many instances directly seeking information as to the system first introduced here.

While ordinary observations of precision are not neglected, the present director, considering the advantage of giving particular attention to some one portion of astronomical science, has aimed to make the Observatory principally useful in physical astronomy, and particularly in solar researches. To this fruitful field of labor, its work is likely to be given chiefly, in the future as in the past ; but it is growing increasingly difficult to carry on such investigations in a site now more than half ringed about with manufactories, and the removal of the Observatory to a purer air will soon become a necessity. Already, in 1881, the prosecution of the most important research became impossible from this cause ; and a special expedition was undertaken from the Observatory to the summit of Mount Whitney in the Sierra Nevada, to complete it. The principal means for the instrumental outfit were furnished by Mr. William Thaw of Pittsburg ; but very essential aid in transportation was obtained from the War Department through Gen. W. B. Hazen, chief signal-officer of the United-States Army, under whose official direction it proceeded in the writer's charge. A full account of the means and results of this expedition will appear this year (1884), in a volume printed at the Government Press.

As no publication fund has ever been created, the Observatory has never published any annals, and the results of its most important original researches or discoveries are to be chiefly found in communications to scientific journals. Of these the principal are, —

1873. "The Solar Photosphere." — *Proceedings of the American Association for the Advancement of Science, August, 1873.*

1874. "On the Minute Structure of the Solar Photosphere." — *American Journal of Science, February, 1874.*

1875. "On the Comparison of Certain Theories of Solar Structure with Observation." — *American Journal of Science, vol. ix., March, 1875.*

1875. "On the Comparison of Certain Theories of Solar Structure with Observation." — *Estratto dalle Memorie degli spettroscopisti Italiani, vol. iv.*

1875. "Sur la température relative des diverses régions du soleil. Première partie : Les noyaux noirs des taches." — *Comptes Rendus de l'Académie des Sciences, vol. 80, 1875.*

1875. "Sur la température relative des diverses régions du soleil. Deuxième partie : Région équatoriale et régions polaires." — *Comptes Rendus de l'Académie des Sciences, vol. 80, 1875.*

1875. "Étude des radiations superficielles du soleil." — *Comptes Rendus de l'Académie des Sciences, September, 1875.*

1875. "The Solar Atmosphere, an Introduction to an Account of Researches made at the Allegheny Observatory." — *American Journal of Science, vol. x., Supplement No. —, 1875.*

1876. " Measurement of the Direct Effect of Sun-spots on Terrestrial Climates." — *Astronomical Society's Monthly Notices, November, 1876.*

1877. " Nouvelle Méthode spectroscopique." — *Comptes Rendus de l'Académie des Sciences, May, 1877.*

1877. " On the Possibility of Transit Observation without Personal Error." — *American Journal of Science, vol. xiv., July, 1877.*

1878. " On the Janssen Solar Photograph and Optical Studies." — *American Journal of Science, vol. xv., April, 1878.*

1878. " Transit of Mercury of May 6, 1878." — *American Journal of Science, vol. xv., June, 1878.*

1878. " On Certain Remarkable Groups in the Lower Spectrum." — *Proceedings American Academy of Arts and Sciences, October, 1878.*

1878. " On the Temperature of the Sun." — *Proceedings American Academy of Arts and Sciences, October, 1878.*

1880. " Observations on Mount Etna." — *American Journal of Science, vol. —, July, 1880.*

1880. " The Bolometer." — *American Metrological Society, December, 1880.*

1881. " The Bolometer and Radiant Energy." — *Proceedings American Academy of Arts and Sciences, January, 1881.*

1881. " The Actinic Balance." — *American Journal of Science, vol. xxi., March, 1881.*

1881. " Sur la distribution de l'énergie dans le spectre solaire normal." — *Comptes Rendus de l'Académie des Sciences, Mars, 1881.*

1881. " Distribution de l'énergie dans le spectre normal." — *Comptes Rendus de l'Académie des Sciences, Juillet, 1881.*

1882. " The Mount Whitney Expedition." — *Nature, Aug. 3, 1882.*

1882. " La distribution de l'énergie dans le spectre normal." — *Ann. de Chimie et de Physique, February, 1882.*

1882. " Observations du spectre solaire." — *Comptes Rendus de l'Académie des Sciences, September, 1882.*

1882. " Sunlight and Skylight at High Altitudes." — *Nature, Oct. 12, 1882.*

1882. " Sunlight and Skylight at High Altitudes." — *Proceedings British Association at Southampton.*

1882. " Sunlight and Skylight at High Altitudes." — *American Journal of Science, vol. xxiv., November, 1882.*

1882. " Observation of the Transit of Venus, 1882, Dec. 6, made at the Allegheny Observatory." — *Monthly Notices Royal Astronomical Society, vol. xliii., No. 3.*

1882. " Observation of the Transit of Venus, 1882, Dec. 6, made at the Allegheny Observatory." — *Astronomische Nachrichten, No. 2481, January, 1883.*

1883. " The Selective Absorption of Solar Energy." — *American Journal of Science, vol. xxv., March, 1883, and London, Edinburgh Phil. Magazine.*

1883. " Die auswählende Absorption der Energie der Sonne." (Same in German.) — *Wiedemann Annalen, April, 1883.*

1883. " Sur l'absorption sélective de l'énergie solaire." (Same in French.) — *Ann. de Chim. et de Phys., September, 1883.*

1883. " The Spectrum of an Argand Burner." — *Science, June 1, 1883.*

1884. " On the Determination of Wave-lengths in the Infra-red Spectrum." *American Journal of Science, vol. xxvi., March, 1884, and London, Edinburgh, and Dublin Philos. Magazine for March.*

It will appear from all that has preceded, that, in the fifteen years since the first equipment, the Observatory has not been inactive; and it may perhaps be felt that the results it has reached, and the work it has accomplished, have been such as the citizens of the great industrial centres in which it is placed have cause to regard as not discreditable to them.

I must recall in this connection the regrettable fact, that, in these wealthy cities, there are not only no museums of art, no libraries of reference, no collections of scientific material, but in general, none of those aids to the investigator which are to be found in so many younger and smaller places; so that an observatory (which lives among such things as its natural medium, and depends upon their association) has here to furnish out of its own means almost every thing outside of its actual apparatus that the ordinary resources of American civilization would provide for it in any large American city but Pittsburg.

This Observatory is an exotic in this community; and that it has been maintained at all during the time I have mentioned, might be, perhaps, supposed to be due to the fact that it represents the sole local channel for contribution to science, in return for those practical results of science on which the prosperity of an industrial community is founded.

But during these fifteen years it should be better known than it is, not only that its existence has been a constant struggle with poverty (its income has at no time till within the past year reached one-fifth that of other American observatories whose reputation abroad is similar) but that this long struggle, during which it has been forced to earn the means to carry on its researches, has never brought it (always with exceptions already gratefully noted) the contribution of a single dollar from an individual in the community in which it exists.

It may perhaps be said that this fact is not publicly known; and that it need only be known, to be a fact no longer.

As I now remain in charge of the Observatory from affection to the place, and my pursuits there, rather than from interest, I can speak freely, and yet the more so, that I remember such constant personal kindness as I have experienced in this community.

I could wish, then, to see better evidence of the community's liberality in the future toward this Observatory, for the community will continue, I hope, to have cause to think it a subject of just local pride; and I can hardly be wrong in speaking with this frankness to respected citizens of Pittsburg and Allegheny, who are interested, not only in its past, but in its future.

S. C. LANGLEY,

Director of the Observatory.

ALLEGHENY, April 1, 1884.

FACTORIES.

GLOBE PLOW WORKS.

THE history of the plough is interesting as well as instructive. Ancient writers, both sacred and profane, speak of it as a well-known implement of agriculture, and frequently illustrate their meaning by reference to its use. Job, in his writings, 1520 B.C., says, "They that plow iniquity, and sow wickedness, reap the same."

In Prov. xxi. 4, Solomon the Wise also says, "The plowing of the wicked is sin."

The ancient plough was a crotched limb of a tree, and frequently fashioned out of the body and root of a sapling. To this, the beam was firmly bound with leather thongs or tough wooden withs.

These primitive implements were made of three pieces, — the beam, handle, and a naturally crooked piece of wood set in the beam, the lower end forming the share, a brace connecting the whole. Iron ploughs, however, were evidently made, and in use, at a very early day.

The quotations above referred to would have had equal force, even if there had been no ploughs other than those made entirely of wood ; but the prophet Joel, 800 B.C., would hardly have used the words, " Beat your plowshares into swords," if the people of that early day would not understand the meaning, and certainly could not have done so if metal ploughs had not been in general use. A complete history of the plough can never be written ; its use ante-dates all records ; nor is it practicable, within the limited space at our disposal, to describe the various improvements in form or mode of manufacture, that have from time to time been made during the present century.

It is but fair to say, that the most valuable improvements in this direction have been made in the United States.

It is said that Thomas Jefferson, the third president of the United States, effected an important improvement in the plough. In his correspondence with the French Institute, he laid down scientific and intelligible rules for shaping the same; and his theory he practically tested by having several ploughs made in accordance with his patterns, and using them profitably on his farms in Virginia as early as 1793.

Charles Newbold, a farmer of New Jersey, made the first cast-iron plough, for which he took out letters-patent: he was, however, in advance of the times; and after spending large sums of money in fruitless attempts to bring his improvement into notoriety and popular favor, he abandoned it in despair. Others followed closely in his wake with like sad results.

Improvements were made in form, but the wooden mould-boards were in common use until the beginning of the present century. The cast-iron share succeeded these: then came the substitution of steel for those parts which came in contact with the soil, and were liable to wear out. Eventually a light, strong, durable, and cheap implement was furnished to the farmer. In no country in the world are so large a number, or so great a variety, manufactured as in the United States, for the simple reason, that in no other land is there so great a variety of soil, or so large an agricultural area, and in no other country has the manufacture of agricultural implements attained such perfection. An exemplification of this is the fact that American ploughs were awarded the highest premiums at the international exhibition, where they were practically tested.

The Globe Plow Works were established on the south-east corner of Penn Street and Cecil's Alley by Samuel Hall in 1828: they were subsequently removed in 1836 to the south-west corner of Ferry Lane (now Beaver Avenue) and Walnut Street (now Greenwood Street), Manchester, now the Fifth Ward of the city of Allegheny.

In 1845 Alexander Speer became a partner in the business, under the name of Hall & Speer. Mr. Speer, being a practical worker at the trade, added much to the credit and success of the business. Mr. Hall died in the year 1852 ; and the business was continued without any change of proprietors, title, or interest until 1858, when John S. Hall, son of the founder of the works, became associated with Mr. Speer in carrying on the enterprise. During these years the business rapidly increased, and the products of the works were greatly in demand throughout the entire south and west, and large shipments made to South America and the island of Cuba.

John S. Hall died in 1873. Previous to his death, he had disposed of his entire interest to Mr. Speer, who subsequently sold an interest in the business to each of his two sons, W. W. Speer and Joseph T. Speer, the style of the firm being Alexander Speer & Sons. These latter gentlemen, like their father, had acquired a thorough knowledge of the business.

In 1870 the works were removed to Pittsburg, to the property bounded by Duquesne Way, Fifth Street, Cecil's Alley, and the property fronting on Penn Street. The works were completed, and ready for occupancy, the same year, and are considered a model in the completeness of machinery, and general arrangement, unsurpassed by any thing of the kind in the country.

The success of the Globe Plow Works may be attributed in some measure to the harmony and good feeling that have always characterized the relations between the proprietors and their employees. Many of the latter have been continuously employed for over forty-seven years.

THE FIRST ROPE WALK.

THE first rope-walk erected west of the Allegheny Mountains, was established in Pittsburg in 1794, and was located on the ground now occupied by the Monongahela House. The business was carried on by Col. John Irwin and wife.

Col. Irwin having been severely wounded in one of the battles of the Revolutionary war (Paoli), and rendered incapable of attending to the details of the business, Mrs. Irwin, — a lady of indomitable courage and perseverance, endowed with rare business qualifications, — with the assistance of her son, then a mere lad, carried on the works successfully.

Immediately following the death of Col. Irwin, Mrs. Irwin gave her son an interest in the business ; and it was carried on under the name and style of Mary and John Irwin.

In the year 1795 the works were removed to the square bounded by Liberty, Third, and Fourth Streets and Redoubt Alley. In view of the increasing demand for their products, and confined limits of this locality, the walk was removed in 1812 to the bank of the Allegheny River between Marbury Street and the point, where the entire rigging for Perry's fleet was manufactured.

The increasing demands induced the junior partner to consider seriously the project of erecting works on a more extensive scale.

Mrs. Irwin, on account of her age, and loss of health, resolved to quit business, in view of which she disposed of her interest to her son, who, in accordance with his preconceived notions on the subject, commenced the erection, in Allegheny, in 1813, of one of the most extensive works in the West, on the ten-acre out-lot bounded by the West Commons, Water Lane (now Western Avenue), out-lots Nos. 275, 29, and 30. It was known and designated as out-lot No. 276 in the "Reserve Tract opposite Pittsburg."

The contract for building the works was awarded to William Delworth, sen.

Mr. Irwin successfully carried on the business until Jan. 1, 1835, when he associated with him his son Henry, under the name of John Irwin & Son. This firm leased for a term of years, from Harmar Denny, out-lot No. 275, over which they extended their walk to within one hundred feet of Allegheny Avenue. In 1847 they became the purchasers.

In the month of July, 1836, a disastrous fire occurred in the factory, resulting in its entire destruction; and after it had been rebuilt, it was again destroyed by fire in the same month. It was again rebuilt, and the business carried on until 1858, when the firm dissolved, and the business at this point abandoned. In 1847 John Irwin, jun., became a partner, and the name of the firm was changed to John Irwin & Sons.

In 1862 Messrs. Fulton, Bollman, & Co., of which Mr. John Irwin, sen., was a member, succeeded the firm of John Irwin & Sons, and commenced the erection of new works on Smoky Island, to which the machinery, etc., of the abandoned works was removed.

These works had but a brief existence. The business of manufacturing had scarcely commenced ere it took fire, and was entirely consumed. This closed the connection of Mr. John Irwin, sen., with the business. Subsequently Mr. A. M. Marshall became associated with Messrs. Fulton & Bollman. The engine and machinery were removed to McKeesport, where they erected new works on a very extensive scale, and continued to do a large and profitable business up to the time it was burned down. From McKeesport it was removed to New Jersey.

During the early operations of rope-making, the machinery was of a rather primitive pattern, and was operated by hand. Subsequently horse-power was introduced, which was hailed as quite an improvement over the old methods.

To the rude and primitive methods of the past, now succeeds the modern improvements in machinery and steam-power.

The manufacture of cordage, etc., was among the early industries established in Pittsburg and Allegheny. And judging from their accessibility to the hemp-growing regions, and the facilities afforded for receiving the raw material, and distribution of the manufactured product, by rail and water, one would reasonably suppose that it would be classed among the most progressive of the industries of our locality: such, however, has not been the fact.

Although the profits accruing to those who have invested capital in the business have been remunerative, yet the manufacture has not been as extensive as might be expected.

THE FIRST GLASS WORKS ERECTED IN ALLEGHENY COUNTY.

It is generally conceded that the first building for the manufacture of green glass was erected on the South Side, in 1797, by Gen. James O'Hara and Major Isaac Craig, prominent and enterprising men of that early day. The works were located at the base of Coal Hill, fronting on the Ohio River, immediately opposite the confluence of the Allegheny and Monongahela, on property purchased from Ephraim Jones and Ephraim Blaine, extending from the river-front to the crest of the hill. The discovery of the great coal-seam underlying the hills south of the Monongahela, determined the location at this point. The proprietors engaged the services of Peter William Eichbaum of the Schuylkill Glass-Works, near Philadelphia, to superintend the construction of the works. They were completed, and commenced blowing glass, in 1797. These works are still standing, and have been successfully carried on for the manufacture of window-glass, etc., up to the present time (1884) by the succeeding firms of Fred Lorenz, William McCully & Co., Lorenz & Wightman, and Thomas Wightman & Co., respectively. It was alleged by one of the original projectors, that, before the first bottle was made, the sum of thirty thousand dollars had been expended.

The manufacture of glass has steadily increased in importance and profit up to the present time, with intervals of depression in common with other industries, and is now one of the leading staples of Pittsburg. But little was known of the coal-deposits in the adjacent hills until the establishment of

these works. The stratum dips towards the south, and at this
point attains an altitude considerably above the level of the
river, about 500 feet, and is about 100 feet below the crest of
the hill. Because of the want of knowledge of this fact, ex-
plorations were confined to the 12-inch seam at the base of the
hill, thereby overlooking the 5-foot seam near the summit: from
the latter the works were supplied with fuel for many years, from
an opening in the hill directly in the rear of the works, delivered
in one-horse skids containing ten bushels; Major Craig having
subsequently withdrawn from the firm. Gen. O'Hara commenced the enlargement of the works with a view to the manufacture of flint glass: this not proving successful, what is
now justly deemed one of the great industries to which the
rise and prosperity of our vicinity is indebted, had to be
abandoned.

Subsequent to the date of the establishment of the works
above described, Messrs. Denny and Beelen commenced the
erection of glass-works on the north side of the Allegheny. It
was located on the bank of the Ohio River, opposite the head
of Alliquippa Island (now called Brunot's), on out-lot No. 15 of
the Reserve Tract, near the mouth of Island Lane (now Washington Street). At this point the current of the river is swift,
and difficult for navigation, and is generally known by river-
men as "Glass-house Ripple." The factory went into operation
about the beginning of the present century, under the superintendence of La Fluer (commonly called "Falure"), a native of
France, who came to this country expressly to take charge of it.
It was, however, after a brief existence, abandoned, on account
of the difficulty in obtaining the necessary supply of fuel.

La Fluer was afterwards employed at the works of Messrs.
O'Hara and Craig, and was subsequently drowned in the Ohio
River immediately in front of the works, in the attempt to ford
the stream from the Gravel Bar below the point of Pittsburg.
He left a widow and several children. Mrs. La Fluer resided
for many years on the north-east corner of out-lot No. 12 and
Ferry Lane (now Beaver Avenue), the dividing line between
out-lots Nos. 11 and 12 being also the dividing line between the
borough of Manchester and McClure township.

THE FIRST IRON ROLLING MILL ERECTED IN THE CITY OF ALLEGHENY.

THE Juniata Rolling Mill was built on the lot extending from Robinson Street along the west side of Darragh Street to the Allegheny River, at the former outlet of the Pennsylvania Canal, by Sylvanus Lothrop, James Anderson, and Henry Blake, in the years 1826 and 1827. Mr. Blake sold his interest to Capt. William Stewart, and removed to Greenup County, Ky., having there purchased two furnaces and a forge from the Messrs. Shreves. Messrs. Lothrop, Anderson, and Stewart sold out their interest in 1834· to John Bissell, William Morrison, and Edward W. Stephens.

The mill, having been constructed for the exclusive use of Juniata blooms, was extended by the latter firm to the manufacture of iron by the puddling and boiling process, and was the first boiling-furnace erected in Allegheny County. Here, too, was also erected the first coffee-mill squeezer, under the personal superintendence of the patentee, Mr. Burden of New York.

The manufacture of iron, nails, and steel of the lowest grade, was successfully carried on by the latter firm and their successors, until the year 1859, when the site becoming too limited for the growing demands of the trade, and the war of the Rebellion threatening in the near future, it was deemed advisable to dismantle the works, and wind up the business. The machinery was sold to Messrs. Reis, Brown, Berger, and James Ward, and was removed to Niles, Ohio.

The above items of information were obtained from William S. Bissell, Esq., who had charge of the Juniata Rolling Mill for nearly sixteen years.

PAPER-MILL.

ONE of the important branches of industry, and the first of the kind established north of the Allegheny River, was the paper manufactory erected by Hind & Howard on the bank of the Ohio River, on part of out-lot No. 20 in the Reserve Tract opposite Pittsburg, which is now embraced within the limits of the Fifth Ward of the city of Allegheny. It was commenced in the fall of 1831, completed, and made ready to commence operations, in the following spring. This, however, was rendered impracticable by the entire demoralization of the building, machinery, etc., of the new enterprise by the disastrous flood in the rivers, of the 10th of February, 1832. By the prompt and energetic measures adopted by the firm in repairing damages, they were enabled after a brief delay to again commence operations.

It was the intention of the proprietors to manufacture what is termed laid writing-paper, in all its varieties. This they practically abandoned in 1837 in consequence of the impurities of the water used in the manufacture.

In this year Mr. Hind disposed of his interest to Mr. Levi Howard, the brother of his partner ; and the business continued under the name and style of James Howard & Co.

The new firm proceeded to introduce into their mill the latest and most approved machinery, in order to enter largely into the manufacture of wall and wrapping paper.

In 1854 the mill was partially destroyed by fire : it was rebuilt, and was again partially destroyed in 1857. It was again repaired, and in 1871[1] was totally destroyed. These repeated disasters so discouraged the proprietors, that they abandoned the further prosecution of the business.

---

[1] Pattersons' saw-mill was also destroyed on these several occasions.

ALLEGHENY GAS COMPANY.

THIS company was organized under a charter granted by the Commonwealth of Pennsylvania, approved March 29, 1852, with a capital of $100,000 divided into 4,000 shares, of the par value of twenty-five dollars, and has been in successful operation to the present time (1881). It was originally located on the northwest corner of Water Lane, now Western Avenue, and Pasture Lane, now Irwin Avenue, being part of out-lot No. 266, having a frontage of 181.4¼ feet on Pasture Lane by 200 feet on Water Lane.

In view of the unsuitable nature of the location, it was, in the year 1860, removed to Bank Lane, now South Avenue, on part of out-lot No. 24.

Over fifty miles of gas-mains have been laid, and the number of public lamps in operation in the city approximates twelve hundred.

The following commissioners were appointed, under the Act of incorporation, to open books, etc. : —

WILLIAM ROBINSON, Jun.
JOHN PRICE.
H. CHILDS.
ALEXANDER CAMERON.
SAMUEL WICKERSHAM.
JOHN T. LOGAN.
JOSIAH KING.
JAMES PARK, Jun.
CHARLES AVERY.

WILLIAM WALKER.
GEORGE R. RIDDLE.
ROBERT B. MOWRY.
JOHN FLEMING.
JOHN IRWIN.
JAMES MARSHALL.
JACOB PAINTER.
WILLIAM COLEMAN.
THOMAS F. DALE.

MANAGERS AND OFFICERS ELECTED IN 1852.

THOMAS F. DALE, M.D., *President.*   JAMES PARK, Jun.
H. CHILDS.   ROBERT DALZELL.
H. P. SCHWARTZ.   JAMES MARSHALL.
JOHN T. LOGAN.   R. H. DAVIS.
JACOB PAINTER.
R. H. DAVIS, *Secretary and Treasurer.*   LEMUEL H. DAVIS, *Contractor.*
H. P. GEMGEMBRE, *Architect and Superintendent.*

These works were erected at a cost of $101,784.53, exclusive of $6,000 paid for the real estate, making the entire expenditure $107,784.53.

The capital stock was subsequently increased to $250,000, then to $500,000, and finally to $800,000; that is to say, 32,000 shares at $25, the present capital.

OFFICERS AND DIRECTORS, 1881.

JAMES McCUTCHEON, *President.*   JAMES LOCKHART.
H. M. BOYLE, *Vice-President.*   HUGH McNEILL.
ADDISON LYSLE, *Secretary.*   JAMES MARSHALL.
WILLIAM WALKER.   JAMES RICHEY, Jun., *Treasurer.*
HAY WALKER.   ROBERT YOUNG, *Superintendent.*
L. McINTOSH.

The company has in successful operation two gasometers: the Eastern has a capacity of 196,000 cubic feet; the Western, 100,000 cubic feet. In order to supply the increasing demand, the latter has recently been reconstructed by increasing the depth of the pit, and erecting an entire new telescopic holder with a capacity of 225,000 cubic feet, thus making the entire capacity 421,000 cubic feet.

CEMETERIES.

THE ORIGINAL BURIAL PLACE IN ALLEGHENY.

THE first place known to be appropriated by common consent of the early citizens for the burial of the dead, was the "Potter's Field," located on the northern slope of what was then known as "Hog-back Hill," immediately in the rear of the present building of the Western Theological Seminary.

After the grant to the seminary, it took the more euphonious title of "Seminary Hill;" but since the erection of the Soldiers' Monument on its crest, it has assumed the appropriate name of "Monumental Hill."

In this once humble locality, about fifty feet from the base of the hill, surrounded by a clump of young forest-trees, many of the early inhabitants of the North Side were interred, of which, unfortunately, there is no record or chiselled stone to mark their humble resting-place.

The excavation caused by the opening of Marshall Street along the base of the hill, left exposed the remains of those buried in the "Potter's Field:" they were carefully collected, and disposed of elsewhere.

In pursuance of a petition of a portion of the commoners in November, A.D. 1825, the Legislature passed an Act approved March 17, A.D. 1827, confirming the title of the seminary to all that portion of the common ground lying south of Ridge Avenue between Marion and Irwin Avenues, extending to the southern boundary of the same, including a large portion of the hill, and containing about eighteen acres: the grant, however, was considered doubtful, as many of the commoners had refused their consent. It was subsequently abrogated, and the same vested in the city by the Act of the Legislature approved March 26, 1867, creating the commission for the improvement of the common grounds, except the part laid off in lots fronting on Ridge Avenue, extending back to Marshall Street, which had been previously disposed of by the city on perpetual lease.

Subsequent to the abandonment of the "Potter's Field," the citizens with commendable zeal determined to provide a more suitable and convenient place for the disposition of the dead, in view of which another portion of the common ground was selected, bounded on the east by Sherman Avenue (formerly Webster Street), on the south by a line corresponding with the northern line of Stockton Avenue, on the west by Marion Avenue, and on the north by a line corresponding with the southern line of Water Alley (now Park Way).

This constituted the only place for the interment of the dead for many years, and until its further use for that purpose was interdicted by the authorities of the city. At this period the congregation of the First Presbyterian Church, through their trustee, Thomas Sample, purchased out-lot No. 251, containing ten acres, a part of which was laid out in convenient size burial-lots, and the balance in building-lots. Many of the dead from the former were removed to the latter. The nature of the ground, however, not proving suitable for the object designed, it was abandoned; and the bodies of the dead were removed to Mount Union Cemetery, and the ground laid out in building-lots, and sold.

The adoption of a generous system for the improvement of the common ground, and subsequent appointment of "Park Commissioners," were wise in conception, as well as glorious in results.

In order to carry out in detail the proposed improvement, it was deemed necessary that every thing calculated to interfere, or mar the general harmony, should as far as practicable be removed. In accordance therewith, the removal of the dead from the old burial-ground, between Sherman and Marion Avenues, to Mount Union Cemetery, was accomplished to the entire satisfaction of all parties.

The members of the Christian Church (Disciples) established a burial-ground on the north side of Jackson Street, a short distance west of Arch Street. It was only maintained for a few years, and then abandoned, as the ground proved entirely unsuited for the purpose. The bodies buried therein were removed to Mount Union Cemetery.

MOUNT UNION CEMETERY.

To the indomitable zeal and efforts of a number of well-known and enterprising citizens of Allegheny, is due the inception and establishment of this beautiful city of the dead. Being impressed with the need of such a place, they made application to the State Legislature for an Act of incorporation, which was granted by the Act of April 14, 1846. In the mean time they acquired by purchase out-lots Nos. 238, 239, situate on the heights north of the city (now Sixth Ward), commanding a view of the valleys of the Ohio, Allegheny, and Mononghela, unequalled in beauty and extent.

Over a third of a century has passed away since it was opened for interment ; and so popular did this necropolis become, that the incorporators began to realize that additional territory would soon be required.

In 1857 Hilldale Cemetery was incorporated ; and an eligible spot of ground, embracing out-lots Nos. 223, 224, immediately adjoining, was purchased, and opened for burial purposes, and was continued for a period of ten years, when the authorities of Mount Union Cemetery became the purchasers of the entire franchise for the sum of forty thousand dollars. Thus the two became merged under the name of Union Dale Cemetery.

There is no essential difference in the nature of the soil, as both are situate on the slopes of adjacent hills, divided by West-End Avenue (formerly New-Brighton Road), by which both are approached.

The soil is generally of a light sandy loam, in some places intermixed with fine gravel, possessing a fertility adapted to give strength and vitality to the exuberant growth of ornamental trees and shrubbery, and keep the surface well covered with a rich coating of grass. The soil, being dry and friable, renders it unsurpassed for burial purposes.

On the occasion of the consolidation, a supplementary Act of the Legislature was obtained, carefully prepared to meet the new condition of affairs ; and on the second day of April, A.D. 1869, the new charter was granted : and the enlarged territory became known to the public as the Union Dale Cemetery, embracing about seventy-five acres of the most beautifully located hill-land, the one sloping gently towards the north, and the other facing towards the south and west.

Looking towards Pittsburg from the crest of Mount Union, a comprehensive panorama of both cities is presented to view, unsurpassed by any other spot in the neighborhood. From the Hilldale side, the view of the cities is entirely cut off, while the country on both sides of the Ohio delights the eye for several miles with a variety of scenery both lovely and picturesque. An additional twenty-five acres of ground adjoining has recently been acquired, and handsomely laid out in lots in accordance with the general plan.

From the time of its organization to the present, it has received assured evidences of popular favor; and a reference had to the several Acts of the Legislature bearing upon the same, will prove that every desirable provision has been made for its protection and permanence. Its government is conducted on principles wholly unselfish, the proprietary rights being vested in the lot-holders.

The land held by the corporation, and thus dedicated, cannot under any circumstances be disposed of for any purpose other than the interment of the dead; it is made exempt from assessment, public taxes, or liability to levy, or execution, for the payment of any debt. The opening of streets through the grounds is prohibited. It is also required, that so much of the funds arising out of the sale of lots as may be required, shall be applied to the liquidation of the purchase-money and the improvement of the grounds, and the residue shall be invested by the trustees in ground-rents, and mortgages on real estate in the county of Allegheny, as a permanent fund to be used for the perpetual maintenance of the cemetery in proper order and security.

By these wise and salutary provisions, it will be observed that the funds cannot be diverted for any other purpose than the purchase, improvement, and preservation of the grounds.

There are natural as well as legal barriers against the encroachment of the almost irresistible march of modern improvements which manifests itself in and around great cities. The "everlasting hills" combine with the plenitude of legislative authority to hold these grounds sacred against any innovation that might mar their beauty, or interfere in any way with thier quiet and seclusion. To the thoughtful, the refined, and the religious, a visit to the silent necropolis is fraught with both profit and pleasure. The tender care of the dead, and the cherishing of the memory of those who have "gone before," are evidences of our civilization and our Christianity. Almost everywhere near the centres of wealth and refinement, these cities of the dead have been established; and as time rolls on, and the "weary pilgrims" find therein a sweet resting-place, these hallowed spots become more attractive and more sacred.

FAMILY RECORD

INTRODUCTION.

AT the instance of some of the surviving members of our family, and particularly at the earnest request of my much-esteemed cousin, William M. Park, of Cornwall, Province Ontario, Canada, as well as the gratification of my own wishes, I have endeavored to compile, as far as possible, a faithful record of the American branch of our family. In the accomplishment of the undertaking, I am largely indebted, for valuable information, to the several kindred family registers and public records preserved intact from casualties and the ever-ceaseless changes of time. Many of the old records, both public and private, connecting the past with the present, having been destroyed by the great fire of the 10th April, 1845, otherwise lost or mislaid in consequence thereof, the void occasioned thereby, if supplied at all, must necessarily be of a traditionary nature, the correctness of which would have been more fully assured had it been accomplished some years ago, when those now deceased were living, and could have supplied information which is now lost forever.

JOHN E. PARKE.

JANUARY, 1878.

RECORD.

JOHN PARK and MARY ANN MAGEE, married in Pittsburg, Allegheny County, Penn., 1797. The former born in Belfast, county Antrim, Ireland, 1760; died in Pittsburg, March 20, 1808. The latter born in the county of Derry, Ireland; died at the old homestead, on the bank of the Ohio River, now in the Fifth Ward, Allegheny, 1819.

Issue.

CLARA M.	Born	, 1798;	died March 19, 1827.
MARGUERITE S.	Born Sept. 10, 1799;	died Sept. 10, 1835.
JAMES C.	Born	;	died	, 1832.
JANE M.	Born	1802;	died Oct. 16, 1872.
ROBERT M.	Born July 14, 1805.
JOHN E.	Born Dec. 12, 1807.

There were two other children, MARY and HENRY, who died in infancy.

CLARA M. PARKE and CHARLES L. ARMSTRONG, married at the old homestead, May 7, 1823. The latter died July 16, 1876. No issue.

MARGUERITE S. PARKE and JONATHAN KIDD, married Nov. 5, 1825.

Issue.

CAROLINE MATILDA	Born Aug. 7, 1826;	died Sept. 13, 1826.
AMANDA MALVENA	Born Aug. 7, 1827;	died May 6, 1828.
CLARA H.	Born March 3, 1829;	died Dec. 31, 1836
MARY EVALINE	Born June 12, 1830;	died Dec. 31, 1836.
CLARENCE N.	Born Nov. 11, 1831;	died March 29, 1848.
JANE H.	Born July 31, 1833;	died Aug. 14, 1833.

JAMES C. PARKE and JANE MATHEWS, married in Pittsburg. Issue, three children, — a son and two daughters. Parents and children all dead.

JANE M. PARKE and ROBERT A. EVANS, married in Pittsburg, 1832. The latter born Dec. 2, 1809; died in Allegheny, Sept. 20, 1862.

Issue.

HENRY	Born Aug. 21, 1832;	died July 2, 1833.
ROBERT A.	Born Dec. 2, 1833;	died Jan. 30, 1837.
MARY P.	Born Dec. 25, 1835;	died Jan. 21, 1852.
ANNIE W.	Born June 2, 1839.

215

ANNIE W. EVANS and JOHN L. RENO, married in Trinity Church, Pittsburg, Nov. 2, 1859.

Issue.

ROBERT E.	Born Oct. 7, 1860.
LEWIS H.	Born Nov. 6, 1861; died Feb. 2, 1870.
ANNIE ELIZA	Born March 9, 1864.
JANE P.	Born Jan. 23, 1867.

ROBERT M. PARKE and JANE W. MILLER, married Dec. 20, 1826. The latter born June 10, 1809.

Issue.

JOHN WESLEY . .	Born Oct. 9, 1829; died Jan. 6, 1861.
HENRY L.	Born April 10, 1831; died July 12, 1869.
MARIAN WALLACE	Born July 11, 1834; died April 30, 1857.
HELEN MARR	Born Jan. 10, 1836.
CHARLES WESLEY	Born Oct. 4, 1838; died April 4, 1860.
EMMA JANE	Born Nov. 15, 1841; died Jan. 10, 1847.
MARGUERITE K.	Born June 8, 1844.

JOHN W. PARKE and MARIA AGGY, married March 13, 1851, in the borough of Manchester, now city of Allegheny. Issue, five children, — three sons and two daughters. Deceased, one son and one daughter.

HENRY L. PARKE and ELVIRA GREENLEE, married April 25, 1855, in the city of Allegheny. No issue.

MARGUERITE K. PARKE and HENRY L. KEAGGY, married June 19, 1865, in the city of Allegheny. Issue, two sons and one daughter.

HELEN M. PARKE and WILLIAM W. ANDERSON, married Feb. 19, 1857, in Allegheny. The latter born in Belfast, Ireland, 1831.

Issue.

HENRY PARKE	Born , 1857.
ALEXANDER V.	Born , 1859.
WILLIAM W.	Born ; died in infancy, aged
JANE M.	Born , 1862; [8 months.
FANNIE W.	Born , 1865.
CHARLES PHILLIPS	Born , 1868.

JOHN E. PARKE and JANE HANNEN, married Dec. 9, 1828, in the city of Allegheny. The latter was born Feb. 4, 1811; the former as above stated.

Issue.

WILLIAM C.	Born Oct. 26, 1829; died Dec. 15, 1830.
EDWIN J.	Born Oct. 16, 1831.

FREDERICK N. . . . . Born Dec. 10, 1833; died Feb. 21, 1834.
FREDERICK A. . . . . Born Feb. 10, 1836.
MARY E.. . . . . Born Sept. 2, 1838.
FRANK H. . . . . Born Feb. 16, 1841; died Sept. 23, 1864.

He was major of the Fourth Cavalry, Sixty-fourth Regiment Pennsylvania Volunteers; was wounded at the battle of Reams Station, on the Weldon Railroad, Virginia, Aug. 23, 1864; died at Philadelphia, as above; buried in Mount Union Cemetery, city of Allegheny.

HENRY D. . . . . Born June 28, 1843; died Nov. 14, 1845.
CLARENCE C. . . . . Born Sept. 19, 1847.
CHARLES L. . . . . Born July 19, 1850; died Dec. 5, 1866.

He was killed on the Pittsburg, Fort Wayne, and Chicago Railway, at Alliance, Ohio; buried in Mount Union Cemetery.

ROBERT M.. . . . . Born Oct. 19, 1852.
GEORGE B. . . . . Born Dec. 3, 1855.

EDWIN J. PARKE and MARY W. DUNHAM, married in the town of Bedford, Aryahogo County, Ohio, Nov. 26, 1855. The latter was born April 28, 1833.

Issue.

JOSEPHINE D. . . . . Born Aug. 5, 1857.
MARY E.. . . . . Born July 11, 1870.
EDWIN . . . . Born April 1, 1876.

MARY E. PARKE and J. S. MORRIS, married July 8, 1858, in New Brighton, Beaver County, Penn.

Issue.

JOHN P. . . . . . Born May 21, 1860; died Jan. 28, 1862.
FREDERICK S.. . . . . Born Nov. 16, 1862.

CLARENCE C. PARKE and ELLA KEECH, married Dec. 22, 1869, in the city of Mansfield, Ohio.

Issue.

EMMA H. . . . . Born May 8, 1871.

ROBERT M. PARKE and LILLIE L. HOUSE, married Dec. 25, 1876, in the city of Toledo, Ohio. The latter born Oct. 27, 1857.

Issue.

JOHN E., jun. . . . Born Nov. 4, 1877.
FRANK H. . . . . . . Born March 12, 1879.

JOHN PARK and ELIZABETH CAMP, married in Pittsburg, 1821. The former born in Pittsburg, 1789, and died in Allegheny, Aug. 13, 1868. The latter born in Norfolk, Va., June 22, 1801; died in Allegheny, March 25, 1875.

A MEMENTO. — To record the merits of the departed soldier may be considered at all times just and proper. The subject of this brief sketch, John Park, was born in Pittsburg, in the year 1789, and resided in Allegheny County all his life. He was actively engaged in mechanical pursuits, and, in early life, connected himself with the Pittsburg Blues, one of the first military organizations in Allegheny County. On the breaking out of the war of 1812,[1] the company, by unanimous consent, tendered their services to the General Government, were accepted, and immediately ordered into active service. The troops, under the command of Capt. James R. Butler and Lieut. Matthew Magee, embarked in boats at Pittsburg, for a point on the Ohio River, late in the autumn of 1812, thence to march over-land to join the North-western army under Gen. William H. Harrison, then engaged in repelling the assaults of the combined forces of the British and Indians, under Gen. Proctor and Tecumseh.

Mr. Park's bravery as a soldier was fully and satisfactorily assured during the memorable siege of Fort Meigs, and at the battle of Mississinewa. He was wounded at the former, May 5, 1813, whilst engaged in a sortie ordered to dislodge the enemy from a position extremely annoying to the garrison.

Those who knew him best could not fail to recognize the gallant soldier, ever ready to assume the responsibilities and dangers attendant upon a faithful and fearless discharge of his military duties. He responded with alacrity to every assignment of duty, and entered upon the work with all the energy of his nature. In one so brave, we naturally look for a noble soul and a generous heart. These qualifications he possessed in an eminent degree, which rendered him exceedingly popular with his officers and associates. He died in Allegheny, Aug. 13, 1868, and was buried in Allegheny cemetery.

Issue.

FANNY B.	Born July 28, 1822.	
THOMAS CAMP	Born Aug. 14, 1824.	
GEORGE	Born , 1826;	died in infancy.
CLARA A.	Born March 26, 1829.	
SARAH R.	Born , 1831;	died Nov. 30, 1868.
WILLIAM H.	Born Oct. 16, 1833.	
ELIZABETH	Born , 1835;	died in infancy.
BELINDA S..	Born April 8, 1839.	

PHILIP WILSON and FANNY B. PARK, married May 27, 1841. The former born in Baltimore, July 15, 1815; died in Allegheny, Aug. 11, 1877. The latter born as stated above.

Issue.

CORNELIA C.	Born May 16, 1842.
JOHN P.	Born Jan. 1, 1847.

HARRY D. RUTTON and CORNELIA C. WILSON, married in Allegheny, Dec. 13, 1866. The former born in Ashford, county Kent, England, April 25, 1834. The latter as above stated.

Issue.

FANNY P. . . . . Born Dec. **22**, 1867; died Oct. 4, 1877.

TO THE MEMORY OF FANNY. — Another tender blossom — another beautiful flower — has gone to mingle its kindred dust with our common mother Earth; another young soul has gone to associate with those departed spirits who have "washed their robes and made them white in the blood of the Lamb." Death has again left the impress of his cold hand upon the loving family circle. Within a few short weeks the aged sire — full of years, and endowed with the glory of Christian hope — answered the summons of his Lord and Master. Oh! who would not wish to have the *finale* of his earthly journey abounding in the grace and glory of the Christian hope, and pass away in light and joy, and, like the falling leaves, put on the brightest robes when about to die? As the brightness of the morning star is absorbed in the splendor of the rising sun, — as the rosy dawn brightens into full day, — so the glorious death of the Christian takes away from the living the terrors of death, and leaves them to say, "The end of a good man is peace. Let my last end be like his."

And now the youthful grand-child has departed on her heavenly journey. In recording the death of the loving and dear little Fanny, our hearts, in moments of sadness and deep thought, can experience no greater comfort than that which we find in the blessed declaration which has brought peace and comfort to the hearts of loving parents and friends in their grief for the loss of the loved ones. When first spoken, the words came forth from human lips, alive and tremulous with the strong love of an affectionate heart: "Suffer little children to come unto me, and forbid them not, for of such is the kingdom of heaven." They are clearly heard amid all the conflicts of human passion, and tell us of the peace that passeth all understanding, and assure us that the Saviour loves our little ones. In this dispensation of providence, we humbly recognize the uncertainty of life, and the necessity for a preparation for that which is to come. The lessons of human frailty come to us by voices as numerous as the falling leaves. God clothes the forests and fields in all the beauties of exuberant life, and then lays their glories in the dust; and all that live and die in the world teach us that we, too, must die. Every flower that fades, every leaf that withers, every return of the melancholy autumnal days, repeats to us the solemn sentence pronounced on all living, "Dust thou art, and unto dust thou shalt return."

The teachings of the solemn lessons of our frail and transitory condition, let us consider with devout hearts and willing minds. Over this the prophets poured their inspired lamentations in ancient days; and in every age and in every land it has been a subject of interest, and a sign to every heart. "We all do fade as the leaf." Those signs are sent us, not to make our earthly journey a melancholy and solemn march to the grave, but rather to create within us longings and preparations to meet our loved ones in the realms of a blessed rest, eternal at God's right hand. It requires not the pen of eulogy to herald forth the character of this loving child. Her kind and gentle manners exhibited an affectionate disposition. "To know her was to love her."

> "So fades the lovely blooming flower,
> Frail, smiling solace of an hour;
> So soon our transient comforts fly,
> And pleasures only bloom to die."

ELIZABETH C.. . . . . Born Sept. 12, 1872.

THOMAS C. PARK and JEMIMA WINGATE, married at Wellsbury, W. V., May 10, 1848.   The latter died July 5, 1873.

Issue.

THOMAS A.. . . . . Born April 14, 1849.

THOMAS A. PARK and LETITIA HOWARD, married in Allegheny, June 1, 1871.   The latter born May, 1849.

Issue.

WILLIAM HOWARD .   Born Aug. 22, 1876.

EDWARD GREGG and CLARA A. PARK, married in Allegheny, July 10, 1849.

Issue.

LIZZIE S.. . . . . Born April 26, 1850; died Oct.   26, 1850.
EVALINE S.. . . . . Born March 1, 1860; died March 20, 1861.
PHILIP W. . . . . Born Feb. 15, 1863; died Aug. 25, 1863.

BIOGRAPHICAL SKETCHES.

REV. WELLS BUSHNELL.

REV. WELLS BUSHNELL was born on the east end of Long Island, N.Y., April 25, 1799. His parents, Alexander and Sarah Wells Bushnell, were natives of the New-England States, both professors of Christianity, and by their earnest prayers and godly example endeavored to bring up their children in the fear of God. In 1816 Mr. Bushnell resided in Pittsburg, and made a public profession of religion, and connected himself with the First Presbyterian Church, under the charge of Rev. Francis Herron, D.D. It was, perhaps, in the year 1817, that Wells Bushnell commenced working at a blacksmith's fire as blower and striker, assisting the late A. Lamont, who was at that time chief blacksmith at the Allegheny Arsenal. In a short time he was able to take charge of a fire, and was considered a fair workman. It was while engaged in that occupation, that he was invited by Dr. Herron to drop his chosen trade, and prepare for the gospel ministry.

After some preparatory study, he entered Jefferson College, where he graduated in 1823. His theological education was completed at Princeton Theological Seminary, after which he was taken under the care of the presbytery of New Brunswick, N.J., and licensed to preach the gospel in 1825. On the twenty-fifth day of April, 1826, he was united in marriage by Rev. Francis Herron, D.D., to Miss Eleanor Hannen, eldest daughter of John and Elizabeth Richards Hannen. He subsequently severed his connection with the presbytery of New Brunswick, with a view to joining the presbytery of Erie. On the twenty-fourth day of May, 1826, his name appears upon the records of the latter as a licentiate. The church of Meadville having made a call for his pastoral labors, he was instructed to prepare his trial Sermon for ordination. He was ordained on the following twenty-second day of June, and regularly installed as pastor of the church of Meadville, on which occasion, Rev. Joseph Stockton, the first pastor of the church, being present, preached the sermon, Rev. Mr. Tait delivered the charge to the pastor, and Rev. Johnston Eaton, the charge to the congregation.   His relation to the church continued until the twenty-sixth day of June, 1833, when, at his own request, it was dissolved, that he might go as a missionary to the Indians. The Western Board of Foreign Missions had been recently established in the city of Pittsburg; and as missions were about to be organized for different points among the heathen, Mr. Bushnell felt impelled to offer himself for the work. His warm and impulsive heart was moved to its depths with a longing desire to engage in this great enterprise.   His firm and earnest conviction was, that the voice of his Master was calling him; and therefore he resolved to sever the tie that bound him to a generous and loving people, to labor and toil as best he could for the welfare of the benighted and degraded. With his family he departed to the wilds of the great West.

But he had over-estimated his strength of constitution, and power of endurance.   With all his self-denial and earnestness, he experienced excessive fatigue, and prolonged sickness of himself and family, until he was almost exhausted.   Notwithstanding these discouragements, he continued his labors in the Indian country over eighteen months, when he felt it his duty to return eastward.

No doubt, his labor and self-sacrifice were approved by the Master, even though he was permitted to see but little fruit. It may, however, be truly said of him, "He hath done what he could."   Upon leaving the Indian country, he came to New Albany, Ind., where his parents resided.   After enjoying a season of rest, he received an invitation to supply the pulpit of the First Presbyterian Church of Louisville, Ky., in the absence of the regular pastor.   His talents and abilities as a Christian minister having produced a marked and favorable impression on the people, he was earnestly solicited to take charge of a new church enterprise, about springing into existence in that city.   His views, however, even at that early day, on the subject of slavery, were so strongly in opposition to the institution, that he could not consistently accept the proposition. He subsequently accepted a call from the church at Greensburg, Ind., in connection with a congregation at Shelbyville in the same State. Here he labored for over a year and a half, when, in consequence of failing health, he returned to Pittsburg to rest and recruit. During his stay in Pittsburg, he accepted an invitation to supply the churches at Gravel Run and Cambridge, Crawford County, Penn.

On the third day of February, 1836, at his request, his connection with the presbytery of Erie was dissolved, that he might connect himself with the presbytery of Indianapolis, Ind. Here he labored for over two years, when, on the eleventh day of April, 1838, he was again received into the presbytery of Erie; and on the eighteenth day of April, 1839, having received a call from the church of New Castle, Penn., he was transferred to the presbytery of Beaver, Penn. Here he labored incessantly and successfully for over fifteen years.

About this time, a change took place in Mr. Bushnell's views in regard to his church relations. He was entirely dissatisfied with the position of the church on the question of slavery. In this matter, he was honest and sincere, and felt that he could no longer, in justice to his feelings, remain in the Presbyterian church. He accordingly severed his connection with the presbytery of Beaver, and united himself with the "Free Presbyterian Church," at the same time feeling the greatest reluctance to separate himself from brethren for whom he always cherished a warm affection. In this new relation, he accepted calls from the congregations of Mount Jackson, Lawrence County, and New Bedford, Mercer County, Penn., in which capacity he labored until the close of his life. The disease that terminated in his death was cholera morbus. He died at Mount Jackson, on the sixteenth day of July, 1863, in the sixty-fifth year of his age, and thirty-eighth year of his ministry. His wife, one son, and four daughters survived him.

Mr. Bushnell's success as a Christian minister was of the highest order. He possessed a warm and somewhat impulsive heart, and his zeal frequently obscured his better judgment. A co-presbyter speaks of him in the following language: " He was a faithful minister of Christ, an excellent preacher, and a watchful and kind-hearted pastor." His ministerial labors throughout bore evidence of his zeal and faithfulness in the cause of his Master. A ready mind and a determined will rendered his conclusions often premature; but those who knew him best, gave him full credit for the goodness of his heart, and devotion to the cause to which he had dedicated his life. One of his elders says of him, "He was courteous and affable in his general intercourse as a Christian. He was zealous and sincere as a minister. His sermons were written carefully, and delivered with a force that carried conviction to the minds of his hearers." Firm and true to his profession, his success was the result of unwavering fidelity and earnest devotion.

To the work of the ministry, he gave the energies of his life; and to fulfil it, he spared no labor. Kind and generous towards all, he spent the entire strength of his nature in doing good, and spreading the glad tidings of salvation. These sterling qualities of character won for him the affection and esteem of all with whom he came in contact. Such a life is itself a lesson, and stimulates our faith in human nature and in the truth and efficacy of the Christian religion. Steadfastness in the faith, the memory of a well-spent life, and a conscience at peace with himself, sustained him to the last; and truly he could say with Paul, "I have fought a good fight, I have finished my course, I have kept the faith. Henceforth there is laid up for me a crown of righteousness, which the Lord, the righteous judge, shall give me at that day; and not to me only, but unto all them also that love his appearing."

REV. DAVID ELLIOTT, D.D., LL.D.

THIS well-known and honored divine was born in Sherman's Valley, Perry County, Penn., Feb. 6, 1787. He was educated at Dickinson College, graduating Sept. 25, 1808 ; was licensed to preach Sept. 26, 1811 ; ordained, and installed pastor of the Presbyterian Church of Mercersburg, Franklin County, Penn., Oct. 7, 1812. In this field, his ministerial duties continued for seventeen years, during which time the congregation largely increased and developed under his zealous labors and unremitting fostering care. He was married May 14, 1812, to Miss Ann, daughter of Edward West of Landisburg, Penn. She was born July 7, 1787, and died July 1, 1870. They had eight children. The first three died in infancy. Thomas H., the eldest, reached maturity, was educated for the medical profession, and died in Allegheny, Nov. 25, 1875. David A. was also educated for the same profession : he died in Brookville, Penn., Dec. 6, 1866. Of the three daughters, the eldest is the wife of I. Patton Lyon ; the youngest, the wife of Rev. A. B. Lowes; and the other one is unmarried, and makes her home in Canonsburg, Penn.

In 1829 he removed to Washington, Penn., and was installed pastor of the Presbyterian church of that place, the duties of which he discharged with rare acceptance. As a pulpit orator, he was celebrated ; his learning, and thorough knowledge of theology, his rhetoric and profound logic, combined to render him one of the most successful preachers of his day.

During this period he was elected by the trustees of Washington College, president of the institution in connection with his pastoral charge. This position he declined, under the impression that the church required his entire time. The board, however, prevailed upon him to consent so far as to assume the duties of temporary president, and professor of moral philosophy, until a permanent president could be secured.

The college at this period was in a condition of complete prostration. To Dr. Elliott's exertions were mainly due its resuscitation and future prosperity.

His connection with the church at Washington terminated in 1836, not by any wish of either himself or the congregation, but rather in obedience to the call of the General Assembly to assume a professorship in the Western Theological Seminary in the city of Allegheny. He was personally averse to the change, and made it with reluctance. His congregation were also unanimously opposed to it, and united with the elders and trustees in an earnest remonstrance. His repeated replies of declination to the directors of the seminary were returned with renewed appeals to him, under Providence, to rescue the institution from its perils, and carry it forward to success.

His compliance, therefore, was a surrender of himself to what he believed to be his duty, indicated by Providence, as expressed in the appeals of his brethren.

His departure from Washington, as at Mercersburg, was viewed with regret; and the affection which marked his intercourse with the people to whom he had endeared himself as a pastor and friend, continued during the remainder of his life. His work as a theological teacher, although the most important, successful, and far-reaching of his many callings, does not require to be elaborated at great length. Its long continuance, his unceasing watching, and assiduous labor belong to the history of that institution. In assuming these duties, he took hold of them with a faithful and trusting heart. His faith soared aloft through the clouds of discouragement, to read the future of his sacrifice in the promises of a covenant-keeping God; upon its altar he laid the offering of his best talents and ability: and, although he is dead, the institution lives to commemorate his efforts in its resuscitation.

Upon his election in 1835, by the General Assembly, he was assigned to the professorship of church history. He was subsequently transferred to the chair of theology, the duties of which he assumed after the close of the session of the

General Assembly of 1836, though still occupying his pulpit until his release in the following October.

The latter chair he held until 1854, when, at his own suggestion, the General Assembly authorized the directors to readjust the professorships. This change met with his cordial approbation : he was elected to the department of polemic and historical theology. During the early period of his teachings, he depended more upon text-books, and less on lectures, than afterwards. His close study of the standard writers qualified him to impart in a clear and lucid manner their treasures to the pupils under his care.

Among the achievements of his later professorship, he delivered a full course of lectures on church government and pastoral theology, the fruits of his patient study and long experience.

To his pupils, he was no less a trusted counsellor and friend than a revered teacher : with paternal care he watched over their interests, and sought at all times their temporal as well as their spiritual welfare. Their poverty or sickness, their doubts and fears in spiritual matters, and all embarrassing questions relating to their future work, found in him a ready ear and a sympathetic heart ; and having acquired the necessary qualification to fit them for the duties to which they were called, and gone out into the world, he was ever solicitous for their welfare, and followed them to their fields of labor with his love and earnest prayers.

To his zealous efforts, great executive ability and personal influence in the management of the seminary, may be justly attributed, in a great measure, its restoration to prosperity. Although it had been established by the General Assembly, backed by public favor, and the influence of the minister of Christ, several important mistakes had, however, somewhat impaired the confidence of the churches in its financial management, and inclined them to withhold, to some extent, further contributions.

The lapse of ten years' experiment ; buildings unfinished ; a faculty incomplete in number ; an inadequate salary, relatively less than he had been receiving, depending solely upon the voluntary support of contributors, whose zeal had become weakened, — these offered but feeble inducements to one of his learning and foresight, in no need of assuming a position of so much embarrassment, except as it appealed to his sense of duty and faith in God. His willingness to serve under this condition of affairs is an honorable exponent of his character.

To his fidelity and indomitable perseverance in contending with embarrassments for over fifteen years, does the Church owe in a great measure the preservation of the life of the institution. By his zeal and faith he inspired the drooping energies of its friends, who would have probably yielded to the force of circumstances had it not been for the interest he manifested in it.

The steadily increasing number of the students confirmed the high estimation in which he was held by the friends of the seminary.

Circumstances having unfortunately arisen during the year 1840, which left him alone and without aid in the faculty, and for a time reduced the number of the students as well as increased the embarrassments, his earnest spirit and abiding faith in an over-ruling Providence gave him assurance of its continuance and final triumph.

His first important literary production was a volume of "Letters on Church Government," a work of merit, and greatly esteemed as a masterly effort. His acknowledged talents and skill in this direction from the first were greatly appreciated, and gave him a prominence in the ecclesiastic courts of the highest importance.

He was noted for his administrative ability as a pastor and moderator of the sessions of the church ; and no opinions were more favorably received than his in the sessions of the presbytery, synod, and General Assembly.

His private as well as his ministerial character was marked by no selfishness: charitable in his judgment, he was indulgent to the weakness and short-comings of others. Those who were intimate with him, admired him for the excellency of his character.

As a pastor, he was firm and true to his obligations, guiding the way to consistent action, striving to do justice to all. His success as a theological teacher, and minister of the gospel, was the result of unity of purpose and perseverance.

He died in Allegheny on the eighteenth day of March, 1874. We close this imperfect record of his virtues and usefulness, with the earnest hope "that our last end may be like his."

REV. JOSEPH KING.

REV. JOSEPH KING was born in Kinsman, Trumbull County, O., July 9, 1831. In his youth he was left without any of the appliances of wealth ; thrown entirely upon his own resources, he was subjected to many privations and severe trials ; yet nevertheless, by patience and indomitable perseverance these were overcome, and became the means of developing a strong character.

The money expended in acquiring an education was earned by his own efforts, in laboring on the farm, and by teaching.

In the eighteenth year of his age, having mastered the common branches of an English education, he entered the college at Bethany, W. Va., from which he received his academic degree of A.B. in 1855.

His early religious training was in the tenets of the Presbyterian church, and he had but a limited knowledge of the Disciples, or the peculiar doctrines entertained by them, until he had arrived at the age of twenty-one ; at this period of his life, he was exceedingly exercised in seeking the way of salvation, was brought to believe in the tenets of this organization, and was immersed in Mahoning County, O., in 1852.

After graduating at college, the first year of his ministry was spent at Warren, O., the next three in the State of New York in connection with the Williamsville Classical Institute. Upon leaving the Institute, he devoted himself to regular ministerial labor, and was chosen pastor of the church in New Lisbon, O., which he served acceptably for four years. He then removed to the city of Allegheny, and took charge of the church in that place, where he has labored successfully for several years.

His general appearance marks him as a man of equitable temper and large benevolence, yet he is, nevertheless, decided and firm.

His teachings are principally practical : his discourses appeal to the conscience of his hearers rather than to their susceptibility to oratorical power.

He possesses very little imagination, and is not, in the popular sense of the term, an orator. His success in the ministry, nevertheless, demonstrates the fact that he wields an influence greater than that which belongs to the most gifted speakers. In all his relations, he is noted for his broad and liberal views, as well as for his labor for the promotion of Christian unity. Wherever he has labored, the divine blessing has attended his teaching.

Mr. King takes a great interest in the cause of education, has been elected for many years a school director from the Second Ward, Allegheny, and during most of the time served as president of the Board of Controllers, being noted for his profound judgment and impartial rulings.

REV. LUTHER HALSEY, D.D., LL.D.

THE subject of this sketch was born in Schenectady, N.Y., Jan. 1, 1794.

His father, also named Luther, had received in his youth a careful and liberal education. He became an officer in the American army of the Revolution. In the early years of the war he was reckless and exceedingly profane.

As adjutant, he was one day forming the battalion. Displeased at something, he burst into blasphemy fearful for force and significance of expression. A soldier called "Wicked Tom," because of his notorious profanity, was seen by the adjutant to tremble, and was overheard to remark, "It makes my blood run cold to hear our adjutant swear."

The comment startled the officer. What was there in his profanity that shocked even "Wicked Tom"?

He began to reflect, and perceived that familiar acquaintance with the Bible and its doctrines enabled him to use, instead of the preposterous profanity of uninstructed men, expressions loaded with the logic and rhetoric of the word of God. His education under Christian influences had done this for him. It had taught him to swear rationally! The skill with which he wove maledictions condemned him. He felt himself to be one of the chief of sinners, a transgressor whose early privileges and light left him without excuse, and aggravated his wickedness. He became a changed man, and was remarkable thenceforth for Christian faith, courage, and devotedness. He was pre-eminently a man of prayer. He believed in the covenant-keeping God of Abraham, and did not for a moment doubt his willingness to accept, and renew by his Spirit, the children of those who believed his promises, and commanded their households in his fear.

Adjutant Halsey had the unspeakable satisfaction of seeing

all his children who arrived at mature years decidedly religious men and women. He lived to see four of his sons graduate at college, and enter the ministry. Of these, Luther was the eldest and the most distinguished.

After the war, Adjutant Halsey engaged in teaching. While the subject of this sketch was still young, the father removed to Whiteborough, in Oneida County, near Utica, N.Y. A few years later he became the principal of the academy at Newburg, on the Hudson. Here Luther, having graduated meanwhile from Union College, was for a brief time his father's assistant. Before 1816 he had studied medicine and law in New-York City, and theology under the Rev. J. Johnston, D.D., of Newburg, and in that year began to preach as stated supply of the Presbyterian church of Blooming Grove, Orange County, N.Y.

On the 1st of January, 1818, he married a young widow, Mrs. Anna G. Smith, daughter of Mr. George Gardner of Newburg.

The same year, or the year before this, he was installed pastor of the church already mentioned. His ministry at Blooming Grove was to an extraordinary degree useful. He soon became widely known, not for talents and unction only, but for learning also.

Excessive labors in a great revival with which the Lord blessed his church, impaired Mr. Halsey's health. The rupture of a blood-vessel made retirement from the pulpit imperatively necessary. In 1824, while his health was still precarious, he was called to the chair of natural history and chemistry in Nassau Hall, Princeton, N.J. He fulfilled the duties of this position until 1829, when the General Assembly of the Presbyterian church elected him professor of ecclesiastical history and church polity in the Western Theological Seminary at Allegheny, Penn. Dr. Janeway was his colleague there for a short time, and afterward the celebrated Dr. Nevin, who, a few years later, joined the German Reformed Church. No interval of distance or time, no denominational diversity of views, could alienate these brethren from each other's affection. Dr. Nevin preached Dr. Halsey's funeral sermon.

From Allegheny, Professor Halsey removed, in 1837, to Auburn, N.Y., to perform, in the theological seminary there, the duties of a similar office.

In July, 1843, while he was still at Auburn, he received from Mr. Michael Allen of Pittsburg, a letter, in which occur some sentences that may interest members of the Second Presbyterian Church of Allegheny, formerly called the Manchester Church. I will quote : —

"I have had a long talk with friend Sampson[1]. A church expressly intended for you will be finished on or before the 1st of October next, seventy feet by forty-three ; Gothic windows eleven and a half feet high ; vestibule twenty feet ; a gallery in front for singers ; eighty-eight pews all complete ; every dollar paid before the church is opened ; Dr. Herron to preach the opening sermon. You see, all is cut and dry for work. Is not this noble for such a small place? But you have some good material at work. All done by a few. I do not think that such an offer should be refused, as it will just place you on your own farm, and in the midst of your best friends, who will endeavor to make you comfortable. Should you refuse it, I well know that the disappointment will go beyond any thing it would be in my power to express."

Dr. Halsey became the first pastor of that church, after some delay, but remained with it only a short time. In 1846 he yielded to Mrs. Halsey's impression that her health would be benefited by residence in the East, and removed to Perth Amboy, N.J.

In 1848 he was in New-York City, delivering a course of lectures to the students of the Union Theological Seminary. There he continued until he was induced by friends and admirers to remove in 1851 to Washingtonville, in Orange County, N.Y., where he preached as stated supply of the Presbyterian Church for many years. Here his congregation included some of the descendants of those who were his parishioners in his first pastorate, Washingtonville being but a few miles from Blooming Grove.

For the last ten years of his life, his home was at Hammon-

[1] Mr. John Sampson of Manchester.

ton, N.J. He and Mrs. Halsey spent much time, however, at the house of Mrs. Halsey's son, Mr. Charles G. Smith, near Pittsburg, Penn. There, on the 22d of February, 1874, more than three years after the death of her son, died Mrs. Halsey, after having been confined to her room for many months by partial paralysis. This affection did not act upon her brain or her spirits. Until the end approached, she enjoyed with even unusual zest the society of her friends, and such literary pursuits as had been, from her childhood, her delight. She was an extraordinary woman. She could repeat word for word, when over fourscore years of age, whole poems of the English classics. Many of her own compositions survive her, and give evidence of both taste and scholarship. Of her poetical productions, perhaps none is superior to verses inscribed " To Lyra," and published in " Putnam's Monthly " for August, 1854. The best known of her prose works is a "Life of Elizabeth Fry." She read six languages besides her own. Her aversions and attachments were equally positive. Persons she disliked were not often encouraged to cultivate her acquaintance. The relatives and friends whom she loved, found her devotion entire and lasting. She had good judgment in all matters of business. Well had it been for her husband to commit to her the management of all his financial affairs! She was deeply interested in all works of Christian benevolence. I am told she was among the first to suggest the founding of an orphan-asylum in Allegheny City, and that she designed its seal, — a nest full of young, open-mouthed birds. She was earnestly interested in all her husband's work, and was supremely desirous to have all whom she loved become true Christians. For more than fifty-six years was she the devoted wife of Dr. Halsey. Her death, and the death in February, 1880, of Mrs. Smith, whom he loved as if she had been his own daughter, caused him to feel the profound loneliness of earth. Very few who had been his friends in the years of his youth and prime then survived.

After the removal of Mrs. Smith from her old homestead, Dr. Halsey had spent a time with one of his grandsons, and then retired to his farm near Hammonton, where he lived with his nephew and tenant, Mr. Abram H. Van Doren. He died in Norristown, Penn., on the 29th of October, 1880, in the eighty-seventh year of his age. He had been called, but a few days before, to attend the funeral of Mrs. Job F. Halsey; had taken cold, and, being extremely weak, was unable to rally.

The personal appearance of Dr. Halsey was impressive. He was fully six feet in height; had very lively eyes of deepest blue, the well-curved brows of which were often knit with an expression of profound thoughtfulness, and were surmounted by a lofty and grandly developed forehead; had brown hair that narrowly missed being auburn; and a mouth very firm when the face was in repose, but very mobile when he was excited by conversation, or interested in any topic that touched his feelings. Ordinarily he was grave and very dignified. In this dignity, there was nothing assumed. It was the result of an ambitious and chivalric nature, earnestness of character, and intellectual force, and was perfectly consistent with the great kindliness of countenance that invariably attracted little children to him. His grandson, the Rev. George G. Smith of Tennent, N.J., thus speaks of him:—

"My first distinct recollection of him takes me back to 1842 or 1843. My parents were living at Dr. Halsey's place below Manchester, where Mr. Bennett lives now. The house was then quite in the country. On a summer afternoon, a stern-wheel steamer that plied between Pittsburg and Beaver 'slowed up' opposite our house, and sent a boat ashore. The steamer was probably the 'Lake Erie' or the 'Beaver,' and made, as nearly all boats did in those days, with every escape of the steam, a tremendous noise, that awakened echoes among the hills for miles on both sides of the Ohio River. I was soon called to the parlor, and led into the presence of a tall, slender gentleman, dressed in black, whose high white cravat, deep, manly voice, thoroughly Christian suavity, and kind notice of me, a little boy, captivated me at once."

Dr. Luther Halsey had come from Auburn to visit his friends in Pittsburg.

He was a man of great learning. I was familiar with his habits of study for more than thirty years. He rose early, and spent more than twelve hours, on an average, each day in close, careful reading of the best books that discriminating scholarship could select. He had a wonderful memory, and readily recollected the substance of all he read. It is not strange, therefore, that such work as he did in the study gave him command of whatever had been written that was best worth remembering in the departments of learning in which he was specially interested.

A justice of the Supreme Court of the United States, and a number of distinguished ministers of the gospel, met at the house of a prominent Presbyterian pastor of Baltimore, were discussing the character and attainments of John Quincy Adams soon after the death of that celebrated scholar. They agreed that America had lost her most learned citizen. "Who is the most learned man left?" asked one of the party. The judge promptly answered, "The Rev. Luther Halsey is now the most learned man known to the public in the United States." In this opinion, all the ministers concurred.

The older citizens of Allegheny remember well the Rev. Dr. Page of the Protestant Episcopal Church, a man of rare erudition. He and Dr. Halsey rode in the same carriage from Maple Grove, the home of the late Rev. A. D. Campbell, D.D., to Allegheny Cemetery, attending Dr. Campbell's funeral. A few days later I met Dr. Page. He said eagerly concerning Dr. Halsey, "He is a wonderful man! A wonderful man! The best-read man I have met for twenty years!"

"He is so full of learning," said Dr. Melanchthon W. Jacobus, "you have only to tap him on any subject, and the stream will flow."

Near the end of his life, Dr. Halsey, while on a visit to Norristown, Penn., was in company with the Rev. J. Grier Ralston, D.D., and Cornelius Baker, M.D., intimate friends of his brother, Dr. Job F. Halsey.

Dr. Baker, who has repeatedly mentioned to me his impression of the extraordinary learning of Luther Halsey, related an incident that particularly struck him.

Dr. Ralston was a scholar and an educator. He knew that Dr. Halsey had once been professor of chemistry in Princeton

College, and inquired whether he kept abreast of the progress of that science. Dr. Halsey, with his usual modesty, felt that he did not, and confessed as much.

"The two talked chemistry," said Dr. Baker, "until Dr. Halsey had drawn out of Dr. Ralston all the latter knew upon the subject, and had overlapped that with evidence of wider and more thorough acquaintance with the science than even Dr. Ralston, learned as he was, possessed."

His knowledge of ecclesiastical history, and of the history of America, was certainly not surpassed by that of any other man of his day.

He bought books to read them. If I mistake not, the number of Dr. Halsey's books, packed and catalogued at Washingtonville, in 1867 or 1868, to be sent to the Allegheny Seminary, exceeded three thousand volumes. He had long before that time given several thousand volumes to the same institution, and thousands more to different relatives and friends. Nearly all of these, excepting books of reference, he had thoroughly read and digested.

In the pulpit, Dr. Halsey was orthodox, instructive, and eloquent. Wendell Phillips was not more eloquent than Dr. Halsey sometimes was in extemporaneous efforts. He was either formally called or privately invited to become the pastor of many of the strongest churches in the land. He was sought by Dr. Payson's congregation in Portland, Me., after the death of that distinguished man, and by the First Presbyterian churches of Utica, N.Y., and Princeton, N.J., as well as by prominent churches in Washington City, and in other centres of intelligence and influence. John Quincy Adams was among those who tried to induce him to go to the national capital.

Dr. Halsey excelled any other man I have ever met in respect of the power he possessed to illuminate a subject by accurate and simple exegesis, and practical adaptation to the minds of his hearers. Many a time in cottage prayer-meetings in Orange County, N.Y., and in the lecture-room of the Second Presbyterian Church in Allegheny, Penn., have I heard from his lips such sweet and edifying conversational comment and discourse upon some passage of Scripture as charmed the scholar, and enlightened and comforted the illiterate. The late Rev. L. L. Conrad was accustomed to say he had never met any one else who equalled Dr. Luther Halsey in a prayer-meeting talk. No other has ever seemed to me to approach him in ability to nourish God's people by running comment upon a chapter, or upon several consecutive verses of Scripture. It was his belief, that no other kind of preaching was so profitable as this exposition of so much of some portion of the Bible as brought out clearly a prominent topic of thought, and its various relations to the minds and spiritual wants of men. To find the central truth of a parable, a miracle, a narrative, a doctrinal statement, and then to irradiate this by bringing to a focus upon it all the converging lines of light revealed by the Holy Spirit in the passage and context, this was his aim in an expository lecture.

His religious character was sincere and exalted, and his habits of devotion and self-examination insured close knowledge of his own heart and of human nature. He endeavored to live in continual remembrance of the presence, precepts, and service of his Lord. A quotation from a memorandum written by him for his own benefit and guidance while he was at Blooming Grove, N.Y., will illustrate the principles, methods, and motives of his ministry.

"Live to-day just as if you were to die to-morrow. *Pingo in æternum.* Live more directly and exclusively for eternity. Let me think, feel, speak, study, act, all for eternity.

"1. The first ministerial qualification is to have a heart warm with desire after the glory of God and the salvation of perishing immortals. It makes the mind fertile, the tongue eloquent, the labor light, and is the surest pledge of a spiritual harvest among the people of one's charge.

"2. The Scripture is the best storehouse for arguments, illustrations, etc. Compose my sermons by the word of God.

"3. Find the subject sabbath evening, think it over through the week, and complete the preparation before the 'next sabbath. Let the morning of the sabbath be spent in devotion, and attention to personal religion.

"4. In my sermons, specially regard the practical application, and endeavor to adapt it to every class of hearers. Let no one go away disappointed, unimproved.   It may be his last opportunity !

"5. If my sermons are not suited to promote *my* spiritual improvement, they will not benefit my hearers.   *Always first preach them to myself.*

"6. Visit the sick and dying once a week.   They are lonely, discouraged, and decaying, and in need.   Visit the tempted and despairing often.   Visit persons who are removing, or who are only transient guests.   This may be my only time.   We separate forever !   Visit the concerned and awakened often. Theirs is a strife with Satan.   Go or send until they are confirmed.   Visit the aged and infirm, and those confined within doors.   Carry to them the ordinances.   They cannot come. Visit those who are under the discipline of the church, to reclaim them while there is hope, and save Christ's kingdom from continued reproach.   Visit the active and apt, to set them upon particular duties while the opportunity lasts.

"N.B. Visit straightway every individual member of the congregation for the spiritual good of each, so that to each one personally may be addressed, once at least in his life, the message of reconciliation.

"7. Take special notice of the religious improvement of the *children* of the congregation.   Pray with them, exhort them, induce them to read, catechise them, inquire whether parents restrain and instruct them.   See that the church pays special regard to *orphans.   Youth is a season of critical importance.*

"8. Poor widows must be sought out, visited, comforted. Strangers must be looked after.

"9. Blacks must be. particularly provided for.   They have no friend but me.   (Harry said, 'Nobody prays for me!')

"10. Let me remember, in all companies and places, that I am a servant of God, a minister of the gospel, officially charged with the salvation of men."

Socially he was one of the most agreeable and delightful of men.   He was a repository, an encyclopædia of facts and anecdotes; and when he was in company that was congenial, his conversation was wonderfully interesting, brilliant, and profitable.   His table-talk was often very sprightly and spicy.   He made all literature tributary to his purpose to inform and please his friends. By the magic wand of memory, he would command into the presence of the company any noted character of history, to speak and act again for the entertainment or instruction of mankind.

I have sat in the society of the celebrated Thomas Marshall of Kentucky, when his brain was stimulated only enough to make it specially active, and have heard him exert himself by the hour to entertain an intelligent circle of college-men. His conversation was not only less instructive, it was less brilliant, than Dr. Halsey's often was.

Frequently when his mind was active, the doctor would pace a room diagonally from corner to corner, his hands under the tails of his coat, or thrust under his study-gown behind. Then was the time to engage him in talk. When he retired to his library, after tea, and lighted his pipe, if you could catch him before he opened his book, he was ready for a long conversation on topics that occupy the thoughts of scholars or earnest-minded men. . The faster he talked, the faster did he smoke, until the blue wreaths encircled his head, and at times half closed his flashing eyes.

His habit of smoking was not formed in boyhood. He was too conscientious and obedient in his youth to do what his father disapproved. While engaged in the severe labors of special services at Blooming Grove, his health suffered from too much preaching. He was attacked by hemorrhages. His physician counselled him to smoke. So repugnant was tobacco to him, that, as Mrs. Halsey assured me, he was nearly two weeks smoking his first cigar. He became an inveterate smoker.

Often he questioned the rightness of indulging himself in the habit. The fact that physicians recommended the use of tobacco, and the fact, also, that it had become a condition upon which he was dependent for quiet nerves and successful study, determined the issue. He smoked the hour before he died.

Whatever good the pipe may have done him, it did him far more harm. To-day physicians and ministers ought to know better than to prescribe or follow the habitual use of tobacco.

Dr. Halsey was entirely free from the ostentation of learning. The simplicity of his manners, and his Christian regard for man as man, often led illiterate people to imagine that his reputation for extensive and profound learning was much exaggerated.

"He's a very plain mon," said an Irish gardener. "He jist talks aboot wur-rums on the cabbage-leaves, an' caterpillars on the ellums, an' sech like."

"Didn't he tell me all about how to make soft-soap!" commented the house-maid.

His knowledge of all the mechanical and agricultural arts; of animals and their habits and diseases; of soils, and the best kinds of treatment for clay, or loam, or slate-land; of the methods of cultivation approved and practised in many different countries; of insects injurious to vegetation, and of insectivorous birds; in short, of all that could interest and help farmers, — made him specially welcome to their homes.

He always contrived, everywhere, to season conversation with grace, as with salt, and was accustomed, after a visit to a family in his parish, to have the household called together to listen to a chapter of the Bible, and to be led by him in prayer.

He was thoroughly in sympathy with all real progress, believing with Tennyson, that, —

> "Through the ages one increasing purpose runs,
> And the thoughts of men are widened with the process of the suns."

So, too, was he heartily in sympathy with young men. He entered enthusiastically into their plans, and encouraged them in study and work. Many are alive to-day who would gladly send, from the four quarters of the globe, testimony to the advantage they derived while students in college or seminary, or while under Dr. Halsey's care in his own household, from his brotherly and fatherly counsels and cheer.

He was a patriot. His descent and his studies intensified his love of country. For sixty years he clung to the purpose of writing a history of the United States, which should make suitable and constant recognition of God's providence, guiding and controlling the affairs of the nation. He left an immense mass of unfinished manuscripts, and inexpansible notes for the book — the results of incredible labor. No one can make any such use of these as he designed to make.

Here it may be well to ask why Dr. Halsey wrote and published so little. I think that only those intimately acquainted with the man can give the answer. *Desire for perfection deterred him.* His ideal was too high ever to be wrought out. He would not write until he had thoroughly mastered the subject. He was so learned as to know, that, while ever learning, he had never attained absolute knowledge of any subject of investigation. He would learn more, *more*, MORE, ALL! He studied incessantly, but never achieved, never could have achieved, what he aimed at. Appalled at the greatness of the work he had conceived, when over fourscore years of age he let the pen fall from a hand unnerved by a glimpse at that which, like God himself, is unsearchable — the immensity of knowledge. He wronged the future by so doing. No other man can do so well what he could have accomplished.

I think his dear namesake, pupil, and friend, the Rev. Luther Halsey Gulick, now in China, could shed much light upon this philosophy of Dr. Halsey's unfruitfulness as an author. No one now living was better acquainted with Dr. Halsey's methods of study.

Although he did not write the proposed history, he did very often deliver at celebrations of the Fourth of July, and on other suitable occasions, remarkable historical addresses. I wonder whether any aged member of the Cincinnati Society, to which he belonged, can give the public some report of Dr. Halsey's reminiscences of characters conspicuous in the military and civil service of the country in the first period of its history? In Norristown, Penn., numbers of members of the First Presbyterian congregation retain vivid impressions of the extraordinary excellence and eloquence of a patriotic discourse delivered by Dr. Halsey in that town.

As a man of business, Dr. Halsey was lamentably deficient. His heart and mind were too much absorbed in his studies, and he was too unworldly, incautious, and visionary, to deal wisely with financial affairs. No man had more physical or moral courage than he had, yet he would allow any poltroon or fool to overreach him in business. This was not the worst of the ill: not only did he often suffer unnecessary loss of property — he was sometimes led to attribute to roguery on the part of others, the inevitable consequences of his own indefiniteness and carelessness. He would give vague directions, and, when these were misunderstood, would sometimes charge mistakes to wilful dishonesty. I fear he once wronged in this way certain brethren who entered with him into a plan to publish a religious newspaper in New-York City. He honestly believed they understood certain moneys advanced by him to be a loan. His own vagueness allowed them to honestly think the payment an investment in stock. So good men were set at variance. One of his relatives, who greatly admired his talents, learning, and piety, said, respecting his unfitness to manage affairs, "He is all right for heaven, but is not worth a cent for earth!" Yet the God in whom he trusted, so overruled his mismanagement, that real estate, part of which was swamp-land below Allegheny City, purchased by him when he was in his prime, did, by its enhancement from the growth of the town, secure to him a sufficient support for the years when he was too old to perform regular pastoral duty. The Marine Hospital stands upon part of that property.

What a man is to his own household and relatives, is the truest test of his character. Those who dwelt at any time in his family circle have the fullest and most delightful impression of Dr. Halsey's magnanimity, unselfishness, courage, fortitude, industry, learning, loyalty to Christ, and devotion to his service. He never had son or daughter of his own ; but he loved little children, dandled them on his keees, and bore them as little kings aloft upon his shoulders as, often and long, he paced the room at tea-time. He made himself their playmate, and liked to have the hand of a little child in his as he took, when he lived in the country, his walk at dewy sunrise. He was never so absent-minded as to disregard the inconsequent prattle of the little ones. Any child that happened to be visiting at his house was as the doctor's shadow wherever he moved.

He had the most reverential regard for woman. From the depths of his pure heart he honored her, and his demeanor toward her was that of a most chivalrous and Christian knight.

He was not merely tolerant of the innocent amusements of young people : he encouraged them. As a boy and young man, he was fond of shooting and fishing. He had many stories to tell of the days when he used to shoot wild turkeys and passenger pigeons in the State of New York.

His presence in the household cheered like sunlight. His equanimity had a calming, peace-breathing power. Old and young went to him naturally with glad tidings or with any anxiety or grief. He had unselfish sympathy for all.

In bringing to a conclusion this inadequate sketch of the life and character of a truly good and great man, it is well to notice last his implicit and triumphant faith in God. No one could be long in his company without perceiving that he habitually lived under the power of things unseen and eternal. To him, God and heaven were realities, — the one his Father, the other his home. To spend a sabbath evening with him in his old age was to enter the vestibule of the upper temple. So high and holy was his joy in the Lord, that his household and friends often seemed to attend him to the summits of the " Delectable Mountains," to catch enrapturing glimpses of the land which to those that are of the earth, earthy, is very far off, and through the telescope of his faith to see "the King in his beauty." Now he sees him as he is, and is like him.

An aged and beloved sister of Dr. Halsey is still living near Springfield, in the State of Ohio ; and many nephews and nieces love and cherish his memory.

REV. JOB FOSTER HALSEY, D.D.

JOB FOSTER HALSEY was born in Schenectady, N.Y., July 12, 1800. He was the youngest brother of the Rev. Luther Halsey, D.D., LL.D.

Job F. Halsey studied theology with his brother Luther, and was licensed by the Hudson-river presbytery in 1820. Subsequently he spent three years in the theological seminary at Princeton, N.J., at the same time rendering his brother, Dr. Luther Halsey, important aid in preparing his illustrations for the lectures delivered by the latter as professor of chemistry and natural history in the College of New Jersey, Princeton.

The pulpit of the Tennent Church, near Freehold, N.J., having become vacant by the death of Dr. Woodhull, Job F. Halsey was invited to preach there, and was ordained and installed the pastor of that church, June 1, 1826.

While he was settled here, he married Miss Elizabeth Parker Brinley, whose strong Christian character, systematic habits, and mental vigor, Dr. Halsey was ever ready to credit with influences which helped and balanced him through all his life thereafter.

Here, also, he began the work which issued in supplying those destitute of it in the United States with the Bible.

First he induced the Monmouth-County Bible Society to supply the county. Then he brought about such action on the part of the Nassau-Hall Bible Society as resulted in supplying the State of New Jersey with the word of God in the short space of two years. Moreover, the society undertook, at his suggestion, to raise forty thousand dollars to be applied to the teaching of those who could not read the Scriptures. After he removed to Albany, N.Y., as agent over sixteen counties of that State for the Sunday School, Tract, and American Bible Societies, he induced the Washington-County Bible

Society to agree to raise five thousand dollars to aid the parent society, on condition that at its next anniversary it would undertake to supply the United States within two years. This it did.

On the failure of his health, Dr. Halsey removed to Pittsburg, Penn., where his brother Luther had been called to serve as professor of ecclesiastical history and church polity in the Western Theological Seminary.

For a time Dr. Job F. Halsey supplied the First Presbyterian Church of Allegheny every other sabbath. In 1830 or 1831 he was called to be its pastor. The congregation then worshipped in a small frame-building. I believe that Dr. Halsey was still pastor of that people when the brick church, afterward destroyed by fire, was erected on Beaver Street (now Arch Street).

In 1835, his health failing, he accepted a professorship in Marion Manual-Labor College, Missouri; and during the absence of its president, the Rev. Dr. Potts, he taught and graduated the first class of that institution.

There he lost his voice, and, turning his back upon Missouri, removed to Perth Amboy, N.J., where he opened the Raritan Seminary for young ladies. Here, as principal, he spent twelve years in teaching.

While educating there the two daughters of his old friend, the Rev. David Nelson, M.D., he was instrumental in inducing that gentleman, who had been, while a practising physician, an undisguised infidel, to write his celebrated work, "Nelson on Infidelity," now owned and published by the American Tract Society. The entire manuscript was sent to Dr. Halsey by mail in letters from Marion, Mo., and Quincy, Ill. He carried it through the press at New York, Mrs. Halsey correcting the proof-sheets. Some years before his death, Dr. Nelson told Dr. Halsey that he had a list of over three hundred persons who had been recovered from infidelity by this book.

In 1848 Dr. Halsey's voice was so far restored that he was able to preach again; and he became pastor of the church in West Bloomfield, N.J., now called Mont Claire. There he remained until a large stone church was nearly completed, when he was compelled to leave on account of the loss of the health of his wife.

In 1856 he received and accepted a call from the First Presbyterian Church of Norristown, Penn., of which he was pastor until July 12, 1880, and from that date until his death "pastor emeritus."

So far, I have made free use of material given by Dr. Halsey to the late Rev. J. G. Ralston, D.D., of Norristown, and used by the latter in his "Historical Sketch of the First Presbyterian Church" of that place.

His pastorate at Norristown was eminently successful. Dr. Ralston's description of Dr. Halsey in 1876 is worthy of being transcribed word for word. "As a man," wrote he, "Dr. Halsey has a commanding presence, a courteous manner, and a kind heart. As a Christian, he is gentle, devout, and evidently sincere. As a minister, he is earnest, and sometimes even impetnous. His style is unpretentious, although studied; while his orthodoxy is undoubted. Christ and Him Crucified finds a place in all his sermons. Now, in the seventy-seventh year of his age, he still preaches with unusual vigor."

A more beautiful and even glorious exemplification of Christian faith, joy, and triumphant hope than Dr. Job F. Halsey presented in the last years of his life, it has never been my privilege to behold. I spent the interval from December, 1880, to June, 1881, under his roof. He was then in his eighty-first year. His tall form was not bowed by age. His blue eyes, which habitually beamed with serenity and charity, could also on occasion flash with fires of enthusiasm, as he addressed the presbytery, or his own congregation, upon some theme that kindled his zeal. His voice was deep, rich, and strong. He was gentle and loving. In his home his presence was like a benediction. To sit in the light of his peaceful and blissful countenance was an honor and a blessing to be remembered through one's life. He was unselfish to a degree which no words can express. His Christ-like life was to very many persons the most beautiful and irrefutable evidence of the divine origin of Christianity. Looking unto Jesus, he had been transformed into his image. He loved little children, and they delighted to play and bask in the sunlight of his presence. His death on the 24th of March, 1882, was like a translation. Having contracted a cold, and feeling unwell, but not seriously ill, he retired early in the evening to rest. His only surviving child, Mrs. J J. Borie, went, with the affection of a devoted daughter, to his room before bed-time, and found him dead. As he lay in his coffin, dressed as he had been accustomed to appear in the pulpit, his dignified, placid, and happy face seemed to be the countenance of one who had laid down to pleasant dreams. He was buried beside his beloved wife at Perth Amboy, N.J.

The inscription upon his memorial tablet in the First Presbyterian Church of Norristown, Penn., closes with this most appropriate quotation : —

"He was a good man, and full of the Holy Ghost and of faith." — Acts xii. 24.

REV. JOHN TAYLOR PRESSLY, D.D.

JOHN TAYLOR PRESSLY was born in South Carolina, in the Abbeville District, March 28, 1795. His ancestors were esteemed the best and most influential citizens of his native State. His parents were distinguished for their intelligence and religious proclivities. In such a home, where Christian instruction and Christian example were combined, in furnishing the best of influences, the subject of our brief sketch was born, and grew up to manhood. Every member of the family — including three brothers who became ministers of Christ, and two others who became distinguished physicians, and two sisters, one of whom became the wife of a minister, the other of a physician — gave to the world an honored Christian life.

The subject of our sketch was esteemed the central figure of the family circle, and became the most distinguished.

Having espoused the cause of religion in early life, and manifested a love of study, he gave promise of his after-eminence in piety and learning.

He connected himself with the Cedar-spring Church of the Associate Reformed Synod of the South, and commenced his studies in a classical school in the immediate vicinity of his home. He subsequently entered Transylvania University, Kentucky, where he graduated in 1812, in the eighteenth year of his age.

During his novitiate, he consecrated himself to the gospel ministry, and, in view of this, determined to acquire the best theological training the country could afford. For this purpose he entered the seminary in New York, then under the charge of the celebrated John Mitchell Mason, D.D.

Having completed the full course of three years' study, he was licensed as a ministerial probationer by the Associate Reformed Presbytery of South Carolina, in the spring of 1815.

For a year he devoted himself to missionary work, travelling on horseback through several of the Southern States, and as far north as Pennsylvania and New York.

He often, in after-years, referred to his missionary tour, especially to the fact of passing through Allegheny, then a forest, and but sparsely inhabited, and which was destined, in the providence of God, to be his future home and the field of his life's labors, and took pleasure in recalling that his journey led him to cross the spot upon which his family residence was afterwards erected.

Returning to his Southern home in the summer of 1816, he received a call to assume the pastoral charge of the church in which he was reared, baptized, and had made a profession of religion.

Having accepted the call, he was ordained and installed its pastor, July 3 of the same year.

For a period of over fifteen years these happy relations were maintained, and he would have gladly spent the remainder of his days in this congenial field. Providence, however, had other and more important work for him to do.

Although pained to sever his connection with a loving people, yet the call was so clear, conclusive, and to his mind imperative, that he felt it his duty to obey. He became celebrated, not only for his eloquence as a Christian minister, but as one eminently qualified to educate others in the gospel ministry. In recognition of his superior abilities in this respect, the members of his own synod had tendered to him the appointment of professor of theology: this he declined to accept, not seeing his way clear to do so. Subsequently, to wit, on the tenth day of October, 1831, the Associate Reformed Synod of the West elected him to the chair of theology in the seminary at Pittsburg, which had been rendered vacant by the decease of its first professor, the Rev. Joseph Kerr, D.D.

The proceedings which resulted in his election, and the causes that led to it, were so manifestly the work of Providence, that he was convinced that the call was directed from above. He at once commenced preparations to enter upon the new work; and on the fifth day of January, 1832, he arrived in Pittsburg with his family, having, in the brief space of two months, decided to change the sphere of his life's work — dissolved his connections with a loving and beloved people, broken up his home, disposed of his property, and made the long and tedious journey from South Carolina to his new field of labor. He entered upon his labors the following week.

His eminent fitness for the work was fully recognized, widely known, and added a new attraction to the merit of the institution. Such was its fame, that students were drawn to it from all parts of the church, north and south.

In addition to his theological duties, he supplied with marked acceptance several of the vacant pulpits in the vicinity, from two of which he received calls to become their pastor, which he declined.

On the 26th of October, 1832, he received a call from the church of Allegheny, which he held under consideration until the following meeting of presbytery. In the mean time, in response to the request of the congregation, he commenced to labor among them as stated supply on the first day of December, 1832, and continued in that capacity until the following April, when he formally accepted the call, and was, on the 27th August of the same year, installed pastor. The Rev. Mr. Cahan delivered the sermon, and the Rev. Mr. Weir made the installation prayer. Thus were constituted relations between pastor and people which continued for thirty-eight years, or until the close of his life, and which proved to be one of the most successful pastorates of modern times.

Possessed of an imposing and stately personal appearance, and endowed with health and great physical strength, he moved with a dignity that commanded attention and admiration wherever he appeared. Endowed by nature with a strong mind, and well trained for the performance of mental work, and methodical in the arrangement of his duties, his labors were abundant and richly productive.

He brought to his work a large experience, and gave to it his whole heart and force of character.

His style of oratory was of that kind that carries conviction to the heart of the truth of the doctrines advocated.

He avoided the sensational in his style of delivery. It was the simple, clear, and earnest declaration of one who knew and felt the object of his teachings to be the salvation of souls.

His great power as a preacher may be attributed to the clearness of conception and expression which characterized his manner of delivery in the presentation of his subject.

His fine personal appearance, strong, sonorous, and well-modulated voice, and suave and dignified manners, gave to his delivery a powerful and lasting effect.

Faithful as a pastor, he was also a tender and sympathizing friend, ever on the alert to do good by counselling the weak and despondent, and soothing the sorrows of the sick and afflicted. In his personal efforts to carry out his benevolent plans, he was warmly aided by his excellent wife.

He was united in marriage to Miss Jane Hearst at Cedar Spring, South Carolina, his native place, July 4, 1816. They had nine children. Mrs. Pressly was born June 10, 1793. Endowed in an eminent degree with all the social and Christian qualifications, she was admired for her modest and unassuming demeanor. Active and zealous in doing good, yet she shrank from the slightest public recognition. She was the light and joy of her own home, and also the welcome visitor in the homes of the members of the congregation. Possessed of a cheerful and happy disposition, a countenance glowing with benevolence, and animated with good nature, she fully exemplified the virtue of the scriptural declaration, " A soft answer turneth away wrath." None were better qualified to assuage the sorrows of a broken heart, and cheer the despondent : to bind up the one, and encourage the other, was her constant aim. Her genial presence and loving words were well calculated to secure the confidence, and win the affections, of all with whom she came in contact. Her whole heart and life were dedicated to the service of God, to her husband and his people in the Lord. Her home was the central object in the congregation, where the meek and lowly received as cheerful a welcome as the rich and honorable. She lived respected, and died lamented, in the city of Allegheny, April 4, 1873.

Dr. Pressly took an active and intelligent interest in every thing that tended to enhance the welfare of his adopted city. In the cause of education his zeal was particularly manifested. He aided with ability in the organization of the first board of school directors elected under the law enacted for the establishment of the present system of public schools, and occupied for many years the position of president. During the year 1842 he established, and ably edited until the year 1845, a religious paper entitled "The Preacher," when the Rev. David R. Kerr became the editor. The name was subsequently changed to that of "The United Presbyterian," and became the acknowledged organ of the church bearing that name. The relations existing between Dr. Pressly and contemporary ministers of his own as well as of other denominations, were of the most friendly nature.

In the spring of 1870, it became painfully apparent to his family and numerous friends, that his health and strength, which had been impaired by a former severe and protracted illness, again exhibited unmistakable evidences of failing. His movements were noticed to be less firm and energetic; his erect and stately form became bowed; pain and suffering were stamped upon his features, and his otherwise clear and sonorous voice rendered tremulous. Notwithstanding these discouraging circumstances, he still continued to fulfil acceptably the duties of his pastorate.

In the hope that travel, and change of scene, would renew his health, accompanied by his two daughters, he was induced by his loving family and friends to make the trip of the lower lakes and the St. Lawrence to Canada, and from thence to Saratoga, N.Y.

The desired relief, however, failed to come. On the contrary, he continued day by day to grow worse, and it was deemed necessary to hasten his return home. He arrived completely prostrated, on the ninth day of August, 1870; and after four days of painful suffering, he ceased from his labors, and passed peacefully to his rest and reward.

He died as he lived, in the hope of a blessed immortality, in the seventy-sixth year of his age, the fifty-fifth of his ministry, and the thirty-eighth of his charge of the first U. P. Church of Allegheny.

To some he may have seemed to be of an austere disposition, as he never lost sight of the dignity of his calling or the manner of a high-toned Christian gentleman; but those who knew him best, gave him great credit for the goodness of his heart, and excellency of his Christian character.

In commemoration of the virtues and faithful services of their beloved pastor, the members of the congregation, among whom he had labored so long and acceptably, erected a mural tablet of white marble to the right of the pulpit, with the following appropriate memorial, inlaid with letters of gold inscribed upon a shield of black marble: —

In Memory of

REV. JNO. T. PRESSLY, D.D.,

FOR 38 YEARS

THE BELOVED AND HONORED PASTOR

OF THIS CHURCH;

A GOOD AND GREAT MAN,

WHOSE PURE LIFE AND TENDER AFFECTION,

WISE COUNSEL AND UNFLINCHING FIDELITY,

AND ABUNDANT LABORS,

ARE ENSHRINED IN THE HEARTS

OF A GRATEFUL PEOPLE.

———

BORN MARCH 22D, 1795.

DIED AUGUST 13TH, 1870.

———

"THE RIGHTEOUS SHALL BE IN
EVERLASTING REMEMBRANCE."

This testimonial of loving and grateful hearts was unveiled on the occasion of the semi-centennial anniversary of the church, held Nov. 8, 1881.

REV. JOSEPH STOCKTON, A.M.

AMONG the early ministers of the Presbyterian church, and the pioneer educators, few, if any, made a more salutary or enduring impression upon the infant communities which in early days were gathered and crystallized in the region lying west and north of the Allegheny River, in Western Pennsylvania, including the now populous city of Allegheny, than the Rev. Joseph Stockton, a very brief epitome of whose life and labors is all that can be given here.

The subject of this memoir was the youngest son of Robert Stockton, a farmer of Franklin County, Penn. He was born on the twenty-fifth day of February, 1779. His mother, Mary McKemy, was a daughter of the Rev. McKemy, one of the earliest Presbyterian ministers in the United States. In 1784 his father removed Westward, and settled on a farm in Washington County, Penn. He acquired his classical education at Jefferson College, Canonsburg, graduating with credit in the nineteenth year of his age. He then entered upon a course of theological studies under the instruction of the celebrated Rev. John McMillan, D.D., and became a licentiate on the twenty-fourth day of June, 1799, he being then in his twenty-first year.

On the 8th of May, 1800, he was married to Miss Esther Clark, daughter of David Clark of Washington County, Penn. In the autumn of the same year, he removed with his wife to Meadville, the county-seat of Crawford County, Penn., then quite a new settlement, where, on the twenty-third day of June, 1801, he was ordained and installed the first pastor of the infant church of Meadville. During the nine years which he occupied that position, he also had charge of the Meadville Academy, which subsequently became Allegheny College, and also ministered regularly to the church at Conneaut Lake, a few miles west of the town.

In 1809 he relinquished his several charges, and removed to Pittsburg, where he was chosen principal of the Pittsburg Academy, which afterwards became the Western University of Pennsylvania, and was formally organized May 10, 1822. Up to this period he held the position, discharging its duties faithfully, and with great acceptance to its patrons.

During those years he published the "Western Spelling-Book" and the "Western Calculator," both of which were extensively used in all the schools of the Western country. Over the problems of the latter, many of the youh of that early day spent many weary hours.

While engaged as principal of the academy, he ministered to an infant congregation, worshipping in a rude log "meeting-house" located in the vicinity of Pine Creek, Indiana township, on the Kittanning road, eight miles from Pittsburg. His time on the sabbath was divided between the Pine-creek congregation and the soldiers of the United-States Arsenal. The latter charge he dropped, and devoted his ministerial labors, up to 1829, equally to Allegheny and Pine Creek.

In the year 1819 he removed from Pittsburg to Allegheny, then an inconsiderable hamlet, having previously purchased property on the north-east corner of Stockton Avenue and Arch Street, upon which he erected a modest frame-dwelling, and to which he built an addition, thus making it a comfortable and pleasant home, in which he resided until his death. Within a few years this venerable landmark has been removed, and the site occupied by the Evangelical Lutheran Church.

The congregation which he organized, and to which his ministerial labors were chiefly directed, is now the First Presbyterian Church of Allegheny. Shortly after his removal to Allegheny, he opened the Allegheny Academy on the north-west corner of Federal and Robinson Streets, where many of the youths of Pittsburg and Allegheny acquired a thorough English, and the rudiments of a classical, education.

He was also óne of the original founders of the Western Theological Seminary, and one of its first professors.

During this period the village of Sharpsburg became a place of some importance, and was embraced within the limits of the Pine-creek congregation. For some years Mr. Stockton divided his labors between Pine Creek and Sharpsburg, at which latter place the Christian people had erected a substantial and convenient brick church. Although the Pine-creek congregation was gathered in 1814, and a house of worship erected (the first brick church built north of the Allegheny River), it was not until the following year that the church was formally organized by the ordination of William D. Hawkins, John Galbraith, and Mathew Crawford, elders, and the administration of the sacrament of the Lord's Supper, at which the communicants numbered seven only. Many of the Christians, however, from Pittsburg and elsewhere united with and encouraged the little band. From year to year this church struggled on until the death of Mr. Stockton, seventeen years afterwards, when the records exhibited that one hundred and thirty-six had been admitted as the fruits of his labors.

During the year 1810 he occupied the pulpit of the First Presbyterian Church of Pittsburg, until the Rev. Francis Herron, D.D., was installed pastor.

In addition to his ministerial labors, he was engaged in preparing a work on theology, evidently intended to fill a void which the early book-trade had not fully supplied. The completed portion of the manuscript is executed in a neat and legible manner, and evidences the attainment and industry of its author.

Before commencing his studies for the ministry, he had read a thorough course of medicine; and many of his friends and neighbors, having unlimited confidence in his knowledge and skill, would call upon him in their seasons of illness, and would be satisfied with none other.

In the year 1831, the church in Allegheny having increased in numbers and importance, it was decided to call a regular pastor, when he ceased to labor there as a stated supply, and devoted the few remaining years of his life to the Pine-creek church. It was his custom, in the preparation of his sermons, to study his subject thoroughly, arrange his matter methodically in brief skeleton notes, and depend entirely, for the expansion of his thoughts, on the prompting of the moment. His notes were briefly and closely written, with no record of the times and places in which his discourses were delivered.

The melancholy circumstances connected with the death of Mr. Stockton imparted additional sadness to that event. It was during the summer of 1832, that that terrible scourge of humanity, the Asiatic cholera, first invaded North America, approaching by way of Quebec and Montreal. It soon broke over the Canada border, and travelled rapidly from city to city, and from village to village, carrying consternation and death in its train. In October of that year, Mr. Stockton was hastily summoned to the city of Baltimore on the occasion of the severe indisposition of one of his sons. While there, he was smitten with cholera; and after an illness of but twenty-four hours, most of which time he suffered intense agony, a merciful death terminated his life and his sufferings on the 29th of October. His dying testimony was a happy close of such a life. "Come, Lord, come quickly; thy servant waits," was his frequent exclamation. Like Paul, he had fought the good fight, he had finished his course, he had kept the faith, and was certain of his reward. Thus departed this good man in the zenith of his powers and usefulness, with his armor on, in the fifty-fourth year of his age.

In 1858 his remains were removed from Baltimore to the Allegheny Cemetery.

His strong sense of personal allegiance to the demands of duty is strongly exemplified in his ministerial career. To it he bent the energies of his whole life; and to fulfil it perfectly, he spared no labor. As a scholar, he ranked high; eloquent as a speaker; and as Christian pastor he had few equals. He possessed rare gifts as a pulpit orator, his style being characterized by unusual earnestness, boldness, and finish, while personally he possessed those rare qualities of the head and heart which invariably attract and fix the affections of all classes and conditions of people. To know him was to love him. It requires not the pen of eulogy to herald forth the excellences of this good man. He exhibited an affectionate disposition towards all, and was ever zealous in his endeavors to promote the moral and intellectual welfare of the city of his adoption.

His success as an educator was well known. The author's recollection and observation enable him to state that his happy methods of inspiring his pupils with his own amiable manner was his highest recommendation as a teacher, while his standing as a Christian minister was a pledge that the morals of those intrusted to his care would not be neglected.

His faithful and loving wife survived him for thirty-six years. She died in the old family mansion, where she had lived for over fifty years a humble and devout Christian life, on the thirteenth day of April, 1868. During the late civil war, this estima ble and venerable lady did what she could for her imperilled country, by a diligent use of her aged hands in knitting stockings for its brave defenders.

Her zealous efforts in this direction, coming to the knowledge of President Lincoln, called forth from him an autograph letter, expressing in grateful and felicitous terms, his approval of the meritorious and patriotic act. This letter is preserved by the surviving members of the family as a precious memento of its illustrious author.

REV. ELISHA P. SWIFT, D.D.

THIS eminent minister of the gospel was the son of the Rev. Seth and Lucy Elliot Swift. His father was the pastor of the church in Williamstown, Mass., where he was born Aug. 12, 1792. He connected himself with the Congregational church in Stockbridge, Mass., in July, 1813. His brother, Rev. Ephraim G. Swift, was pastor of that church at that time. He graduated at Williams College, Mass., Sept. 1, 1813, and his theological training was received in Princeton Theological Seminary. He was licensed by the presbytery of New Brunswick, at Lawrenceville, N.J., April 24, 1816, and was ordained by a Congregational Council held in the Park-street Church, Boston, Mass., with a view to the foreign missionary work, Sept. 3, 1817. He was accepted by the American Board of Missions, but providential events interfered with the execution of his purpose. He commenced his ministerial labors in the Second Presbyterian Church of Pittsburg, Oct. 10, 1819, and continued its pastor until Feb. 26, 1833, when he was released, in order that he might devote his entire time to the Western Foreign Missionary Society, of which he had been appointed the corresponding secretary.

On the 1st of July, 1835, the First Presbyterian Church of Allegheny extended to him a call, which he accepted, and continued the pastor of this church for nearly thirty years, the duties of which he discharged with rare fidelity and marked acceptance. He was united in marriage in Hanover, N.J., to Miss Eliza Darling Beach, Oct. 2, 1817, by the Rev. Aaron Condit. Mrs. Swift was born in Hanover, N.J., Feb. 16, 1791. They had nine children, — five sons and four daughters, — named respectively, Henrietta Mary, Asbel Green, Samuel Beach, Elliot Elisha, Henry Martin, Catherine Wilhelmina,

Joseph Patterson, Edward Payson, and Lucy Elizabeth.   Asbel, Samuel, and Joseph died very early.

The subject of our brief memoir died April 3, 1865. For five years previous to his death, the indications of failing health and strength were observed with solicitude by his people, among whom he had labored so faithfully and acceptably. The times on which he was unable to occupy his accustomed place in the sanctuary were occurring with painful frequency. Under these circumstances, the congregation, with an intelligent and generous appreciation, called his son, the Rev. Elliot E. Swift, then pastor of a church at Newcastle, Penn., for the purpose of relieving their tried and feeble pastor. Under this new arrangement, the father was enabled to occupy the pulpit with more or less frequency until within a few months of his decease. He delivered his final discourse on the 18th of September, 1864. From this time onward, through the autumn and winter months, he was confined to his room. At noon·on the day above indicated, while sitting in his chair, his spirit departed from earthly scenes to enter the heavenly rest.

It was his habit, from the commencement of his ministry, to preach without notes; he had evidently trained himself upon the principle that memory loves to be trusted : it was, therefore, only on special occasions, such as the installation of professors, pastors, elders, or deacons, that he would sometimes read the charges he had been called upon to deliver. It must not be supposed from this fact, that his sermons were prepared without the use of the pen. On the contrary, they were mostly fully written out, and gave evidence of deep thought and research, and were delivered with a pathos that riveted the attention, and moved the hearts, of his hearers, and were considered among the grandest specimens of effective pulpit oratory.

His tall and commanding person aided the effectiveness of his delivery ; his large and well-developed head and expansive forehead gave evidence of a superior mind ; and his large and luminous eyes, fixed upon the hearer, imparted to his delivery an almost irresistible power.

His faithful wife survived him for nearly six years : she died Jan. 30, 1871. They rest side by side in Allegheny Cemetery.

Dr. Swift was the author of the following publications : —

"The Sacred Manual, containing a Series of Questions, Historical, Doctrinal, and Preceptive, on the Sacred Scriptures," published January, 1821.

A Sermon delivered in the college-hall at Canonsburg, Washington County, Penn., Sept. 19, 1820, before the Female Education Society of Jefferson College.

"Duties and Responsibilities of the Professorial Office in Theological Seminaries," a sermon delivered in the First Presbyterian Church of Pittsburg, Oct. 16, 1828, on the occasion of the inauguration of the Rev. Jacob J. Janeway, D.D., as professor of theology in the Western Theological Seminary.

"The Character of God," a sermon published in "The Presbyterian Preacher," July, 1832.

An Address delivered to the congregation of the Second Presbyterian Church of Pittsburg, March 3, 1833, on the sabbath following the dissolution of the author's pastoral relations to that church, by the presbytery of Ohio, at the request of the executive committee of the Western Foreign Missionary Society.

A Sermon on Isa. xviii. 1, "Woe to the land shadowing with wings," preached before the synod of Pittsburg, in Washington, Penn., Oct. 16, 1825.

He edited "The Western Foreign Missionary Chronicle," in 1833 and 1834, which contains a full account of the proceedings of the Western Foreign Missionary Society.

"The Misdirection of Physical and Intellectual Effort," an address delivered to the Franklin and Philo Literary Societies of Jefferson College, on the occasion of the annual commencement, Sept. 28, 1837.

"The Nature and Importance of a Revival of Religion," a sermon published in "The Presbyterian Preacher," March, 1837.

"Semi-centennial Retrospect," a sermon delivered in the First Presbyterian Church of Allegheny, Dec. 8, 1839, being the day appointed to be observed as the fiftieth anniversary of the General Assembly of the Presbyterian Church in the United States.

"The Calamity of Pittsburg," a sermon delivered in the

First Presbyterian Church of Allegheny, April 24, 1845, being the day appointed by the mayor of the city as a season of fasting, humiliation, and prayer, in consequence of the appalling destruction of a large portion of the city of Pittsburg, on the 10th of the month.

A Funeral Sermon, delivered on the death of the Rev. Robert Dunlap, A.M., March 28, 1847, to which is prefixed an address delivered at his interment, March 23, 1847.

A Charge delivered at the inauguration of the Rev. William J. Plumer, D.D., as professor of didactic and pastoral theology in the Western Theological Seminary, Oct. 19, 1854.

" Judah's Mercies and Transgressions," illustrative of the duties and dangers of the American nation : a discourse delivered on the fortieth anniversary of the author's ministry in Pittsburg and Allegheny, Nov. 6, 1859.

" The Prophets, do they live forever ? " a discourse commemorative of the character and labors of the Rev. Robert Johnston, delivered before the synod of Allegheny, in session at New Castle, Penn., Sept. 29, 1861.

He had the degree of A.B. conferred upon him at Williams College, Mass., and that of A.M. at Yale, Conn. He was a member of the first faculty connected with the Western University of Pennsylvania, organized in 1822 ; and occupied the chair of moral science and general evidence of Christianity.

WILLIAM B. ADAMS.

WILLIAM B. ADAMS was elected mayor of Allegheny, and served in that position from 1854 to 1856. The history of Mr. Adams is quite an eventful one. He was born in the State of New York in 1822, and was a cooper by trade.

He commenced his political career in Allegheny as constable in the Third Ward, and was subsequently employed on the police-force, and in 1852 was appointed its chief. He then became conductor on the P., F. W., & C. Railway.

In the contest for the mayoralty in 1854, he was taken up as the citizens' candidate, in opposition to H. Campbell and R. W. Park, both Whigs. The delegates from the four wards were equally divided between the regular nominees, neither of which would yield : the consequence was a triangular fight, which resulted in the election of Mr. Adams. He had the reputation of having made a faithful and efficient officer. The popularity of his administration was fully demonstrated by the fact of his succeeding elections.

Some time after his retirement from the mayor's office, he unfortunately became involved in complications of a very serious nature, over which, in view of his subsequent merit as a gallant soldier, let us cast the mantle of charity.

He went West at the beginning of the late war, and was recruited in one of the Illinois regiments of volunteers, and commissioned a lieutenant in one of the companies attached to the same. This regiment took part in the sanguinary battles of Chattanooga and Stone River, and was highly complimented for its bravery on these occasions.

Lieut. Adams served honorably throughout the whole war, and was wounded in the engagement at Stone River.

After having been mustered out of the volunteer service, he immediately enlisted in the regular United-States Army for three years, and was ranked as quartermaster-sergeant in the Thirteenth Infantry. At the expiration of his term of enlistment, he took up his residence near Cleveland, O.

HERMAN DE HAVEN.

HERMAN DE HAVEN was chosen mayor of Allegheny in 1857. He was born in 1806, near the head waters of Conestoga Creek, Lancaster County, Penn. He served an apprenticeship to the blacksmith business, and came to Allegheny in 1831, and there kept the principal hotel, located on the west side of Federal Street, between the Diamond and Water Alley (now Park Way). He was subsequently engaged in the manufacture of linseed-oil in the old mill on the west side of Middle Alley, between Gay Alley and Park Way.

In 1840 he removed to Trumbull County, O., and in the autumn of 1845 returned to Allegheny. In the spring of 1858 he removed to his farm in Shaler township.

Prior to the Presidential campaign of 1840, he was an ardent and devoted Democrat. Since then he has been identified with the Whig and Republican parties.

During the contest at which he, as the nominee of the "bolters" from the Republican convention, became mayor, there was a fierce triangular struggle for the supremacy, in which B. C. Sawyer and R. P. McDowell were his opponents. The latter, however, withdrew; and Tony Haslitt took his place as the Democratic candidate. The voting on the day of the election was close and exciting, resulting in the choice of Mr. De Haven by a majority of twenty-seven. He was much admired for his sterling integrity, and highly respected by the citizens generally.

He died June 20, 1880, in the seventy-fourth year of his age. He was married to Miss Diana C. Lightner, sister of the late J. Lightner, Nov. 9, 1830, who died May 28, 1837. The fruit of this marriage was a son and daughter. In 1839 he married Miss Jane Mager, who also died, Feb. 6, 1872. There are five children living of the latter marriage, two sons and three daughters.

JACOB STRICKRATH.

JACOB STRICKRATH was elected mayor of Allegheny in 1858. He was born in Sinsheim, in the Grand Duchy of Baden, a quiet village, about eighteen miles east of the city of Heidelberg, on the 3d of December, 1809.

He came to the United States, arriving at New York in 1829 : from there he went direct to York, Penn., where he remained for a few years, working at his trade of a tanner and currier. From York he went to Philadelphia ; from the latter city he came to Westmoreland County; and in 1833 he arrived in Pittsburg, and was employed in the tannery of the late John Caldwell, on the south-east corner of Second Street and Redoubt Alley. He continued with Mr. Caldwell until 1835, when he removed to Allegheny, and was employed as foreman in James B. Irwin's tannery, located on the north-east corner of North Avenue and Race Street, formerly Middle Alley. After the close of his engagement with Mr. Irwin, he formed a partnership with Mr. John Taggart, and with him carried on the tanning business for over eight years on the east side of Pasture Lane (now Irwin Avenue).

On the dissolution of the partnership, he bought out Mr. Irwin, and carried on the business for himself for a number of years.

In politics he was an old-line Whig, and was the ardent advocate of the principles of that party, especially the doctrine of a protective tariff. The drifting of his old party friends, however, towards Native Americanism, induced him to cease acting with them as long as they advocated doctrines so prejudicial to citizens of foreign birth. Without having expressed any feeling, or pronounced any views, in favor of the Democracy, he was taken up as their candidate for mayor without effort or solicitation on his part ; indeed, he was rather opposed to it, feeling assured that no one could be elected by them on strictly party grounds ; he was therefore by no means sanguine of success. But the high estimation in which he was held by his old party friends, gained for him their hearty co-operation, and insured his election.

To this feeling may be justly attributed his election to the office of county commissioner in 1871.

These important trusts he discharged with rare fidelity, and in a most acceptable and efficient manner. His social and unassuming nature won for him a wide-spread popularity, and his executive ability and general business qualifications are freely acknowledged by his fellow-citizens. He was married, in 1835, to Miss Rebecca Wicklim. On the breaking out of the war he had five children living, — four sons and one daughter. His eldest son, Lewis, at the commencement of hostilities, was residing in Hartsville, Tenn., and was compelled, much against his inclination, to do service in the Home Guards : he, however, fled North with his family on the first opportunity. His other three sons joined the Union army. John became a member of Company K, Thirty-eighth Regiment, Ninth Pennsylvania Reserves ; he was taken prisoner at the battle of James River, Va. ; was exchanged and transferred to a Missouri battery, commissioned lieutenant ; he was severely wounded in action, from the effects of which he died, and was buried at Vicksburg, Miss. William joined the Two Hundred and Twelfth Regiment, and was a member of Company L. Silas belonged to Company G, One Hundred and Twenty-third Regiment. Their merits as gallant soldiers were fully attested upon the several battle-fields in which their regiments were engaged.

In all the relations of life, Mr. Strickrath proved himself true to his professions, always courteous in his manners, but firm in what he deemed right, doing justice to all. He placed himself squarely on the doctrines of our national creed, that "all men are created equal," and repudiated all political distinctions based upon the accident of birth.

There are few men who possess more fully the confidence and esteem of their fellow-men. His chief characteristics are those of honesty and integrity, and a conscientious discharge of the duties of life. He received an ordinary German education in his native land, and since he became an American citizen, has acquired a pretty fair knowledge of an English one. He is versed not only in the common topics of the day, but may be also regarded as well read in history and politics. His career presents a record which proves conclusively that the only road to success in life is pre-eminently that of unceasing industry and undeviating integrity.

SIMON DRUM.

SIMON DRUM was elected mayor of Allegheny in 1861, 1862, and also in 1868 and 1869. He was born in Westmoreland County, Penn., in 1824, and was brought up on his father's farm. In 1834 he went with his parents to the State of Ohio, and in 1835 to Wheeling, W. Va. Here he remained until 1840, when he came to Allegheny, and was apprenticed to Brown & Carothers, to learn the carpenter-trade.

He was married in 1846 to Miss Elizabeth Workman. In 1852 he commenced business on his own account on the northeast corner of Cedar Avenue and Avery Street.

The undertaking, however, proved unfortunate ; as his shops, together with his implements of trade, lumber, etc., were entirely destroyed by fire on three different occasions during the same year. These repeated disasters having greatly discouraged him, he removed with his family to Indianapolis, Ind. : here he remained for a year, when he again returned to Allegheny, and recommenced his former business, which he continued until 1859. He was elected to the Common Council from the Third Ward in 1856, 1857, 1858, 1859, and 1865. He was chosen president of the same in the latter year. In 1866 he was chosen to represent the First Ward in the select branch.

On the breaking out of the war, inspired with becoming patriotic zeal, he resigned his position as mayor, with a view to entering the army. He forthwith commenced to recruit for the nine-months' service, Company H of the One Hundred and Twenty-third Regiment, Rev. J. B. Clark, colonel, commanding. He was commissioned captain of Company H, and mustered into the service, Aug. 9, 1862, and mustered out with the company, May 12, 1863, having served the full term for which the regiment was recruited. The gallantry of the regiment during its service was fully attested in many well-contested battle-fields. In 1864 he went into the hardware business on Ohio Street; sold out his interest in 1868, and bought a planing-mill. In 1873 he recommenced the hardware trade, and continued in the same until 1876, when he again sold out, and is now engaged as general agent of the Ben Franklin Insurance Company. His military record is that of a brave and gallant soldier, and he is esteemed as one of our best citizens.

ALEXANDER C. ALEXANDER.

ALEXANDER C. ALEXANDER was elected mayor of Allegheny in 1863 and 1864. His parents settled in Allegheny County at Buffington's Ferry, on the Allegheny River, in 1801. On the 31st December, 1802, the subject of our sketch was born. His parents subsequently removed to Pittsburg, and located on the east side of Fifth Street (now Fifth Avenue), between Wood and Smithfield Streets. At this point his father commenced the business of nail-making. The site of the old factory is now covered by Masonic Hall. Here the son was taught the art and mystery of the trade of nail-making, and continued to assist in conducting the business until his marriage in 1827. He afterwards was employed as chief nail-cutter in the Juniata Iron Works, on the north-west corner of Penn and Cecil Alley, carried on by Smith, Roger, & McDowell, subsequently by Turbett, Roger, & McDowell. On the suspension of the latter firm in 1844, he removed to Allegheny, and engaged in the grocery-trade on Ohio Street. This he abandoned in a short time, having received the appointment of general tax-collector for the city, which position he held for over eleven years. He served for several years in the council of the city, and his liberal and progressive views gave him an influence in that body that was always exerted for the promotion of improvements and the advancement of good government.

During his administration as mayor, his health began to fail: he continued an invalid until his death, which occurred on the twenty-eighth day of May, 1868. He acquired an ordinary education, and was always acknowledged as a gentleman of worth and ability, and was much admired for his integrity and correct business qualifications.

In all the relations of life he proved himself a man of sterling worth, faithfully discharging the duties committed to his care, wise in counsel, and firm in his friendship.

A. P. CALLOW.

A. P. CALLOW was elected mayor of Allegheny for the term covering the years from 1870 to 1872, and was re-elected for a second term in 1873, and died during the same year.

His occupation was that of a printer, and he was formerly engaged as pressman on "The Gazette" and "Commercial Journal."

On the breaking out of the war, moved by becoming patriotism, he enlisted as a private in the three-months' service in Company C, Thirteenth Regiment, commanded by Col. Thomas A. Rowley. He was mustered in with the company, April 25, 1861, and mustered out Aug. 6, 1861. Previous to the abandonment of the Thirteenth, it had been determined to organize a new regiment for three years, which in a short time had the requisite number of men in camp. The regiment, although among the first recruited, was not recognized by the State authorities, nor its officers commissioned, until a large number of the three-years' regiments had been placed in service. The number was consequently changed to One Hundred and Second. He was a member of Company F, and was mustered into service with the regiment, Aug. 16, 1861. For gallantry and meritorious conduct he was promoted to adjutant of the regiment, July 1, 1863. He was severely wounded in the battles of Malvern Hill, July 1, 1862, and Wilderness, Va., May 5, 1864, from the effects of which he partially recovered. He was mustered out with the regiment, Sept. 3, 1864, their term of service having expired.

Adjutant Callow was subsequently seriously injured in a railroad disaster, which occurred on the P. R.R. on a western-bound train, near New Florence: from the effects of these injuries he was rendered a cripple for life, and was compelled to use crutches during the balance of his days. He acquired a liberal education, and was considered a gentleman of superior natural ability, courteous and affable in his manner towards all, endowed in an eminent degree with those moral and social qualities which rendered intercourse with him agreeable, and his friendship desirable. He carved out his own fortune, and his success as a civil and military officer is due to his courage and indomitable zeal and energy. He died in 1873, highly respected and lamented; and his remains lay in state at City Hall amid demonstrations of profound sorrow and regret.

THOMAS MEGRAW.

THOMAS MEGRAW was elected mayor of Allegheny for the term covering the years 1878, 1879, 1880, to expire in April, 1881. He was born in the village of Grange, county Down, Ireland, on the 27th June, 1835. His parents emigrated to the United States while he was quite a youth, and settled in the Fourth Ward of the city of Allegheny in 1842. He was educated in our public schools, and was by trade a stone-cutter.

At the commencement of the late civil war he enlisted in Company A, Capt. J. Heron Foster, of the One Hundred and Second Regiment Pennsylvania Volunteers, commanded by Col. Thomas A. Rowley, and was mustered into the service, Aug. 29, 1861, as first sergeant; was wounded at Fisher's Hill, Sept. 22, and at Cedar Creek, Va., October 19, 1864, and was yet an invalid confined in hospital when the regiment was mustered out of service.

On his return from the army he was enrolled as a veteran, and was elected street-commissioner of his adopted city for many years, the duties of which he faithfully discharged. Upon his retirement from his official position as street-commissioner in 1874, he entered into partnership with his brother John, who was extensively engaged in the business of general contractor. During his association with his brother, he accumulated a competence. In consequence, however, of failing health, superinduced by the inhalation of the dust and sharp particles of stone to which he was exposed whilst engaged in the occupation of stone-cutting, he retired from active business life to a farm in Beaver County. Returning to Allegheny in the autumn of 1877, he received the Republican nomination, and was elected mayor of the city in the following year.

The three years of his administration were remarkable for the peace and quiet of the city. His skill as a mechanic was of the highest order: his record for gallantry as a soldier adorns the pages of his country's history. As a citizen he was highly respected for his courteous and affable manners, as well as for his stern and unyielding integrity as a magistrate. He was married Aug. 19, 1868, to Miss Harriet Gray, who was born in the Fifth Ward, Pittsburg, Oct. 2, 1848. They have no children living. He died at his home on Perrysville Avenue, after a painful and lingering illness, which he bore with patience and Christian fortitude, on the twenty-second day of August, 1882, and was laid to rest in Union Dale Cemetery, where his loving friends and comrades may indulge in the melancholy pleasure upon the return of each succeeding Decoration Day, of strewing his grave with flowers as an outward evidence of the inward truth, "Though dead, he is not forgotten."

JAMES ANDERSON.

JAMES ANDERSON, iron-manufacturer and philanthropist, was born in Shippensburg, Cumberland County, Penn., Aug. 3, 1785. His parents removed to Allegheny County in 1801. In early life he was engaged extensively with his brother-in-law, Richard Gray, in the manufacture of brick, subsequently in the manufacture of iron.

He was one of the projectors of the first iron-mill erected within the limits of the city of Allegheny. It was built on the west side of Darragh Street, extending from Robinson Street to the Allegheny River, near the Columbus-outlet lock of the Pennsylvania Canal. It was finished and commenced operations in 1827 by the projectors, Messrs. Sylvanus Lothrop, James Anderson, and Henry Blake. The latter having disposed of his interest to William Stewart, the new firm continued the business until 1834, when they sold out to Messrs. John Bissell, William Morrison, and Edward W. Stephens. He subsequently became involuntarily engaged a second time in the iron-business. The iron-mills erected and operated by the Messrs. Lippincott on the north-east and south-west corners of Thirteenth and Etna (formerly Walnut) Streets, Pittsburg, were purchased by Messrs. King, Higby, and Anderson, the latter being a son of the subject of this sketch. The firm having become financially involved, and Col. Anderson being largely on their business paper, he was compelled against his inclination to assume again the *rôle* of an iron-master. He operated these works for about five years, and having during that time made good the losses incurred by the failure of the late firm, he then sold out his entire interest to Messrs. Graff, Lindsay, & Co.

In order to establish his two sons in business, he was induced to purchase an interest in the machine-works of J. H. Jenks in Allegheny. This unfortunately, however, proved a total loss, owing to complications and misunderstandings between the parties. His next venture was the manufacture of paper at Canton, O. This also not proving remunerative, he sold out, and retired from the more active pursuits of life. For the last years of his life he devoted his entire time and talents to the various bridge, banking, and benevolent institutions, in whose management he was from time to time engaged.

He was one of the corporators and managers of the Exchange Bank, also of the Western Pennsylvania Hospital, and House of Refuge, and was president of the Board of Directors of the latter for many years.

He was also one of the founders of the old Allegheny Bridge, in the management of which he continued up to the time of his death. In the bridges on the Monongahela he was largely concerned, and was for many years president of the Manchester Savings Bank.

For twenty-three years he occupied the office of Inspector of the Western Penitentiary, having been appointed in 1832, and served until 1855, when he retired. He was re-appointed in 1859, and continued to act until 1867. He held the responsible position of president for fifteen years.

Well-executed portraits of this philanthropist adorn the halls of the Western Penitentiary, Western Pennsylvania Hospital, and Pennsylvania Reform School at Morganza, Washington County, Penn.

On the breaking out of the war with England in 1812, he joined the North-western army, under Gen. Harrison. During his service he acquired among his comrades a reputation for soldierly conduct of a highly commendable character.

Col. Anderson, having acquired considerable property on the north side of Ohio Lane (now Pennsylvania Avenue), erected a substantial and commodious mansion on the avenue, between Manhattan and Chartiers Streets, Allegheny, where he resided from 1830 up to the time of his decease.

He was the architect of his own fortune. In public as in private life, he was firm and true to his professions. His success in life was the result of a determined and earnest purpose, prompt to act, and just in his business relations, zealous in carrying out his promises, and a faithful discharge of his obligations, with a determination to do right, regardless of consequences.

His strong sense of personal loyalty to the demands of duty is forcibly illustrated in his career. To it he devoted the energies of his life; to accomplish it he spared no labor; always kind and affable in his intercourse with all, he was ever zealous in his endeavors to do good, and advance the cause of religion. His excellent qualities won the confidence and respect of all his acquaintances. He evinced a deep interest in the cause of education, and the intellectual improvement of the youth of our city. Generous to a fault, he was active in the promotion of all charitable and benevolent enterprises, always ready to aid and support the efforts made for the mitigation of suffering, and good of humanity.

As an evidence of his praiseworthy intentions in this direction, we note the fact that he donated to the city of Allegheny over fifteen hundred volumes of religious, scientific, and historical standard works, and over four hundred similar volumes to the authorities of the borough of Manchester, in order to establish public libraries for the youth whose opportunities for obtaining useful reading-matter were somewhat limited. Unfortunately, the contents of these works not proving suitable to the taste of the youthful patrons, the two benevolent projects were suffered to die out. The volumes donated to the city of Allegheny form a part of the present valuable library: those donated to the borough of Manchester were sold to the Independent Order of Odd Fellows. For these, and his other benevolent acts, his fellow-citizens remember him with gratitude.

He was married on the 6th June, 1811, to Miss Ann Miller, who died in May, 1859. His own death occurred March 11, 1869. There were three children living at the time of his death, two sons and a daughter; viz., William G. Anderson (since deceased), Henry L. Anderson, and Isabella Burnett. Henry resides at Fair Oaks, on the Pittsburg, Fort Wayne, and Chicago Railway, and the latter at Philadelphia.

CHARLES AVERY.

CHARLES AVERY, the distinguished philanthropist and subject of this brief sketch, was born in the county of West Chester, New York, Dec. 10, 1784. In early youth he determined to seek his fortune in the metropolis of his native State. With this object in view, and having completed his arrangements, he left his rural home full of hope, and arrived in New York, a stranger in a strange land. His exemplary moral deportment, however, soon gained him friends, who assisted him in the furtherance of his wishes by obtaining for him a situation in a drug-house, in which he served faithfully as an apprentice until he became master of the business. Having honorably and creditably completed his engagement, and being endowed with the full vigor of youth, though with a limited education, he gave evidence of no ordinary ability. By a systematic course of reading, and embracing every opportunity to attend night-school, he added much to his mental culture. Generous in all his dealings with his fellow-men, possessor of a happy and genial disposition, he rapidly acquired friends, and advanced steadily in the estimation of those who were fortunate enough to obtain the knowledge of his moral worth.

He determined to seek his fortune in the West, and came to Pittsburg, Aug. 28, 1812, and at once commenced the drug-business with Mr. Van Zandt, and subsequently with the late James S. Stevenson (at one time a representative in Congress from this district), who was then engaged in the manufacture of white and red lead, in which Mr. Avery also subsequently became interested. This partnership continued until the death of Mr. Stevenson, when Mr. George Ogden became a partner in the lead and drug business.

For a number of years Mr. Avery was a partner in the Eagle Cotton Mill, in connection with John and Thomas Arbuckle,

Josiah King, and J. M. Pennock. To the cotton-business may be justly attributed the foundation of his ample wealth. His investment in the copper regions of Lake Superior was highly profitable. He was among the few who were willing to credit the wonderful wealth concealed in the upper peninsula of Michigan, and was, with Messrs. Howe, Hussey, and others, considered a pioneer in its development, they sinking the first shaft for copper in all that vast region.

He prospered in an eminent degree in all his undertakings, and was classed among the enterprising and solid men of the city of his adoption. His wealth was acquired by an honorable and legitimate method. Averse to speculation, a greedy and selfish speculator he could never tolerate. He persevered in a conscientious discharge of the duties he owed to the Church, to the State, and to his fellow-men. In every relation of life he received the approval of all, and "though dead, the memory of his good deeds liveth." Prudent and careful in all his business transactions, he avoided running in debt, or overburdening himself with complications ; and he was always esteemed a genial, social, and happy man. In early life he espoused the cause of religion, and connected himself with the " Methodist-Episcopal Church." At this time an important and influential element entered into his youthful and earnest life, by his conversion and self-dedication to the cause of Christianity. He had grave doubts as to his duty and the best interest of the church, whether to enter it as a regularly ordained minister, or serve it to the best of his ability in connection with his business vocations, in the capacity of a "local preacher." After counselling with his friends and his own heart, he determined to adopt the latter.

It is the pleasing duty of the living to record the deeds, and cherish the memory, of those whose death we mourn, and whose acts of benevolence and Christian unselfishness we acknowledge and admire. Mr. Avery accumulated his own fortune. It was here he acquired his wealth, and it was here he dispensed it with a liberal hand ; here he proclaimed the doctrine of salvation, and pointed the way to obtain it ; here he died, and is lamented. The leading and ruling idea of his whole life was, that he was only the steward of God's bounty, and, as a faithful trustee, he was accountable to him for its proper disposition, which he held should inure to the welfare of his fellow-man and the glory of God. He was not one who would ever violate his own judgment, or honest convictions, nor was he one of those who defer their charities and intentions until death separates them from their wealth, and thus condone for life's neglects by a posthumous benevolence. On the contrary, he was the dispenser of his own charities, frugal, temperate, and unselfish in his habits in order that he might dispense the more to the needy. His benevolence was as much a part of his daily life as was his religion. He was a liberal and constant giver to the poor, without regard to color, nationality, or denomination. Modest and retiring in his habits and disposition, he avoided notoriety ; and his philanthropy was so quietly exercised, that it was only known through its comprehensiveness and bounty. He was devoted to the doctrine of free grace for all, and the advocate of the rights of the laity in the matter of church government. His views in regard to the latter induced him to withdraw from the Methodist-Episcopal Church, and become prominently identified with the movement to establish the Methodist-Protestant Church, in which he was engaged up to the time of his death.

On the question of slavery, he always espoused the cause of the oppressed and much-abused black race, and became thoroughly anti-slavery in sentiment and practice. His generous heart required no outward prompting to duty in the premises : he was intuitively the defender of the cause of the despised and friendless negroes. It was sufficient for him to know they were poor, uneducated, degraded, and socially ostracised, to excite his sympathy and earnest efforts in their behalf. Confiding in the justice of the cause, he committed himself to the work of ameliorating their condition. To the black people of his own section, his benevolence was most liberal ; acknowledging them as men, and socially equal in all respects, at a time, too, when it was unsafe to do so. In order to test his convictions by actual experiment, he caused to be erected on his own ground in the Fourth Ward, Allegheny, exclusively at his own cost, a commodious college edifice, dedicated to the education of black people, and which now bears his name. The design of the institution was to afford the youth of this race an opportunity to obtain a thorough classical education; and in order to fit students for the classical course, he established a preparatory school under the superintendence of a competent teacher. Mr. Avery died before the college went into actual operation, leaving a special bequest of twenty-five thousand dollars to aid in its maintenance.

In all his business transactions, Mr. Avery was eminently successful, and was ever ready to aid by his counsel and active assistance the poor and struggling classes. He was admired for the purity and excellence of his Christian character, and was never known, even in the most unguarded moments, to give utterance to a word or sentiment that did not indicate true nobleness, or that cannot now be remembered with satisfaction. As a minister of Christ he was firm and true to his profession. His strong sense of personal allegiance to his Lord was characteristic of his life.

Mr. Avery's fortune at his death was estimated at eight hundred thousand dollars, a large portion of which was given to charitable objects. During his life a sum probably equal was expended by him in public and private benefactions. Having no children to inherit his large estate, after liberally providing for his widow, and his own and wife's relatives, he left the residue for the good of his fellow-men. His chosen executors, Thomas M. Howe, William M. Shinn, and Josiah King, in whose integrity and business qualification he had the utmost confidence, he devised to dispose of his residuary estate, estimated by the testator at about one hundred and fifty thousand dollars, by devoting a portion to be used for the "dissemination of the gospel of Christ among the tribes of Africa;" also another portion for a perpetual fund, the interest thereof to be applied "to the education and elevation of the colored people of the United States and Canada."

The faithful and efficient management of the trust confided to their care has been such, that they have accounted for an amount more than double the maximum estimate of the testator, and have partially or wholly endowed normal and other schools in Pennsylvania, Ohio, Virginia, North Carolina, Canada, etc., for black people.

Before closing this imperfect memoir, we will simply add, it requires not the pen of eulogy to herald forth the virtues of this humble and devoted Christian : those who knew him best gave him full credit for the goodness of his heart, and beauty of his character.   He died in the city of Allegheny, Jan. 17, 1858.   Over his grave in the beautiful ("God's Acre") Allegheny Cemetery, his executors have caused to be erected a stately and costly mausoleum, worthy of the character it commemorates.   This monument is surmounted by a colossal marble statue of Mr. Avery, and has on one side the figure of *Charity*, and on the other the figure of *Justice*, and on the other opposite sides the following appropriate mottoes : "The tree is known by its fruit." — *Matt. xii.* 33.   "He hath dispersed abroad ; he hath given to the poor : his righteousness remaineth forever." — *2 Cor. ix.* 9.   "Remember the words of the Lord Jesus, how he said, It is more blessed to give than to receive." — *Acts xx.* 35.   "The memory of the just is blessed." — *Prov. x. 7.*

HENRY BALDWIN EARLE.

HENRY BALDWIN EARLE, as his name indicates, was called for one of the brightest luminaries of the Allegheny bar, who was a warm personal friend of the family : he was born in the borough of Pittsburg, on the north of Market Street, between Fourth Avenue and the Diamond, June 16, 1803, and died March 28, 1883. He was educated at the Moravian College, Bethlehem, Penn., and was married Aug. 22, 1830, to Miss Jane Douglass Kirkpatrick by the late Bishop John H. Hopkins, at the latter's residence on Western Avenue, Allegheny. They had ten children, seven of whom were boys, and three were girls : his wife and five children — four sons and one daughter — survived him.

The family originally came from England, settled in New Jersey, and subsequently in Pittsburg, and were among its first settlers ; his father, William Earle, being mentioned in Breckenridge's " History of the Western Insurrection," as one of the committee of twenty-one appointed by the loyal citizens to manage the part which the citizens should act in order to avoid the threatening complications.

The subject of our sketch was at one time extensively engaged as a dry-goods merchant. In his early manhood he espoused the political doctrines of the old Whig party, and subsequently the principles of the Republicans ; was elected a member of councils from his native ward, and was appointed treasurer of the fund raised for the relief of the sufferers at the great fire of April 10, 1845. He was also elected by the city councils to the position of wharf-master on the Allegheny, and held it for quite a number of years. The duties of these several positions he discharged with the strictest honor and fidelity. The high estimation in which he was held politically and socially, is evidenced by the fact that during the year (1844) of the great Presidential contest between Henry Clay and James K. Polk, he received the unanimous Whig nomination for mayor of his native city : the result, however, of the election, proved the success of Alexander Hay the Independent candidate.

He possessed in an eminent degree a mind well disciplined by a liberal education, endowed by nature with the strength of a Hercules, quick and agile in his movements ; and to these excellences were added those rare qualities of the heart that make many and warm friends. Kind and unassuming in his intercourse with all, possessed of a generous and happy disposition, modest and retiring in his habits, and being entirely trustworthy, he won the friendship and esteem of all who had the good fortune to enjoy his acquaintance.

He was a self-made man. In all his business and social relations he was firm and true to his professions ; and his success in life was the result of unswerving fidelity, virile energy, and diligent application.

Some years before his death, he became afflicted with acute rheumatism, which subsequently assumed the chronic form : from this he suffered intensely, and his hitherto robust and vigorous physique became emaciated and feeble. Although his last days were marred with suffering, he gave evidence of his faith in a merciful Providence and the immortality of the soul. His character, like his frame, was established in the ardor of youth ; and a determined ambition to lead an honest life was succeeded by the cool, matured resolution of manhood, — powerful to will, prompt to execute, and patient to endure. He was proof against idle hopes and the temptations of the world no less than against groundless fears, and the common vexations of life took less hold of his mind than the toils and suffering of his body.

He was an enthusiastic lover and patron of the fine arts. In early youth he exhibited a talent for drawing and painting of no ordinary ability : these he studied under the teaching and auspices of his friend, the late Bishop John H. Hopkins. One of his sons inherited in an eminent degree the talent of the father, and is now a professional artist of considerable ability. He was also fond of piscatorial pursuits, and was an active member of the old Isaak Walton Club.

CHARLES BREWER.

CHARLES BREWER, late of the city of Allegheny, was born in Taunton, Mass., in 1784. He came to Pittsburg in 1814, and was engaged for a number of years as a successful dry-goods merchant on the property which he owned, situated on the corner of Market Street and Fifth Avenue. In 1832 he removed to the city of Allegheny, and entered his new mansion, erected in 1830 on the south side of Western Avenue, between Allegheny Avenue and Fulton Street. He died in 1860, in the seventy-sixth year of his age, leaving no issue.

The following information is derived from a manuscript volume of over fifty pages super-royal duo. size, containing a copy of his will, and a synopsis of the account of his executors, — William Holmes and Franklin H. Eaton. This manuscript was compiled by Mr. Thomas Marshall of the First Ward of the city of Allegheny, from the records of the court of Allegheny County, filed in the register's office, and was prepared solely in the interest of philanthropy, in order to preserve and perpetuate in a convenient form the voluminous evidence relative to the settlement of the estate that encumber the records, and is virtually entombed in the archives of the court.

It is the first attempt that has been made to convey to the public mind a knowledge of the extraordinary benefits that were conferred, through Mr. Brewer's liberality, upon various benevolent institutions in this and other communities. It is more especially designed to give publicity to the origin of the noble charity which he founded, and which is known (only to a limited extent) as the "Brewer Fuel Fund." With this object in view, the author dedicated his book to his friend, the late John B. McFadden, one of the managers of the Western Pennsylvania Hospital ; and it was by him formally presented to William Holmes, one of the executors of Mr. Brewer's estate, who, in turn, donated it to the managers of the Western Pennsylvania

Hospital, who were by Mr. Brewer's direction constituted trustees perpetually of the " Brewer Fuel Fund," and who are, by Mr. Holmes's mandate inscribed on the book, required to " preserve and keep it in close connection with the account-book of the Brewer Fuel Fund." It is thus that the managers of the Western Pennsylvania Hospital, and their successors for all time to come, will be in possession of the history of the distribution of the " Brewer estate," and the origin and intention of the greatest of Allegheny County's individual charities. Strange as it may appear, there is no other memorial of the man, save the sepulchral structure erected to his memory in the Allegheny Cemetery, with the vague inscription, " Brewer," chiselled upon it.

By direction of a clause in his will, the receptacle which contains all that was mortal of him has recently been permanently closed, "never again to be opened." It is thus that he has willed that his charity shall continue, and that the recipients of his bounty shall not know whence it came.

The following clippings from Pittsburg papers of March 27, 1882, are of interest in this connection : —

"A SEALED SEPULCHRE, THE KEY OF WHICH IS TO BE THROWN INTO THE ALLEGHENY RIVER.

Singular Request of the Late Charles Brewer to be complied with To-day.

To-day a very singular request in the will of the late Charles Brewer will be complied with at the Allégheny Cemetery in Lawrenceville. All old residenters in Pittsburg remember Mr. Brewer ; and his name is also quite familiar to our younger people, owing to the many charitable bequests he left behind him. Among these there are still in existence the Brewer Alcove in the Mercantile Library, and the Brewer Coal Fund, which has perpetuated his memory among the poor people of Pittsburg. At the time of his death he was very wealthy.

THE BREWER VAULT.

The particular feature of the will, to which we refer, will require some words of explanation to be properly understood. The details are full of interest. The private Brewer burial-vault in the Allegheny Cemetery is familiar to many who have visited the place. It is situated just off the main road leading from the Butler-street entrance, and a short distance from the gate. It is one of the oldest sepulchres in the beautiful city of the dead, having been constructed shortly after the cemetery was established. When the vault was completed, the first bodies deposited within its walls were those of the father and mother of Mr. Brewer's wife, Mr. and Mrs. William Cecil, a venerable couple well known in the early days of Pittsburg, after whom Cecil Alley in the First Ward was named. Then other members of the Cecil family, and Mr. and Mrs. Brewer, and descendants of both families, were buried there, and the marble shelves in the vault rapidly filled up.

MR. BREWER'S STRANGE REQUEST.

When Mr. Brewer made his will, he inserted a clause in relation to this vault, which was regarded as very singular. It was to the effect, that when the death of his niece, Miss Mary C. Hern of Allegheny, occurred, and her body was placed in his vault, it should be the last corpse deposited therein, and that, no matter how many vacant coffin-shelves remained, the lock on the door of the vault should then be hermetically sealed, and *the key be thrown into the Allegheny River.* It is said the words requiring the key " to be thrown into the Allegheny River," really occur in the will ; but whether they do, or not, his executors say he certainly meant that the key should be destroyed or lost. It is, of course, a matter of curiosity to know what motives led Mr. Brewer to make this requirement. Our informant, a reliable gentleman who was a close friend of Mr. Brewer, and who knows the history of his affairs and family, told the reporter of the POST last night, that it was probably a whimsical freak of Mr. Brewer, who had become somewhat childish as his death approached. He did not desire to have too many of the Herns buried in the vault, and perhaps concluded to prevent any further interments after Miss Mary's death.

THE VAULT TO BE SEALED TO-DAY.

Miss Mary C. Hern, the lady mentioned in the will, died in Allegheny on the 15th of September, 1877, and was buried in

the Brewer vault three days later.   Mr. F. H. Eaton, an exec-
utor of Mr. Brewer, took the responsibility of not complying
with the request of the deceased about closing the vault forever.
There are twelve shelves in the vault; and as only eleven
were occupied, Mr. Eaton concluded to hold it open until the
twelfth shelf should be taken.   That shelf will be filled to-day.

The corpse of Mrs. Frances Hern Burnside, who died in Allegheny on Sunday, will be deposited there.   She was also a
niece of Charles Brewer, sister of Mary Hern.   The cemetery
officials have been notified to have a supply of cement at the
vault; and before the carriages leave the spot, the queer request
of the founder of the vault will be carried out, — the lock will
be securely sealed, and Mr. Eaton, who has always had the key
(a large brass one) in his possession, will throw it into the Allegheny River, or dispose of it in some equally effectual manner.

The funeral services over Mrs. Burnside's remains will be
held at Trinity Church on Sixth Avenue, this afternoon, at 2.30
o'clock, after which the funeral will proceed to the cemetery.
The pall-bearers will be Messrs. H. J. Lynch, John Porterfield,
Andrew Peebles, and Kinder Blair.

It was mentioned yesterday that Isabella Martis of Lake,
Brook County, Ill., wrote to Mayor Lyon asking for information concerning Mrs. Burnside, who is her aunt.   It is said she
wanted to get hold of some property Mrs. Burnside leaves; but
it is not very valuable, and she will not get it."

After making liberal provision in legacies and annuities to
individuals, he bequeathed large sums of money to various
benevolent institutions as follows: —

"To the Protestant Orphan Asylum of Pittsburg and Allegheny, in five annual payments of $500 each,	$2,500 00
To the Protestant Orphan Asylum of Pittsburg and Allegheny, on their failure to realize a legacy made by the late Dr. Hartford	5,000 00
To the Protestant Orphan Asylum of Pittsburg and Allegheny, for a new location and buildings for asylum	10,000 00
To the Western Pennsylvania Hospital . . .	1,000 00
To the Western Pennsylvania Hospital, for the depart-ment of the insane	1,000 00

To the Western Pennsylvania Hospital, in trust for the Brewer Fuel Fund	$10,000 00
To the Church Home Association of Pittsburg, for a permanent asylum for the aged, infirm, and helpless members of the Protestant Episcopal Church,	2,500 00
To the Protestant Deaconesses' Institute (Passavants Hospital)	5,000 00
To the Orphan Farm School, Zelienople (Passavants),	5,000 00
To the Pennsylvania Colonization Society, to send colored people to Africa	5,000 00
To the Pennsylvania Colonization Society, to acclimate colored people in Africa	2,500 00
To the Seamen's Aid Society, to advance the moral condition of the seamen of the port of Philadelphia	5,000 00
To the Young Men's Bible Society of Pittsburg and Allegheny	1,000 00
To Associate Missions among the Indians of Minnesota	2,500 00
	$58,000 00

The executors were invested by the terms of the will with unlimited powers and discretion in the management of the estate, extending over a period of eighteen years; viz., from April 7, 1860, to March 4, 1878. During that period they filed in court sworn statements of their accounts at intervals of from two to four years, all of which were confirmed by order of the court. The seventh and final account was confirmed by the court on the date above stated, March 4, 1878.

By extraordinarily good management, the executors were enabled to realize $492,046.75 from the estate, being more than three and three-fourths times its appraised value.

A clause in the will provides, that, after the payment of the legacies and bequests enumerated in it, the remainder of the estate in the hands of the executors shall be distributed *pro rata* among the institutions that were entitled to the original bequests. This intention was carried out by the executors, and, as will be seen by the reader, has resulted in an extraordinary benefaction to each of the institutions in question.

*The Pittsburg and Allegheny Orphan Asylum has received	$112,917 40
*The Western Pennsylvania Hospital has received	12,904 78
*The Brewer Fuel Fund has received .	64,524 12
*The Church Home Association has received . .	16,131 10
*Passavants Hospital has received . . .	32,262 13
The Orphan Farm School has received	32,262 13

The Pennsylvania Colonization Society has received	$48,393 60
The Seamen's Aid Society has received .	32,262 13
*The Young Men's Bible Society has received	6,452 45
The Indian Missions of Minnesota have received .	16,131 10
Total	$374,240 94

Each institution has been paid 6.45¼ times, or nearly six and one-half times, as much as was bequeathed to it.

The amount bequeathed to institutions of Allegheny County (*) is $38,000. The aggregate amount which they received is $245,191.98 (two hundred and forty-five thousand one hundred and ninety-one dollars ninety-eight cents).

Respectfully submitted.

THOS. MARSHELL.

"243 REBECCA STREET, ALLEGHENY."

JAMES C. BUTLER.

IN early days the "Commons" of Allegheny were quite celebrated for the military parades held there on those memorable
days, so dear to the hearts of every American citizen, when
hoary-headed men and unsophisticated youth mingled in the
joyous throng, gazing with amazement on the "pomp and circumstance of war."

On one of these occasions the writer was present when the
following affecting incident occurred, resulting in the death of
a gallant officer : —

Col. James C. Butler, the subject of this brief sketch, was
born in the State of Connecticut in 1789. During his minor-
ity he became inspired with the glowing tales told of the
country made memorable by the struggles for supremacy between the legions of France and the battalions of England,
where the gorgeous *Fleur-de-lis* and the royal banner of St.
George waved successively over the battlements of old Fort
Duquesne.

To this region, hallowed by the military services of the good
and faithful Washington, his youthful ambition was directed :
and having completed his arrangements, he left his Eastern
home, launching his bark on the sea of uncertainty, freighted
with the blessing of his parents, and kindness of friends ; he
arrived in Pittsburg in 1810.

After a careful examination of the locality, he resolved to
settle here, and make it his future home. He was then in the
full vigor of youth, endowed with a liberal education ; he gave
evidence of abilities of no ordinary degree ; generous to a fault,
possessed of a genial and happy disposition, he soon made for
himself friends, and rose rapidly in the estimation of all who
had the good fortune to become acquainted with his merits.

Shortly after his advent in Pittsburg, and in accordance

with the scriptural declaration, "it is not good for man to be alone," he wooed and won the affections of one of Pittsburg's fair daughters, Miss Jerusha McKinney, to whom he was united in wedlock on the twenty-eighth day of April, 1813.

Extensive as the pursuits of civil life are, it failed to afford a sufficient field for his enlarged views and laudable ambition. His genius soared aloft into the empyrean of military tactics; and having thoroughly mastered the science, he felt himself competent to serve his country in war whenever she might require his services.

It was with the citizen soldiery that he chose to exercise his genius, and from the ranks he rapidly rose to the command of a regiment. The bright example of the heroes of the Revolution fired his youthful ardor, and impelled to follow in their brilliant footsteps. But alas! he fell a victim to that science in which he so much gloried.

In response to the pressing invitation of a volunteer company about springing into existence, he consented to act as their commander; and on that fatal tenth day of September, 1821, whilst instructing his command in military evolutions, and firing by platoons, he met with his sad fate.

Full of ardor, he stood in his proper position, on the right, giving the order to fire, etc. After the first fire, and subsequent order to prepare for the second round, an unfortunate member of the first platoon, in loading up, discovered, to his dismay, that his former load had failed to explode; and fearing the recoil of his musket, it was inadvertently swerved from the right direction, and in a line with the brave but unfortunate commander; the unexploded cartridge taking fatal effect, shattering his left temple, and killing him almost instantly. Thus perished the gallant Butler in the thirty-second year of his age.

In all his intercourse with his fellow-men, he zealously maintained a character for strict integrity, faithfully discharging every duty: wise in counsel, strong in his friendship, as citizen and soldier he left behind him an untarnished reputation and an honored name.

His remains were followed to the place of interment — the

First Presbyterian Church burying-ground, Pittsburg — by his weeping relatives and sorrowing friends, preceded by the military and Masonic order. The solemn ceremonies on the occasion were conducted by the latter in the beautiful and impressive ritual of the fraternity; and amid the deep and imposing silence of the scene, arose clear and distinct the voice of the grand master in the touching and solemn declaration of the Scripture, "And I heard a voice from heaven saying unto me, Write, Blessed are the dead which die in the Lord from henceforth: Yea, saith the Spirit, that they may rest from their labours; and their works do follow them."

His three daughters, Mrs. Minot Holmes, Mrs. J. M. Burchfield, and Mrs. Capt. William Dean, survived him.

HENRY CAMPBELL.

CAMPBELL — Oct. 6, 1881, HENRY CAMPBELL, in the 78th year of his age.

Funeral services at his late residence, No. 370 Ridge Avenue, Allegheny, Saturday, Oct. 8, at 2 o'clock P.M.   Interment private at a later hour.

HENRY CAMPBELL was elected mayor in 1847 and 1848.   He was born in the borough of Pittsburg, Oct. 17, 1803, on the west side of Fifth Street (now Fifth Avenue), between Market and Wood Streets.   The building in which he was born is still standing, and is one of the few remaining landmarks of the olden time.   It was at one time occupied as a hotel by John McClintock, and rendered famous for the good cheer and hospitalities dispensed by its worthy host.   Its sign — a ship under full sail, with the significant motto of "Don't give up the ship" — will doubtless be remembered by many of our older citizens.

Mr. Campbell's parents were among the early settlers of Pittsburg.   On April 13, 1813, they removed to Allegheny, to the west side of Middle Alley, between North and Strawberry Alleys (the latter now North Diamond Street): from here they removed to the south-east corner of Federal Street and North Alley.   From this point they removed in 1817 to the west side of Federal, between the Diamond Square and Water Alley (now Park Way), and lived on property he owned and maintained as a hotel.   In 1829 they removed to the south-east corner of Ohio Street and the Diamond Square.

He was variously employed in commercial and manufacturing pursuits.   In 1831 he was extensively engaged with his brother-in-law, Capt. John Hay, in the manufacture of flint glass, under the name of Hay & Campbell.   In 1834 he purchased his partner's interest, and formed a partnership with John E. Parke and James P. Hanna, under the name of Parke,

Campbell, & Hanna. This firm was dissolved in 1838, and the business abandoned. He subsequently was engaged in steam-boating on the Ohio River.

In politics he was formerly a leading Whig, and was afterward an ardent supporter of the Republican cause.

In 1840 and 1841 he was elected to the city councils. He was also elected city treasurer, and served in that capacity during the years 1854–57.

Mr. Campbell acquired a fair education under the care of the early educators of Allegheny, — Thomas Salters and the Rev. Joseph Stockton. He is in a certain sense a "self-made man," and has established for himself an honorable distinction among his contemporaries. He possessed many warm personal friends, and enjoyed in an eminent degree the confidence and esteem of all who know him. As a business man he evinced commendable enterprise, ability, and uprightness, and as a public officer won many commendations for his zeal and loyalty under all circumstances.

He was married on the 18th of May, 1828, to Miss Sarah Anderson.

ROBERT S. CASSATT.

ROBERT S. CASSATT was chosen mayor of the city of Allegheny in 1846, succeeding Hezekiah Nixon. He was a resident of the First Ward. He was born in the city of Wheeling, W.Va., in the year 1805. His father died in that city in 1807: during the same year his mother removed to Pittsburg, where she subsequently married the late Paul Morrow. She was a lady of more than ordinary culture and intelligence, and possessed all the virtues that adorn the female character: in short, she was considered a model matron, one of the excellent of earth.

The subject of our sketch was highly educated, and possessed a fine personal appearance. Courteous and gentlemanly in his manners, these qualities won for him the confidence and esteem of the citizens generally. In the years 1847 and 1848 he was chosen president of the select council, the duties of which he discharged with manifest ability.

Although his administration as mayor was unmarked by any event requiring special notice, he always sustained the reputation of being a good and faithful officer.

He was extensively engaged in the mercantile trade, cotton-manufacture, and the banking and broker business, the latter with George H. Cooke, on Wood Street, Pittsburg, under the name of Cooke & Cassatt. During the year 1848 he removed to Pittsburg, and resided on the corner of Penn Avenue and Marbury Street. He subsequently removed to Philadelphia, and afterwards to Europe for the purpose of educating his children: he remained in Europe six years, and, returning to his native land, he located again in Philadelphia.

During his residence in Pittsburg and Allegheny, he was regarded as an intelligent and enterprising business man by all who had the pleasure of his acquaintance. Mr. Cassatt is a descendant of a family of French origin, who emigrated to this country at an early day, and settled in Bergen County, N.J. Subsequently they removed to York County, Penn., and located in a portion of the county now embraced within the limits of Adams County.

He married Catherine, the only daughter of the late Alexander Johnston, the first cashier of the bank of Pittsburg, who was a descendant of Alexander Johnston of the Chester-county family of that name.

His son, A. J. Cassatt, who has recently been elected one of the vice-presidents of the Pennsylvania Railroad, was born in the city of Pittsburg in the year 1846. He married a daughter of the Rev. Edward Y. Buchanan of Philadelphia. Although comparatively young in years, he has acquired a high reputation among railroad officials for intelligence and executive ability.

WILLIAM COCHRAN.

THE subject of this brief sketch was born in the county of Derry, Ireland, on the 9th of November, 1777. He came to the United States in the year 1791, and settled in the city of Philadelphia. In 1795 he left Philadelphia on account of the yellow-fever, which prevailed there at the time to an alarming extent. The fearful mortality and the fleeing, panic-stricken inhabitants left the city in an almost depopulated state.

He came to Allegheny County the same year, and purchased from the government twelve hundred acres of unimproved lands in Pine township, which he divided into three farms of four hundred acres each. One of these he disposed of to his father, one to his brother George, the other he occupied himself. Upon it all his children were born.

He was married June 8, 1808, to Miss Mary Davis, by the Rev. Robert Steel, pastor of the First Presbyterian Church of Pittsburg.

The lady was the sister of the late Judge Hugh Davis: she was born in the county Tyrone, Ireland, April 7, 1780. Her parents, with the family, came to this country in 1801, and settled on a part of a large tract of land which had previously been purchased by her father in Pine township, fronting on the Ohio River, and extending back so as to embrace the Ninth and Eleventh Wards of the city of Allegheny. She died at the residence of her daughter, Mrs. Jane Lecky, Jan. 28, 1877. In life she was highly esteemed as a devout Christian, and in her death deeply lamented by a large circle of loving friends and relatives.

During the year 1809 Mr. Cochran was appointed a justice of the peace in and for the county of Allegheny, his residence being in Pine township.

In 1815 he was elected a member of the Legislature, and

was re-elected the following year. In the session of 1815 he had charge of the bill for the charter of the Allegheny Bridge Company (St. Clair Street), which passed both Houses, and was approved by the governor.

He was the warm personal friend of the late President James Buchanan, who was also a member of the session of 1815, and who greatly aided him in his efforts to have the application for that charter favorably considered.

In 1826 he removed to Allegheny, and was appointed assistant warden of the Western Penitentiary. In 1831 he resigned the position; and in 1832 he returned to his farm in Pine township, where he resided until 1859, when he again removed to Allegheny.

He died in the city of Allegheny at the residence of his daughter, Mrs. Jane C. Lecky, May 12, 1867, aged ninety years, and was interred in the Allegheny Cemetery.

Mr. Cochran and his wife in early life espoused the cause of religion, and always proved themselves humble and devout Christians.

They united with the Highland Presbyterian Church of Ross township, afterwards by certificate with the Cross-roads Church of Pine township, and subsequently with the First Presbyterian Church of Allegheny, Rev. Joseph Stockton, pastor.

They had five children, — two sons and three daughters, — viz., Robert D., George W., Mrs. Jane C. Lecky, Mrs. Sarah Ann McGonnigle, and Mrs. Eliza Davis.

Mr. Cochran traced his Scottish ancestry as far back as the beginning of the seventeenth century. They were associated with the fearless signers of the "Solemn League and Covenant," and on account of the religious persecution, headed by the notorious "Claverhouse," fled to Ireland. The history of these eventful times must ever be associated with that of civil and religious liberty.

HUGH DAVIS.

HUGH DAVIS, late of the city of Allegheny, was elected burgess May 10, 1830, and served in that capacity until 1838.

He was born in the county Tyrone, Ireland, in 1777, and was a descendant of a Scotch-Irish stock.

Enthused with the glowing tales related of the transatlantic Eldorado, he determined to leave his friends and native land, to seek his fortune in it. With this object in view, he came to the United States in 1801, and settled in what was then Pine township, Allegheny County, on a farm fronting on the Ohio River, now embraced within the limits of the Ninth and Eleventh Wards of the city of Allegheny.

He was married in the borough of Pittsburg in 1805, to Miss Elizabeth, daughter of Robert Henderson, a prominent citizen of Pittsburg at that early day, by whom he had five children, three of which are now living, — two sons and one daughter, — viz., R. H. and H. E. Davis, and Hannah Morrison.

He was a kind and affectionate parent, courteous and affable in his habits and disposition, and was marked for his strict integrity of purpose. He prospered in an eminent degree in all his business transactions, and by honest industry acquired a large and valuable property in the city of his adoption.

The various positions of honor and trust conferred upon him from time to time without solicitation, afford the strongest testimony that could be offered of his sterling worth as a citizen. Whether as a public officer, merchant, or gentleman, he leaves behind the enviable record of an untarnished reputation and successful career.

In 1810 he received the appointment of deputy, under William Wasthoff, high sheriff of Allegheny County, and served with ability and fidelity.

On the eighth day of April, 1822, he was duly commissioned

by James Monroe, President of the United States, marshal for the Western District of Pennsylvania, and on the twenty-second day of December, 1825, was re-appointed by President John Quincy Adams, as will more fully appear in the following correspondence had on the subject : —

DEPARTMENT OF STATE, WASHINGTON, 16th April, 1822.

JONATHAN H. WILKINS, Esq., *Judge of the United States for the Western District of Pennsylvania, Pittsburg.*

SIR, — I have the honor to enclose you herewith a commission appointing Hugh Davis, marshal of the United States for the Western District of Pennsylvania, and to request the favor of you, to deliver it over to him after he shall have given the official bond required by law, and complied with the usual forms in such cases.

I am very respectfully, sir, your obedient servant,

JOHN QUINCY ADAMS.

DEPARTMENT OF STATE, WASHINGTON, 2d Feb., 1826.

HUGH DAVIS, Esq., *Marshal of the United States for the Western District of Pennsylvania, Pittsburg.*

SIR, — I have the honor to inform you that a commission appointing you marshal of the United States for the Western District of Pennsylvania has just been forwarded from this office to Mr. Wilkins, judge of the said district, with a request to him to deliver it over to you when you shall have given the official bond required by law, and complied with the established forms in similar cases: you will be pleased to acknowledge to this department the receipt of your commission so soon as it reaches you.

I am very respectfully sir your obedient servant,

H. CLAY.

In 1838 he was appointed by his Excellency Joseph Ritner, Governor of the State, associate judge of the Courts of Common Pleas, Quarter Sessions, Oyer and Terminer, and Orphans, of the county of Allegheny. In this position he served for three years, giving entire satisfaction.

In politics he consistently adhered to the principles of the Whig and Republican parties.

He was ever loyal to his party and convictions, and expressed his opinions upon all proper occasions, though never offensively or unnecessarily obtruding them.

His wife died at the family residence, north-west corner of Federal Street and Water Alley (now Park Way), in 1852; and on the 17th of February, 1862, he died at his mansion on Stockton Avenue, highly esteemed and much lamented by a large number of affectionate friends.

HUGH S. FLEMING.

HUGH S. FLEMING was elected mayor, and served in that capacity during the years 1850, 1851, and 1852. He was born in Ross township, Allegheny County, now Third Ward, Allegheny, March 26, 1820; has resided therein all his life, and is prominently identified with its local history.

He acquired an ordinary academic education under the Rev. Joseph Stockton and John Kelly. In 1835 he entered the drug-store of H. P. Schwartz, and continued in the business until 1839.

He early took an active part in the politics of the city and county, and was elected to the common council from the Third Ward in 1841, 1842, and also in 1859. During the latter term he was chosen its president. In 1853 he received the nomination for county treasurer, and was elected on the Whig ticket. In 1861 he recruited Company K of the Thirty-eighth Regiment, Ninth Pennsylvania Reserves, Col. Conrad Jackson commanding; was mustered into the service with the company, May 4, 1861, and commissioned as captain. He resigned June 27, 1862, on account of impaired health. In 1870 he received the Republican nomination for sheriff, and was elected to succeed Samuel B. Cluley. This position he held for seven years. In 1872 he was chosen to serve out the unexpired term of the late Mayor A. P. Callow: the emoluments of the office he generously gave to his predecessor's widow.

In all the various positions he held, he proved himself a gentleman of ability, integrity, and indomitable courage: prompt and energetic in his movements, he was eminently qualified to discharge the duties of his civil as well as his military appointments. As an illustration of his efficiency as an executive officer, it may not be considered out of place to relate the following incidents.

During his administration as mayor in 1851, he had occasion to issue a warrant for the arrest of a certain well-known des-perado (Jack Aldrich), who had evaded the vigilance of his police. Meeting his man accidentally on the street, he at once approached him, and, placing his hand upon his shoulder, said, "Come along, I want you," and after a short struggle suc-ceeded in taking him to the mayor's office, a feat which would scarcely have been attempted single-handed by any one know-ing the desperado.

At a public meeting held in front of City Hall on Sunday afternoon on the occasion of the railroad riots in 1877, to adopt measures for the protection of the peace of the city, Mr. Fleming, with his characteristic promptness, was among the first to step to the front, and say, "Come, boys." His courage and calm determination with others on that eventful night served much to secure the city's safety. He also assumed the responsibility of stopping and searching the street-cars as they emerged from the suspension bridge, for suspicious characters and contraband articles, explaining to the conductors and drivers, that, if any objections were made by the authorities of the road, he would be personally responsible for results.

On the occasion of the cotton-factory riots in 1850, word came to his office that considerable disorder and intense excite-ment prevailed among the employees of the cotton-mills, and that great danger to the Eagle Mill was apprehended. The entire police-force at that time consisted of six men. Mayor Fleming was not long in deciding his course of action: he immediately impressed into service a number of citizens, cloth-ing them with authority to act as special police. A load of wagon-spokes passing at the time, he stopped and ordered the driver to unload instanter. He did so unwillingly, but was somewhat re-assured by the fact that Mayor Fleming made himself personally responsible to the owner. These spokes served as formidable weapons in the hands of the "specials," whose numbers and martial appearance overawed the turbu-lent crowd, who, upon the conclusion of the mayor's address, quietly dispersed.

In the year 1877 he was chosen president of the Third

National Bank of Allegheny, and in 1879 he was elected a member of the select council from the Second Ward.

He is still an active citizen, and, although pretty well up in years, retains the vigor of his early manhood. He mingles as usual in the busy whirlpool of politics, and is warmly and ardently attached to the doctrines of the Republican party, ever ready to advocate or defend them to the utmost of his ability.

He was married in 1856 to Miss Julia H. Bollman.

ROBERT W. PARK.

ROBERT W. PARK was elected mayor of Allegheny in 1853. He was born in the city of Pittsburg, on the west side of Third Street (now Third Avenue), between Wood and Smithfield Streets, in the year 1822. In 1826 his parents removed to Allegheny, and occupied the house on the north-west corner of the Diamond Square and Federal Street.

Mr. Park is a gentleman of culture and refinement: having received a liberal education, he is well qualified to take a prominent position in all the relations of life. His genial manners, and kind and generous disposition, endeared him to all who had the pleasure of his acquaintance. In his youth he took an active and intelligent part in acquiring a knowledge of mechanics, and is the author of several ingenious and useful inventions, for which he has taken out patents.

He married Miss Catherine, eldest daughter of the late William Robinson, who, during the latter part of his life, resided on the south-east corner of Cedar Avenue and Liberty Street, Allegheny, and who was generally termed Irish William, in contra-distinction to Gen. William Robinson, who claims to be to the "manor born."

Mrs. Park is a lineal descendant of Gen. John Wilkins, who was prominently identified with the early history of Western Pennsylvania.

Mr. Park removed to Philadelphia in 1852.

HUGH GALLAGHER

WAS born in the city of Philadelphia, Aug. 12, 1779; was married to Miss Margaret Hawk, a native of Ligonier Valley, Penn. She was born in 1783, and died in the city of Allegheny in 1837. Her father was a soldier in the British army during the French and Indian war, and also served with credit under Gen. Washington in the Revolution. He had three brothers who also served creditably in the same wars.

The subject of this short sketch settled in Pittsburg in 1811, and in 1826 took up his permanent residence in Allegheny, where he lived continuously until his death, which occurred Sept. 6, 1875, having reached the advanced age of ninety-six years. He was a moulder by trade, and was at one time connected as a partner in the foundery and engine-shop carried on by Stackhouse and Tomlinson on the corner of Liberty and Short Streets, Pittsburg, where the engines were constructed for the first steamboats built at Pittsburg. He was celebrated among his friends and acquaintances for the intelligent interest he manifested in all matters connected with the history of the noble qualities of the horse, especially the racer. He was an ardent student of the diseases incident to them, and *modus operandi* of their cure : his services as an expert amateur veterinary surgeon were frequently called into requisition with marked success.

RICHARD GRAY.

RICHARD GRAY was a native of Ireland.   He was born in the town of Drumgumberland, in the county of Donegal, in the year 1781.   When in his eighteenth year, he came to the United States in search of better opportunities for making his way in the world, than were offered in his native land.

Having acquired a liberal education in the schools of his native village, and being endowed with a hopeful and cheerful spirit, he felt himself fully qualified and willing to commence the active struggles of life, depending alone on his personal efforts for success; and for this purpose he left his native land to seek a more congenial home in the Western World.

He landed at the port of Philadelphia in 1789, where he re-sided for a year : he then decided to come westward, and arrived in Pittsburg in 1801.   He determined, after a full examination of the surroundings, to make it his future home.

His cheerful and buoyant spirit, his pleasant countenance, genial and agreeable manners, rendered him a pleasant com-panion.   He evinced more than ordinary ability as a conversa-tionalist, ever ready, either in relation to Church or State, to give a reason for the hope he enjoyed.

He was married in 1807 to Sarah, eldest daughter of Col. William Anderson of Revolutionary fame.

In 1810 he removed to Allegheny, and was engaged exten-sively in the manufacture of brick.   The town at that early day was a mere hamlet of log cabins.

His first residence on the north side was on the north-east corner of what is now called Anderson Street and River Ave-nue, where he established a ferry, and operated it for several years.   It was at this point that the troops under Gen. Tanne-hill crossed the Allegheny River on their way to Black Rock in the war of 1812.   Subsequently he erected the third brick house in Allegheny on Cedar Avenue, between Avery and Liberty Streets, on the site now occupied by "Gray's Row." Here he resided during his latter days.

All the territory now embraced within the limits of the populous city of Allegheny was then a part of Ross township, and constituted but one election district: the place of voting was at the Green Tree tavern on the Perrysville road.

Mr. Gray served in the council of the borough of Allegheny from its organization in 1828 to 1831, also in 1836, and in both branches of the city councils. He was one of the corporators for the erection of the Pittsburg and Allegheny Bridge, and was for many years connected with its management. In all the various positions to which he had been called, he took an active and intelligent part, and was always found faithful in guarding the interests committed to his care.

He was a consistent and efficient member of the First Presbyterian Church of Allegheny during the pastorates of the Rev. Joseph Stockton and Rev. E. P. Swift, and was a ruling elder under the latter at the time of his decease.

Eminently successful in all his business transactions, he was always ready and willing to give his counsel and material aid to the misfortunate. He was charitable in his judgment of the weakness and shortcomings of others. Those who knew him best gave him full credit for his goodness of heart and integrity of purpose. In no instance, even when most unguarded, did he utter a sentiment that did not indicate the noble Christian character of the man.

His success in life was the result of an earnest purpose to do right: to it he devoted the energies of a whole life, — to accomplish it, he spared no labor.

His faithful and loving wife survived him four years: she died highly respected and much lamented in the year 1853.

Five children were the fruits of this marriage; viz., Elinor Gray, James A. Gray, William C. Gray, Richard C. Gray, and Sarah Gray (now Mrs. James Park, jun.). Elinor died in 1833, in the twenty-fourth year of her age. Her premature death cast a gloom over a wide circle of relatives and personal friends, who loved her for the beauty of her character, her purity, unselfishness, and freedom from vanity. James A., prominent in politics and business circles, died in 1876.

The grandsire, Col. William Anderson, a soldier in the Revolutionary army, joined the patriot forces shortly after his arrival in the country in 1776; thus evincing, by the trials and sufferings encountered during that eventful period, his devotion to the cause of his adopted land. He remained in the service until the surrender of Lord Cornwallis, at the siege of Yorktown; after which he settled in Cumberland County, near Carlisle, Penn., where he married, and where all his children were born, except the youngest, — three sons and four daughters, — viz., Paul, James, William, Sarah (Mrs. Gray), Letitia (Mrs. Caldwell), Mary (Mrs. Way), and Clarissa (Mrs. Hender). Mrs. Way is the only one of this large family now living (1881): she resides in the family mansion near Sewickly, full of years and hopes of a blessed immortality.

In addition to Col. Anderson's fame as a gallant soldier, his ability as a mechanic was considered of the highest order. He erected the first Presidential mansion at Washington, D.C., which was subsequently destroyed by the British troops under Gen. Ross, Aug. 24, 1814. He was the personal friend of Gen. James O'Hara, upon whose invitation he determined to come to Pittsburg with a view of superintending the erection of the public buildings in Allegheny County. On his route, with this object in view, he was detained at Bedford in consequence of the troubles arising out of the Whiskey Insurrection. At this point his youngest daughter, Clarissa, was born.

On his arrival in Pittsburg, he connected himself with the First Presbyterian Church, and was one of the principal contributors to the erection of the brick church on the site of the then log edifice, and which was afterwards taken down, and the present magnificent structure erected. His three sons served in the war of 1812 with credit. The records of their military services prove them worthy scions of their patriotic sire.

JOHN HANNEN.

Sketch of the Builder and First Warden of the Western Penitentiary.

In preparing this brief memoir of the late John Hannen, how far I may be able to do justice to his memory, I will leave to others who knew him best while living, to decide.

Writers, as a general thing, are more apt to confine themselves to the memoirs of heroes and statesmen, whose love of country and high-toned courage have justly adorned the pages of our national history; and this may be considered just and proper, provided it does not cast in the shade the merits of those in humbler life. The passion for military glory, or fame won by eloquence, induces the people of all countries to devour with avidity any fact recorded upon these fruitful themes, because both are calculated to excite a proper ambition, as well as a love of country. But while we are willing to accord the meed of praise justly due these great men, let us not forget that others have arisen from comparative obscurity, who for usefulness, goodness, and philanthropy, are equally entitled to our favorable recognition.

The deceased was born in Strasburg, Lancaster County, Penn., on the 26th of January, 1777. He was married in Stoystown, Somerset County, Penn., to Elizabeth Richards, Jan. 1, 1800. Shortly after his marriage he removed to Pittsburg, Penn. He was a brick-mason by trade, and followed it up to the time of the completion of the Western Penitentiary, on which he was engaged, in connection with the late Thomas Fairman, as contractor.

On the completion of the penitentiary, in 1826, he was appointed its first warden, which position he held until the year 1829. His first residence was on Sixth Avenue, Pittsburg, on the site now occupied by the Cumberland Presbyterian Church. On the twenty-second day of July, 1823, he had the misfortune to lose his beloved consort, who died at the old homestead, full of hope in the promises of a blessed immortality. Subsequently, on the 30th of January, 1827, he was married to Mrs. Clarissa Caldwell, who survived him a few years, and died at Meadville, Crawford County, Penn., full of years and Christian hopes. By his first marriage he had nine children, — two sons and seven daughters; one son and two daughters died in early life; the others reached their majority. Mrs. Eleanor Bushnell, Mrs. Jane H. Parke, and Mrs. Sarah E. Blake are the only ones living of this family. By the second marriage he had two children, a son and daughter, who are also living, and reside at Meadville. Subsequently he resided on the corner of Ohio and Sandusky Streets, Allegheny. About this time he carried on the drug-business on the south-west corner of Market and Liberty Streets, Pittsburg, and also, in connection therewith, the manufacturing of white and red lead on Sandusky Street, Allegheny, on the site now occupied by the Covenanter Church.

During his residence in Pittsburg, he received the appointment of justice of the peace, the duties of which he discharged with rare integrity. He early connected himself with the First Presbyterian Church of Pittsburg, and for many years exercised the office of ruling elder. In the year 1830 he was chosen one of the three elders at the organization of the First Church of Allegheny.

The Rev. E. P. Swift says of him, "For years he stood among the eldership of these cities, and I may say of this synod, as pre-eminent for the depth and vigor of his piety, the consistency of his Christian life, and the abundance of his evangelical efforts to do good. The lineaments of his countenance bore the impress of the tranquillity of his mind and the kindness of his heart."

The Rev. Elliot E. Swift thus speaks of him: "It was his custom to linger, particularly at the close of the evening service, to enjoy the company of his pastor on their homeward way. Often by the help of their lantern they would pick their steps along the street, conferring together of the interest of the church. He carried the old-time ivory-headed cane, and

walked with careful and deliberate tread. No better conception of his character can be obtained than is derived from the
fact that he was called the 'beloved disciple.' He was particularly solemn and impressive in prayer; and in leading the devo-
tions of the communicants' meeting, he seemed to have a lofty
conception of what it was capable of being made."

Mr. James McKain, who was associated with him in the
eldership for nearly forty years, says, "In all my association
and intercourse with this godly man, I can truthfully say, in
the fullest meaning of the words, he was a righteous man, certainly one of the purest Christians I have ever met. I vener-
ate his memory. He was truly a man of God, and has made
for himself a record superior to the wisest and greatest states-
man or soldier with his military renown. He has been the
means, in the hands of God, of the salvation of many souls,
who are now brilliant gems in his celestial crown of glory.
. . . He was ever active and faithful in the discharge of his
duty as ruling elder, until the mysterious, afflicting hand of
Providence was laid upon him, rendering a continuance of
these duties impracticable. Although his last days were
marked with extreme suffering, he died in the triumph of faith
in the promises of his blessed Master."

He continued to exercise his office in the church until the
year 1843, when he removed to Manchester (now embraced in
the Fifth and Sixth Wards of the city of Allegheny), and there
became an elder in what is now called the Second Presbyterian
Church of Allegheny. Subsequently he removed to Meadville,
Penn., where he died on the fifteenth day of December, 1854,
aged seventy-seven years and ten months.

His character, like his frame, was established in youth. Under
every circumstance of life — like a clear water-drop in amber —
there ever abode within him the tenderness of heart he acquired from the gentle teaching received in his early youth.

Those who knew him best gave him full credit for his many
Christian virtues.

His heart was attentive to the cry of the helpless and oppressed. To assist the one, and uphold the other, was his
constant aim.

He early espoused the cause of the colored race in their struggles for freedom, and often expressed his abiding faith that God in his own good time would raise up a second Moses to lead this down-trodden people from their dark and gloomy condition, to the light of freedom and their rights as men.

A warm and zealous advocate of the cause of temperance, he early took an active and intelligent interest in all questions bearing upon the movement, believing its opposite to be the fruitful source of crime and unhappiness. He manifested by his walk and conversation his hostility to the demoralizing habit, and he was ever ready to counsel and encourage the repentant inebriate. Many revere his memory for the good they realized from his kind and gentle admonitions.

In the sabbath school he always took an active part, believing it to be the nursery of the church, leading souls to Christ. Many of the young have abundant reasons to be thankful for the good derived from his labor of love. In every relation of life, either in Church or State, he proved himself a man of sterling integrity, conscientiously performing the duties committed to his care. Wise in counsel, and true in his friendship, he leaves behind him, as a parent, citizen, and Christian, the best of all legacies, — a blameless reputation and an honored name.

It may not be considered irrelevant to this imperfect sketch, to introduce a few incidents illustrative of prison life experienced by John Hannen during his official relation of warden. His kind and considerate treatment of the unfortunate prisoners had the happy effect, in a certain degree, to soften the asperities of their confinement. Notwithstanding their misfortune aroused the sympathetic feeling of his nature, he never for a moment relaxed his vigilance in guarding the trusts committed to his care. His confidence in their repentance and good behavior was rarely betrayed. One of the incidents referred to was of an alarming nature, and bade fair to result in serious consequences. Although fifty years have passed away, yet the scenes of that fearful night left an impression on the writer's memory, enduring as life itself.

An organized effort by the prisoners of one of the wards to escape, was betrayed to the warden by one of their number, who was far gone in consumption, and whose death was daily expected. On the information thus obtained, the authorities went gently to work, so as not to alarm the other prisoners, to organize a volunteer force in addition to the regular guard, to meet the exigency of the contemplated outbreak, the writer being one of the volunteers. On the first regular nightly round, we were quietly introduced into the ward, and took our stations under cover of an out-house. The guard having made their examination, and finding all apparently right, retired, locking us in. Silence reigned supreme for a while, then the novelty and danger of our position became apparent. True, we were armed; but what could four novices expect to accomplish against twenty or thirty desperate men in their struggle for liberty, limited by the order of the warden that under no circumstances should we kill?

At length the silence was broken by calling softly to each other, and the desperate struggling of some one immediately opposite our concealment, indicated by his curses and laborious breathing. The night being dark, and no light in the ward, we had to depend solely on the sense of hearing. Silence having again been restored, we remained concealed until about midnight, the pre-arranged time for the guard to again appear. The examination of each prisoner disclosed the fact that all were prepared for the bold attempt. A large and powerful mulatto, in whom the officers had reposed the most confidence, was the ringleader in the plot. He had fashioned a key out of some filched material; and in his intense eagerness to accomplish his purpose, had broken it short in the lock, thus dissipating all hope of escape at the time.

The incident connected with the notorious and successful escape of Lindsay and Garrabrants partook, in some degree, of the nature of a romance. The former was an extraordinary man, and had often asserted that the prison had not been built, nor the irons forged, that could hold him a prisoner. In view of these bold and defiant declarations, he was guarded with more than ordinary care. Notwithstanding, he effected his escape (taking Garrabrants along with him), by the aid of a key ingeniously manufactured out of the copper spouting, and which he left with a message to the warden, stating that he had started for Washington City to take out a new patent for an old Yankee trick. He was arrested in Canada; and the warden was instructed to go there at once, and claim the fugitive. On the return to the United States, while crossing the lake, he contrived to free himself of his irons; and to the astonishment of the warden, he found his prisoner promenading the deck free from his shackles. Upon inquiring how he did it, and what he did with the irons, to the former he replied that that was another Yankee trick, for which he had not yet taken out a patent: the latter he would answer, provided a promise was given not to put them on until near port. The required promise having been given, he told where he had ingeniously hidden them about the machinery of the boat. As the vessel was entering the port of Erie, he quietly submitted to be ironed again, and was safely returned to his old quarters.

John Hannen died as he lived, a devoted and humble Christian: although pain and suffering marked his latter days, his faith in the divine declaration, "Whom the Lord loveth, he chasteneth," never forsook him. The privations of the body had the effect of rendering his mind somewhat inert; yet from time to time, by a mighty effort, he would arouse himself to act as vigorously as ever.

Who would not desire to have the ending of their earthly journey adorned with the surpassing grace and glory of the dying Christian? As the brightness of the morning star pales before the superior glory of the rising sun, as the rosy dawn brightens into full day, so does the Christian's hope take away the terrors of death, and leaves for the living a day of glory. "Let my last end be like his."

GEN. ALEXANDER HAYS.

THIS gallant officer was born in Franklin, Venango County, Penn., on the eighth day of July, 1819. He was the son of Gen. Samuel Hays and Agnes Hays, whose maiden name was Broadfoot. In 1840 he graduated at Allegheny College, Meadville, Penn., and in the same year entered the West Point Military Academy, in which institution he also graduated in 1844, and was breveted second lieutenant in the Fourth Infantry. His regiment was among the first to advance upon the enemy's territory in the late war with Mexico. In the memorable engagements of Palo Alto and Resaca de la Palma, he displayed great bravery and undaunted courage, capturing, in connection with Lieut. Woods, the first gun taken from the Mexicans. In the latter action, he was seriously wounded. In recognition of his gallant and meritorious conduct on these occasions, he was promoted to the rank of first lieutenant, and was transferred to the Eighth Infantry. The painful nature of his wound, however, rendered him unfit for active duty, in view of which he was ordered on recruiting service, but soon rejoined the army at Vera Cruz, with over two hundred recruits. He participated in all the principal battles of the war, and for his gallant and efficient services received the earnest commendation of the commander-in-chief.

In 1846 he was married to Miss Annie, daughter of the late John B. McFadden. In 1848 he resigned his commission in the regular army. The education he acquired at West Point made him an efficient civil engineer; and at this period the importance of railroad construction was agitating the country, and it had need of talents of this kind.

In California he first found employment, and subsequently in Western Pennsylvania. He was employed as chief in making the preliminary survey for the Allegheny Valley Railroad, and making draughts for the construction of bridges, etc. In 1856 he was appointed by councils, chief engineer of the city of Allegheny.

Fired with becoming zeal and military ardor, at the commencement of the late civil war, he cast aside the implements of his profession, and recruited a military company in Pittsburg, under the call for the three-months' service, called the City Guards, of which he was chosen captain.

They were soon on their way to Harrisburg, to join the other troops concentrating there for assignment to duty. In a short time he was commissioned major of the Twelfth Regiment, Pennsylvania Volunteers.

During the summer of 1861 he was tendered the position of captain in the Sixteenth United-States Infantry, but declined the honor; and at the close of the term of service of the Twelfth, he returned to his home, and immediately commenced recruiting a regiment for the war.

His comrades of the City Guards, in whom he had infused his own military ardor, followed him, thus forming the nucleus of the Sixty-third Regiment, of which he was commissioned colonel. The regiment, having been thoroughly drilled and disciplined at Camp Wilkins, departed for the war.

The military record of this regiment is full of heroic deeds, brilliant achievements, and laurels gathered on many battlefields, hallowed and made memorable by the blood of its decimated ranks.

Col. Hays possessed a warm friend and comrade in the brave and heroic Gen. Kearney, who took occasion on several well-contested battle-fields to highly compliment him for his cool and indomitable courage, and skill in handling his regiment.

During the interim occurring between the engagement at Fair Oaks and the seven-days' battle, the Sixty-third occupied the front facing Richmond, and was frequently engaged in attacks with the enemy, and was the last to leave the intrenchments upon the retreat to the James, and, when in the vicinity of Charles-city Cross-roads, was attacked with determined force and earnestness by the enemy. Col. Hays, however, was fully prepared with his well-disciplined regiment to give them a warm reception. It was here that the intrepid Hays with the Sixty-third Pennsylvania and a part of the Thirty-seventh New York were advanced to the line of the battery; and amidst the carnage of that eventful period, the gallant colonel and his noble regiment won for Pennsylvania laurels of imperishable fame. What grape and canister failed to accomplish, was effected by the determined charge and raking volleys of the indomitable infantry. Checked by the raking fire of the rifles, the foe sullenly retired, disputing every inch of ground: the space between the opposing forces having been cleared, orders were issued to the Sixty-third to "lie low," and the artillery again commenced its terrible work of destruction.

At the second battle of Bull Run, the Sixty-third and the Fortieth New York suffered severely: it was in this engagement that Col. Hays, while leading his command up to the breast-work occupied by the enemy, was shot in the ankle, terribly shattering the limb. For the heroism manifested on this occasion, he was promoted and confirmed a brigadier-general of volunteers, and lieutenant-colonel in the regular army.

His command captured during the war twelve banners and battle-flags, and over three thousand stand of arms. He participated in all the engagements of the Army of the Potomac up to the day of his death, which occurred at the battle of the Wilderness, May 5, 1864. Whilst advancing in line through its labyrinthian mazes, he suddenly encountered the enemy's forces. In the early part of the battle, amid the smoke and roar of the artillery, and rattle of musketry, he had ridden along his entire front; pausing on his return for a moment in front of his favorite regiment, the Sixty-third, he was struck with a minie ball, which penetrated the brain; he sank unconscious to the ground; in the brief space of two hours he expired in the arms of his sorrowing comrades, who, whilst the storm of battle still raged, bore his body to the rear; from thence it was conveyed to his home in Pittsburg.

The day of his funeral was a sad one to the citizens generally. The trappings of mourning, and evidence of sorrow, everywhere met the eye, and roused a response in every heart. All that was mortal of this gallant soldier repose in the Allegheny Cemetery, over which an appropriate and beautiful monument has been erected by loving friends as an appropriate memorial.

He possessed all the qualifications for a commander; thoroughly educated in all the theories as well as the sterner praetice of war, he had omitted nothing that would enable him to defend his post as a man of courage; a soldier by profession and name, to his natural and acquired abilities he added a clear judgment, a strong mind, and the courage of a hero.

His orders were few, but they were always to the point, marked by brevity; they were obeyed with alacrity, and carried out with a perfect reliance upon his sagacity and bravery: with his trusty sword he has established his fame, and fenced it around by his gallant deeds.

He leaves to his widow and orphan children the proud legacy of a brilliant record of military achievements.

GEORGE S. HAY, M.D.,

WAS born on his father's farm in St. Claire township, Allegheny County, Sept. 28, 1807. After acquiring a rudimentary education in the schools of his native place, he entered the Western University of Pennsylvania, and devoted himself zealously to an academic course of studies.

At an early age he evinced a decided inclination towards the profession of medicine. With this object in view, he entered the office of the late Peter Mowry, M.D., under whose instruction he evidenced the possession of eminent abilities, which ultimately enabled him to take a prominent and enviable position among his contemporaries.

Thoroughly inspired with an ardent desire to perfect himself in all the principles and manifold details involved in the study of the profession, he attended two courses of lectures in the Medical University of Pennsylvania, in which he graduated, and had the degree of M.D. conferred upon him.

On his return to the rugged hills and valleys of his native place, he commenced the active practice of his profession, meeting with marked success. The high position to which he attained, in a great measure was won by his indomitable perseverance, promptness, and professional ability.

He was married three times, in the following order: To Miss Mary Taylor of Hobbestown, Allegheny County, Penn., on the twenty-second day of May, 1835, who died April 1, 1839. The issue of this union were two daughters, Elizabeth and Margaret. The former died in infancy: the latter is still living, married, and with her husband, Mr. Hernott, resides at Redwood, Minnesota.

Early in the year 1844 he was again united in marriage to Mrs. Rachel Montgomery, *née* Arthur, of the city of Pittsburg, who died in the latter part of the same year. She and her infant occupy the same grave.

He married his third wife, Maria Thompson, *née* Beltzhoover, of Allegheny County, Feb. 5, 1846, who died in the city of Allegheny, March 16, 1882. The fruits of this marriage were two sons and one daughter, named respectively Robert, George S., and Maria, wife of Addison Lysle.

In 1847 he was elected on the Whig ticket, prothonotary of Allegheny County; held office until 1851, the duties of which he discharged to the satisfaction of his fellow-citizens.

At the commencement of the late civil war he recruited a company, and was elected its captain, which subsequently became united with the Eighth Pennsylvania Reserves, Thirty-seventh Regiment, as Company C.

The Eighth Reserves were formed from companies recruited for the three-months' service, but were not accepted, the quota having been filled, and who were rendezvoused at Camp Wright on the bank of the Allegheny, under the command of Col. J. W. Lane. There were at that time forty-three companies here assembled, and only those from Erie County had a regimental organization. In June, 1861, Gen. McCall visited Camp Wright, and selected the companies to form the Eighth Reserves, who were ordered to Camp Wilkins, and there organized on the 28th of June, the subject of our sketch being placed in command. He being well versed in military science, having commanded the Duquesne Grays, an organization of considerable notoriety, it was considered a wise selection. The regiment being now armed, uniformed, and thoroughly drilled by battalions, the camp was placed under the command of Col. Hay until the 20th of July, when the regiment was ordered to Washington, arriving there on the 23d of July, and went into camp on Meriden Hill. From hence it was transferred on the 2d of August to the Reserve Camp at Tennalytown, and assigned to the first brigade, Gen. John F. Reynolds, commandant. From the latter position the regiment, on the 9th of October, crossed the Potomac to Langley, Va., and went into winter quarters.

In forming the line of battle at Charles-city Cross-roads, the first brigade was held in reserve; but as the struggle became desperate and doubtful, the Eighth was ordered to advance to a position opposite the Sixth Georgia, which was on the point of charging. Here the gallant Eighth, under an impetuous onset led by their intrepid colonel, forced the Georgians to retreat: the enemy, however, massing their forces on that point of the field, the Eighth was reluctantly compelled to retire, until it reached support from a new line. In this engagement, Col. Hay had his horse killed under him, and was himself severely injured. Notwithstanding, he immediately mounted another horse, and remained on duty to the close of the conflict. This was the last battle he was engaged in: owing to loss of health, he was compelled to resign his command on the eleventh day of July, 1862.

His medical knowledge and experience, especially as a surgeon, were frequently called into requisition for consultation during his command of the regiment.

Courteous and affable towards all in his private and public life, he was esteemed for the goodness of his heart, suave and gentlemanly manners.

He died at the home of his son Robert in the city of Allegheny, on the twenty-fourth day of February, 1884. As a Christian parent and friend, he was highly esteemed. To his children he bequeaths the legacy of an honorable professional and military career.

JOHN IRWIN.

THE subject of this brief sketch had the honor of being chosen May 10, 1828, first burgess of the borough of Allegheny, in pursuance of the Act of incorporation approved April 14, 1828. He was born in the borough of Pittsburg, July 1, 1787. His father, Col. John Irwin, was an officer in the Revolutionary army, who was severely wounded in the sanguinary night attack on the American camp at Paoli.

Col. Irwin was a prominent member of the Cincinnati Society, an order established in the United States by the officers of the army in 1783, "to perpetuate their friendship, and raise a fund for the relief of the widows and orphans of those who had fallen in defence of their country." The State society is still in existence, and meets annually in the city of Philadelphia.

It was so named in honor of Lucius Quintius Cincinnatus, the Roman sage and warrior. Its membership included patriots headed by Washington, who, like the great Roman, left their rural pursuits in order to serve their country, and at the close of hostilities returned to them.

The emblem of the society is an eagle suspended by a blue ribbon with a white border, symbolical of the friendship then existing between France and the United States. On the shield covering the breast of the eagle is the figure of Cincinnatus receiving the military ensign from the Roman senators, with the plough and other implements of agriculture in the background. Surrounding the whole is the motto, *Omnia reliquit servare rem-publicam.* The society is hereditary in its operations, the membership descending from father to son to the latest generation.

Mr. Irwin was a rope-manufacturer, a knowledge of which he acquired when a mere lad under the teachings of his father and mother, who carried on the business under the name of

John Irwin & Wife, and who were the successors of the firm that established the first ropewalk in Western Pennsylvania, in 1794, on the ground now occupied by the Monongahela House.

The wounds received by his father rendered him unable to attend to the details of the business: the management was therefore entirely left to the mother and son. At his death, the son became a partner in the business, and it was continued under the style of Mary Irwin & Son.

Col. Irwin died May 5, 1808, in the fiftieth year of his age. His remains were interred in the First Presbyterian burying-ground, with military and Masonic honors, in the presence of a large concourse of his fellow-citizens.

In 1795 the works were removed to the square bounded by Liberty, Third, and Fourth Streets and Redoubt Alley. His mother, on account of her advanced age and loss of health, sold out her interest to her son, and retired to private life.

The works were subsequently removed to the bank of the Allegheny River between Marbury Street and the Point, where the entire rigging for Perry's fleet was prepared.

In the year 1813 he commenced the erection of works in Allegheny, on a more extensive scale. In July, 1836, they were destroyed by fire twice in the same month. They were promptly rebuilt, and the business continued until 1858, when he ceased business, and retired to private life.

He acquired a liberal English education in the schools of his native city, and was for a number of years before his death a director of the bank of Pittsburg.

High as his business qualification ranked in the branch of industry with which he had so long been connected, it stood no higher than his personal reputation in the estimation of the community generally. Many places of political preferment had been tendered him; but he uniformly declined such distinction, believing, that, by diligently caring for the extensive manufacturing interest in which he was engaged, he could better serve the public than by the acceptance of a political position.

In 1810 he was married by the Rev. Joseph Stockton to Miss Hannah, daughter of the late Rev. John Taylor, rector of the Episcopal (Round) Church, then located on the triangular lot bounded by Wood Liberty, and Sixth Avenue, Pittsburg.

His wife died in 1844. He was subsequently married to Mrs. Abigail Paul, daughter of the late Rev. Elisha McCurdy, in the year 1847.

He was a man of fine personal appearance, firm in posture, and elastic in his movements, courteous and affable in his manners, and was remarkable for his strict integrity. He was a consistent member of the First Presbyterian Church of Allegheny, and always took an active and intelligent part in all its movements, and was ever faithful in his attendance, and zealous in promoting its welfare. He died at his residence in Sewickly, Penn., June 30, 1863.

JOSIAH KING.

Josiah King was born Oct. 3, 1807, in Waterford, Erie County, Penn., on the site of Fort Le Bœuf, one of the chain of forts established by the French, from the lakes to the head waters of the Ohio, and died in Allegheny, Dec. 18, 1882. He descended from an Anglo-Irish stock on the paternal side, and Scotch-Irish on the maternal.

His grandfather was a soldier of the Revolution, served with distinction, and was promoted to a captaincy for his gallantry at the storming of Yorktown.

On the occasion of the visit of Gen. Lafayette to this country in 1825, the general called upon Capt. King, whose acquaintance he had made during the war.

The captain, being a surveyor, spent a large portion of his time, after the close of the war, in regulating property lines in the then wild lands of that section. He also carried on an extensive trade with the Indian tribes on the borders of Lake Superior.

He was educated at the academy of his native place, and improved his time and opportunities as fully as circumstances would permit.

At the age of twelve years he was apprenticed for seven years to the mercantile business.

Having reached his majority, he determined to seek his fortune in a more extensive field of operation than his native place afforded; in view of which, he selected the city of Pittsburg as his future home. He commenced his journey in 1827, by the then usual mode of conveyance between the lakes and the Ohio, — in a flat-boat, by French Creek to the Allegheny River and thence to the point of destination.

Immediately on his arrival in the city, a stranger in a strange land, he sought and obtained a situation in the commercial establishment of the late Isaac Harris, one of the most prominent and widely known business men of the West; and was subse-sequently appointed the first agent of the line of freight and passenger boats on the Pennsylvania Canal.

In 1831 he became associated with the late John Dalzell in the wholesale grocery and produce business: in 1836 the part-nership was dissolved by the death of Mr. Dalzell, and was immediately re-organized under the title of King and Holmes. The firm carried on an extensive trade, East and West, for over nine years.

Mr. King had now become generally and favorably known as a thorough business man, and his services were sought for in municipal matters.

He was for several years elected a member of the city coun-cils, during which time he took an active and intelligent part in all questions bearing upon the improvement of his adopted city.   Among the important measures advocated by him was the paving of the Monongahela Wharf.

In 1846 he turned his attention to the manufacture of cotton goods, and formed a partnership with Isaac Pennock, under the name and style of King, Pennock, & Co.   Under their auspices the Eagle Cotton Mill was erected in the Fourth Ward of the city of Allegheny.

The firm was eminently successful: during the civil war the profits were very large, the raw material having advanced from ten cents to one dollar per pound.

Mr. King spent the greater part of two years at Cairo, Mem-phis, and other Southern points, purchasing cotton, and caring for the interests of the firm generally.   From this fact, it became, in a financial point of view, one of the strongest in the two cities; but alas! a change soon came over the spirit of their pleasant dreams.

During the great petroleum excitement which swept over the Western counties, and proved so disastrous in its effects, the firm, like many others, were involved in the enticing tempta-tion to invest largely in the product, the consequence of which was a most disastrous failure; Mr. King retiring without a dollar, when he supposed he was worth a half a million.

Notwithstanding this sudden and unexpected reverse of fortune, he still maintained his courage, his tact, and his integrity unimpaired, important factors in the struggle for a new business life.

In May, 1866, he, in connection with F. B. Penniman, A. P. Reed, and Thomas P. Houston, purchased "The Pittsburg Gazette," established in 1786 by John Scull, the oldest journal published west of the Alleghenies.

The new firm operated under the name of Penniman, Reed, & Co. In 1870 the senior partner retired, when George W. Reed and David L. Fleming were associated, and the name changed to King, Reed, & Co.: of this firm he was an active member up to the time of his death.

In addition to his having served in the city councils, he was called upon to fill other places of trust, and was noted for the interest he took in the cause of education and scientific investigations. He was for several years elected a school director in the Third Ward, Allegheny; was chosen a member of the board of trustees of the Western University of Pennsylvania; and was for many years an active member of the board of managers of the House of Refuge (now Pennsylvania Reform School); member of the Board of Trade, and also of the Commercial National Bank; and was one of the projectors of the Allegheny Observatory, which has become a scientific school of wide reputation; was president of the old reliable Pittsburg Insurance Company, the only office that withstood the shock, and weathered the storm, of the disastrous fire of the 10th of April, 1845.

He was also a prominent member of the Philological Institute, established in 1828, and took a prominent part in all its deliberations. Politically he was an ardent Whig, and subsequently a Republican; was chosen chairman of the Allegheny Clay Club in 1844, and presided at several of the annual nominating conventions of the party. As a trustee of the "Avery" estate, Mr. King brought into requisition that rare tact and foresight which so eminently characterized his course in all his fiduciary relations.

This estate was devised for the benefit and advancement of the interests of the negro race. A large number of institutions were assisted, and some established.   Conspicuous among the latter was the Hampton Normal and Industrial School in the vicinity of Fortress Monroe, which owes its existence to the forethought of Mr. King, and generosity of Mr. Avery.

Quite a number of ministers and teachers have been educated at this institution, and are now spread over the South and elsewhere, engaged in the work of elevating the freedmen, physically, intellectually, and morally.

Mr. King was esteemed a sincere and devoted Christian, a strict observer of all the sacred ordinances of the Protestant-Episcopal Church, and served for over twenty-five years as one of the vestry-men of Trinity Church, and was noted for his zeal and intelligence in all matters bearing upon the welfare of the church and the cause of Christianity generally.

He was married in Pittsburg to Miss Mary Earle Holdship, daughter of the late Henry Holdship.   They had six children : his widow and three children survived him.

Henry, the eldest, resides at Plainfield, N.J.   Wilson, the second son, has been in the consular service of the United States for over twelve years, and is now stationed at Birmingham, England.

His eldest daughter, Frances K., is the wife of Joseph Brown of the Wayne Iron Works.   His second daughter, Estella, who died some years ago, was the wife of Joseph G. Seibenick of "The Chronicle."   Two of his children died in infancy.   He died in Allegheny, Penn., Dec. 18, 1882, aged seventy-six.

GEORGE LEICHTENBERGER.

GEORGE LEICHTENBERGER, anglicized " Lighthill," was born in Würtemberg, Germany, Jan. 22, 1737. He came to this country during the French and English contest for supremacy on the American continent, about the middle of the eighteenth century, and settled in Pittsburg, on the west side of Fifth Street (now Fifth Avenue), on a large lot between Wood and Market Streets, extending in depth to Diamond Alley. He is mentioned in Craig's " History of Pittsburg."

He was married twice. The marital relations between him and his first wife were not of a happy nature : they were legally separated.

By his subsequent marriage he had three children, — one son and two daughters, — named respectively, John George, Margaret, and Catherine. Margaret intermarried with John Donly, and Catherine with Frank Rudolph.

He had two children by his first wife, — Thomas, and Elizabeth, who became the wife of the late Mr. Glancy.

Mr. Leichtenberger was a teamster by occupation, and was the principal operator in that line in the vicinity of Pittsburg.

He removed to the North Side in the year 1794, having purchased from the late West Elliot, out-lots Nos. 23, 24, and 272, in the " Reserve Tract opposite Pittsburg," and erected a substantial though humble log cabin on out-lot No. 23.

He died in June, 1814; his wife shortly after. His will, which is dated Jan. 12, 1814, made a liberal disposition of his property to his widow and children, including those of his first marriage.

His son, John George Leichtenberger, was born in Pittsburg in 1780. He was married in Ross township, in 1807, to Sarah Adams, daughter of the late Robert Adams. They had nine children, — five sons and four daughters, — all deceased except two sons, John and Christopher.

During the war of 1812 he was employed as a teamster and scout, and, when necessity required it, fought in the ranks, and was noted for his coolness under fire, and bravery in danger.

After the close of the war he followed the occupation of a fisherman. He was esteemed a man of the strictest honor and integrity, but took little interest in religious matters, until, awakened to its importance through the influence and conversation of the late Elder Samuel Church, he was brought to seek an interest in Christ, and connected himself with the Christian Church (formerly Disciples) of Allegheny, and became a devout and humble Christian. He died on the old homestead lot, July 10, 1865.

What has been said of the father may be truly said of his son John: through the same influence, aided by his faithful Christian wife, he was also brought within the Christian fold.

Sarah Leichtenberger, *née* Adams, died Jan. 2, 1844.

John Leichtenberger, son of the latter, also a fisherman, was born in the old homestead, Aug. 22, 1809.

He was married by the Rev. John Taylor to Miss Nancy Kelso, daughter of the late Charles Kelso, Dec. 20, 1832. Miss Kelso was born in Pittsburg, Oct. 6, 1813.

They had twelve children, — six sons and six daughters. Five died in infancy.

Charles Kelso, the father of Nancy Leichtenberger, was born in Belfast, County Antrim, Ireland, and came to America in his youth: love for his native land, however, after a short sojourn in this country, induced him to return. He afterwards resolved to return to the United States, with a view to making it his future home.

He settled in Portland, Me., and there married Miss Sarah Staples, a native of the place, in 1799.

In 1804 he came West, and settled in Pittsburg: subsequently he removed to the North Side.

He was a sailor and ship-carpenter, and assisted in building and rigging the schooner "Amity" and other sailing-vessels among the first cleared at the port of Pittsburg.

Ten children were the fruit of this union, — four sons and six daughters, — all deceased except Nancy, wife of John Leichtenberger.

Mr. Kelso was for many years engaged in the rope-manufactory of the late John Irwin, and was esteemed for his intelligence, and probity of character.

He died in Allegheny, 1850. His wife died November, 1854.

H. H. McCULLOUGH.

H. H. McCULLOUGH, the subject of this brief sketch, was born in the city of New York, Feb. 17, 1807, and was the son of a soldier of the war of 1812.

His parents at an early date came West, and settled in Georgetown, Beaver County, Penn. Here he acquired a liberal English education in all the branches commonly taught in the schools of his day.

He arrived in Pittsburg about the year 1830, and obtained temporary employment in the grocery establishment of Miss Rachel Watson, on the west side of Diamond Alley, between Wood Street and the Diamond Square. Whilst here engaged, he was stricken down with a severe attack of small-pox, and his life at one time was despaired of ; but by the care and attention of his kind employer, he was ushered back to health.

His predilections were in favor of acquiring a knowledge of the drug-business.

Immediately on his restoration to health, he sought and obtained a situation in the White and Red Lead Factory and drug-establishment of John Hannen & Co., of which firm the writer of this sketch was the junior and active partner. This position Mr. McCullough retained, and enjoyed the confidence and esteem of the firm to the fullest extent ; and upon its dissolution in 1834, they were succeeded by Dr. Henry Hannen (a son of the senior partner of the retiring firm) and Mr. McCullough in the drug-business, under the name and style of Hannen & McCullough ; from which he subsequently retired in 1838 or 1839, and purchased the drug-establishment of Mr. Bourne, doing business on the north-east corner of Wood and Fourth Streets, and successfully carried on the same until the event of the great fire of the 10th April, 1845.

Mr. McCullough was largely interested in the stock of the

Pittsburg and Isle Royal Copper Mining Company in the Lake Superior regions, and was induced to accept the position of agent and general manager of the company to conduct the business at the mines. This position he held until about the year 1863, the duties of which he discharged to the entire satisfaction of the company.

During his sojourn in the Lake Superior regions, he established and carried on an extensive fishery, in which he engaged the services of the Indian inhabitants of the island, to whom he became endeared for his proverbial kindness and honorable dealings, and so far won their confidence and friendship as to receive the exclusive right to trade with them. From this source, in connection with the mining and fishing operations, he acquired considerable wealth.

In all his business and social relations, he was esteemed a gentleman in the fullest meaning of the term, and was noted for his enterprise, promptness, and conservatism, qualifications that enabled him to withstand the various panics and commercial distresses which periodically arose during the many years of his active business life.

In politics he was an ardent Democrat : although he never sought political preferment, he nevertheless was always ready and willing, in a modest and unassuming manner, to discuss the principles of his political faith.

In 1835 he espoused the cause of religion, and connected himself with the First Presbyterian Church of Allegheny. Subsequently, on his removal to Newark, N. J., he united with the First Reformed Church of that city, and was noted for his liberal benefactions and unobtrusive charities.

From his advent in Newark to the close of his life, he was extensively engaged in the manufacture of shoes, etc., carried on by Miller, McCullough, & Ober, he being the principal capitalist of the concern.

He was united in marriage, in Newark, to Miss Justin of that city.

They had three children, who all died in infancy. Mrs. McCullough died in July, 1875.

Mr. McCullough died May 3, 1883, highly respected and

much lamented. He left an only sister, Mrs. Mary J. Dawson of Georgetown, Beaver County, whose daughter, Mrs. Jennie Spence, wife of the Hon. Edward Spence of Beaver County, was present with him during his illness, and bestowed upon him the constant attention and loving care of a most affectionate daughter.

Suffering marked his last days. He was conscious of his approaching dissolution; and his faith in the divine promises, and his hopes of a blessed immortality, never for one moment forsook him.

JOHN MORRISON

WAS elected mayor of Allegheny in 1859, 1860, 1865, and 1867. He was born in May, 1805, in the old red ferry-house kept by his father on the north-east corner of Anderson Street and Bank Lane (now River Avenue), and who subsequently removed to the equally ancient log ferry-house on the north-east corner of Federal Street and Bank Lane.

Mr. Morrison, in his youth, exhibited evidence of intelligence far beyond his years. His age and general appearance, resembling a deceased son of the late Judge Hugh Davis, attracted the notice of the latter, and led to the youth's adoption in his family, and subsequent employment in his store. So happy were the relations between the judge and his *protégé*, that he was rapidly promoted to the dignity of clerk and general business manager. In 1827 he was married to the judge's only daughter.

He became one of the leading Whig politicians of the day, and was the ardent advocate of the doctrines of his party: generous to a fault, frequently he ignored his own political claims and aspirations for the benefit of others. At one period of his life he occupied a very enviable position in politics, which, if taken at the flood, would have led to fame and fortune far above his contemporaries. He acquired a liberal education under the tutelage of the late Thomas Salters, then one of the principal educators of Allegheny.

At the organization of the borough of Allegheny, in 1828, he was elected by council chief clerk, and subsequently elected burgess.

He was also elected county commissioner during the time of the issue and circulation of the county scrip. In 1849 he was elected county treasurer. The duties of these various positions he discharged with ability and integrity, and retired from them in the full enjoyment of the confidence and esteem of the citizens generally.

He was largely engaged in the lumber-trade, and, as long as he confined his operations to its purchase and sale, he prospered in an eminent degree ; but unfortunately he became involved in extensive manufacturing operations in the pine regions on the upper Allegheny, which proved a failure. If, however, the same amount of energy and care had been applied to conducting the business at the mills as had been given by him in the management of affairs in Allegheny, it would have doubtless turned out differently.

He was honest in all his dealings with his fellow-men, ever ready to aid by his advice and material assistance those who were commencing the more active duties of a business life, and struggles with adversity ; charitable in his judgments, and indulgent to the shortcomings of others; and those who knew him best honored him for his goodness of heart, and the true nobleness of his nature.

He died at his late home on California Avenue, Ninth Ward, Allegheny, on Thursday, the 19th of April, 1883, after a lingering and painful illness superinduced by injuries received by falling through a hatchway on Park Way, and was interred in Allegheny Cemetery.

There were nine children the result of this union ; viz., Elizabeth H., Eleanor G. (deceased), Hugh D. (deceased), Martha M., Hannah W., Robert S., Mary T., Annie C., and William D. (who died in infancy).

HEZEKIAH NIXON.

HEZEKIAH NIXON was elected mayor of Allegheny in 1844 and in 1845. He was born on the South Side in Scott (formerly St. Clair) township, Allegheny County, Penn., on the twenty-first day of May, 1802. His father, Thomas Nixon, was a blacksmith by trade. He came from New Jersey, and settled on the farm on which Leasdale Station of the Chartiers Valley Railroad is located. He married Miss Jane Lea, daughter of the late Col. William Lea.

On the death of his father, young Nixon, then nine years of age, was left to his own resources. He first went to live with Mr. Robert Bell, a neighboring farmer, and when of sufficient age to learn a trade, chose that of a carpenter, and went to live with his uncle, Robert Lea, with whom he learned the art and mystery of the trade he had chosen. On the fulfilment of his engagement with his uncle, he started out as a journeyman, and worked for several years in the rural districts. In 1824 he settled in Allegheny.

His first engagement after he came to Allegheny was the building of the rolling-mill of Messrs. Cowan & Brown on the north-west corner of Penn Avenue and Cecil Alley, Pittsburg, the site of which is now covered by the Fourth Ward Public School House. His next important work was the erection of Messrs. Blake & Anderson's Rolling-Mill on the bank of the Allegheny River between Darragh Street and the outlet of the Pennsylvania Canal. This was the first rolling-mill erected in Allegheny.

He also built the Hurd & Howard Paper Mill on the bank of the Ohio River, on part of out-lot No. 20, in the "Reserve Tract opposite Pittsburg," now embraced within the limits of the Fifth Ward of the city of Allegheny.

For a number of years he was associated with Richard

Dewhurst in the prosecution of the business under the name and style of Nixon & Dewhurst.

In all the varied operations in which he was engaged, he rendered entire satisfaction to all, both as to the kind of workmanship and the quality of the materials furnished.

He subsequently leased for a number of years a lot of ground on the bank of the Allegheny River, from the late Neville B. Craig, on the west side of the outlet of the Pennsylvania Canal, and erected a saw-mill thereon, generally known as the "Outlet Saw-mill." This he operated for about ten years, when it was destroyed by fire.

He was one of the first select councilmen elected in Allegheny, and was chosen president of that body in 1842. During his administration as mayor he was the first to establish a police-court in connection with that office. On his retirement from the office of mayor, he was again elected to the select council, which position he held for nine years.

In 1848 he was elected recorder of deeds, etc., for Allegheny County; and after the expiration of his term of office, he engaged in the business of steamboating on the Ohio River.

A few years before his death he became aware that his eye-sight was rapidly failing, which unfortunately culminated, in 1856, in total blindness, and he was obliged to relinquish all work. He died on the twelfth day of December, 1858.

When quite a young man, he was a member of a military company called the Jackson Independent Volunteers, and was elected their captain. In politics Mr. Nixon was at first a Federalist, then a Whig and Anti-mason, and lastly a Republican.

He was a member of the first temperance organization in the county. He was strongly impressed with feelings averse to the system of domestic slavery. In early life he took an active and intelligent part in opposition to these great moral and social evils. Although modest and unassuming in his manners, yet he was ever ready to fearlessly disclaim against the destroying influence of the one, and the manifest injustice of the other.

He was a devout and humble lifelong Christian, connected

with the Associate Reformed, afterwards United Presbyterian, Church.

He assisted in the organization, and was one of the first elders, of the Rev. John T. Pressly's congregation, the First Associate Reformed, now the First United Presbyterian, Church of Allegheny.

In 1851 he, with other members of the congregation, organized the Second Associate Reformed Church, now the Third United Presbyterian.

Although Mr. Nixon possessed considerable natural ability, and was intelligent to a remarkable degree, he was a wholly elf-educated man. The world was his school, and time his tutor.

He was married March 3, 1831, to Miss Rose Anna, daughter of Charles Frow, late of Union township, Allegheny County. He had seven children, — two sons and five daughters. Two of his children, a son and daughter, died in infancy. His wife and five children — a son and four daughters — survived him. His eldest daughter, Harriet H., now deceased, was married to Col. Levi Bird Duff, formerly of the One Hundred and Fifth Regiment Pennsylvania Volunteers. He was severely wounded at Petersburg, Va., losing a leg.

His second daughter, Mary C., is the wife of the Rev. Hunter Corbett, a Presbyterian missionary, who resides at Chefoo, China. The third, Cornelia C., is the wife of Samuel O. McKee, who is engaged in the railroad business at Wichita, Kan. The fourth, Agnes S., now deceased, was married to the Rev. Cyrus B. Hatch of the United Presbyterian Church, formerly of Allegheny, now a resident of Irwin, Westmoreland County, Penn.

His son, Thomas L. Nixon, is a surveyor and civil engineer, and resides in Wichita, Kan.

In all the phases of his eventful life, both in Church and State, he was much admired for the goodness of his heart and the excellent qualities of his mind.

JOHN PARK.

WRITING the memoirs of those who have long since passed away, especially in the absence of written testimony to guide in making up a truthful record, is a task by no means easy to accomplish.   Facts collected from tradition, or gleaned from the unreliable recollections of others, must necessarily be received with some degree of caution.   The writer is well aware of the extreme difficulty of avoiding mistakes ; and if any palpable errors in the computation of time should have crept into these memoirs, he can only plead guilty beforehand, offering in extenuation, the assurance that he has at least done the best he could under the circumstances.

The subject of this sketch was born in the city of Belfast, county Antrim, Ireland, in the year 1760, and died in the borough of Pittsburg, March 20, 1808, in the forty-eighth year of his age.   The writer was then in his infancy, consequently it is not to be supposed he could have any recollection of him. His knowledge is therefore derived from those who were best qualified to impart the necessary information.   When a youth of fourteen years, he embarked with his father at the port of Belfast, some time during the year 1774, on a merchant-vessel owned by the latter, bound on a voyage to one of the West-India Islands (Curaçoa).   Notwithstanding his extreme youth, he exhibited unusual abilities, which induced the father to appoint him his private secretary and supercargo of the vessel ; and when we take into consideration that the father was then engaged extensively in the commerce of Europe with the West-India Islands, the appointment of one so young to a position so responsible evinced a confidence highly creditable to the recipient.

A change, however, soon took place.   During the voyage an unhappy misunderstanding occurred between the imperious father and impetuous son, growing out of a mere difference of opinion in regard to some unimportant matter. This unpleasant state of affairs continued with no hope of a reconciliation; and for this reason the father determined to change the course of the vessel, so as to touch at some convenient point on the American coast (probably New York), and there to cast adrift his youthful son. This unnatural and inexorable determination was fully carried out. The boy never forgot the treatment received, and to the day of his death repudiated all and every attempt towards a reconciliation, as will more fully appear as we progress in these memoirs.

All nature seemed alive with joy: the stately ship glided through the bright waters of the broad Atlantic. The sun lit up with superior brilliancy the glorious scene, and not a cloud obscured the clear blue sky.

There was one, however, who occupied the quarter-deck, to whom nature's beauty seemed to have no charms, if we may judge from the gloomy frown upon his brow, and the apparent anger that gleamed from his eye as it roamed over surrounding objects.

The father had scarcely reached the age of fifty years. His face had evidently been at one time handsome, but the fierce struggles with the world had imparted lines which marred the traces of the comeliness of youth. As his experience increased, it seemed to impress him differently from others. There appeared but few signs of declining strength in his countenance; imagination could scarcely picture that those stern features could ever soften into a smile : and time, instead of lessening his energies, had rather added additional force; and the violent impulses of the man were more indomitable at fifty than they had been at an earlier age.

The vicissitudes of an eventful life, while they affected him intensely, failed to have that salutary influence upon his disposition so desirable in the parent; and, like the impetuous mountain torrent, his passions gathered strength and fierceness as they rushed on unchecked.

The frequent and impatient looks he directed towards the companion-way, gave evidence that he was expecting some one. Twice he essayed to enter, but as often paused : at length, however, when his patience had become well-nigh exhausted, the proud and impetuous son made his appearance.

For a brief space they mutually gazed upon each other in silence, the elder frowning with anger, and the son looking him calmly and respectfully in the face. The son had too often detected the angry cloud upon the parent's brow, to be awed by the tempest it portended ; and he stood up before him, collected almost to indifference, with a composure that irritated the sire more than, perhaps, the offence for which he was arraigned. The boy desired to know if he wished to see him. "No, sir, I do not wish to see you," replied the sire, in a hot and sarcastic manner. "I never wish to see you again. I would rather you were removed to some remote corner of the world, where your presence could never offend my eyes, and where reports of you rwayward conduct could never reach my ears."

To this unfeeling remark, there was no reply made. The son well knew that nothing he could say would mitigate the wrath of his unreasonable father. "By your waywardness and disobedience you have crushed out the confidence and affection I had for you," continued the proud parent. "Your conduct is alike disgraceful to yourself and to me." — "I have not disobeyed you or violated your confidence in this matter. You accuse me unjustly and without proper thought ; and if you will do me the favor to listen patiently for a moment, I think I can convince you that I am entirely innocent." — "I will not hear you : I cannot believe you, sir. You are guilty of this offence, as well as many others. Innocence, with you, was never considered a minute. Your whole life has been one of insubordination." — "But, sir, although I may have committed grave errors, I may be innocent of this one," replied the son. "Do not attempt to palliate your conduct, or reason with me !" exclaimed the imperious sire. "Bear it in mind, sir, when in after-years your shortcomings shall have involved you in trouble, that I have not caused your ruin ; that I have taken all the pains a parent could bestow upon a most obedient child, and what has been the result ? How have you requited me ?" — "But, father, if you would permit me to explain"—"Call me not 'father'!" interrupted the parent. "You are no son of mine: from henceforth I disown you. There runs not a drop of my blood in your veins, no, not one drop! The tie between us is forever severed!" and as he concluded, he commenced pacing the deck, muttering the incoherent ravings of uncontrollable passion. This outburst of a father's wrath was borne at first by the son with the utmost humility; but when the father disowned and denied him, his blood boiled, and he trembled in every limb from excessive agitation. His features worked convulsively, and the great tears sprang up in his clear blue eyes; but with one mighty effort he controlled his feelings; and though appearances indicated repose, it was an ominous stillness that obliterated the color from his cheek until long after that eventful interview.

The father at first failed to observe the struggles of the sensitive son, and continued his perambulations of the deck for some time. When his rage had well-nigh exhausted itself, and he had discovered the effect which his conduct had aroused in the breast of his son, he became more considerate, and his countenance assumed a milder, but still gloomy, expression. Whether it was that he was softened by the appearance of penitence which his wayward boy had never evinced on former occasions, or whether it was that his conscience rebuked him for his unnecessary and unfeeling violence, is a problem that none but himself could have determined. There is no doubt but that one or the other exerted a powerful influence over him at the time.

In a much milder tone than he had previously used, he said, "You proposed to explain away your recent offence; I hope you will be able to do so; you have now the opportunity; proceed, sir." The son answered, "The time for explanation has passed away. I cannot now oblige you. I could have cleared up the matter to your entire satisfaction had you permitted me when I first proposed it. I do not deem it my duty to attempt it now." The father, as if in doubt as to the proper course to pursue, pondered a while. At first he was disposed to exhibit his former anger; but when he encountered the calm, defiant spirit of his son, he became convinced that such a course would be productive of disastrous consequences. Veiling his vexation as much as possible, he again requested an explanation of the cause of their misunderstanding, and promised that he would accord to him his sincere forgiveness. This proposition was met on the part of the youth with a ghastly smile. Said he, "Forgiveness? And for what, sir?" It was not in the power of the father at that moment to reply to the calm though withering interrogatory had his life depended upon the effort. He was confounded; and the color even came to that cheek, hardened by the storms of fifty winters. A painful silence obtained which he was unable to break. Twice he strove to do so, but the words died upon his lips; and the proud, haughty, iron-hearted parent stood humbled before his injured son.

The son saw the anguish of the father. He felt his own triumph too; and although it was a proud moment, he was too generous to take advantage of his position. He could not injure the feelings of a father who had failed to spare his. He was affected, however, and in a proper spirit resumed, "In consideration of the declaration you have made at this time, I can no longer remain under your care and protection. The obligations I am under to you are very great, and can never be obliterated from my memory. I feel that the debt can never be repaid. Yet I am not wanting in gratitude, though I have seemingly been in rectitude; and that my unfortunate though involuntary errors may not in the future disturb your equanimity, I shall perpetrate them in another clime. It has been my misfortune to offend you, never my intention, sir. My every wish was to please you. I would have ultimately done better: it has been my study to please you; and if I have failed, it is not that I am unwilling. The events of to-day, however, render it unnecessary for me to continue in trying to please you. I feel that I can have no further claim on your affection. Every consideration in our relation except the feeling that binds one man to another, you have disowned." As he concluded, he withdrew from the quarter-deck, to mingle with the sailors, leaving his father motionless with amazement.

The son, although a youth in years and experience, yet possessed all the feelings and qualities of one of maturer years;

and had these been more fully developed, age could only con-
firm them, not change their general nature in any other manner. Like all youths who are restrained in their actions, he
was wild and irregular when freed from the immediate influence of thraldom, and had frequently indulged in a series of
frolicsome and mischievous pranks, one of which gave rise to
the scene just described, and in which he was entirely innocent
of intentional wrong. These erratic ebullitions were more the
momentary caprice of a sanguine and happy temperament than
the exercise of vitiated and corrupt impulses.

In fact, there were so many contradictions in his character,
that it took a long acquaintance and some penetration to understand him. Of a restless disposition, there were times when
he settled down in a thoughtful and studious mood; and when
he took hold of a subject that involved a difficulty, it was not
laid aside until it was thoroughly understood. It would naturally be supposed that a youth so ardent would be habitually
social and communicative, but with him it was entirely the
reverse. He avoided company, indulged in long and solitary
rambles, and was remarkable for his taciturnity: nor was he,
as might be inferred, selfish, vain, or cold-hearted; for there
never existed a more generous, disinterested, or affectionate
being when events transpired to call these virtues into action.
His taciturnity did not arise from any want of those social feelings that endear us to each other, but rather from the failure to
meet with those whose disposition harmonized with his own.
His reticence was not caused by a dislike to meet with others,
but rather from an inclination to commune with his own
thoughts; and if he avoided society, it was not from any an-
tipathy to it, but rather that solitude had more to interest his
thoughts, and less to annoy his tender sensibilities.

These distinctions may be considered too finely drawn, but
those who study human nature will not deny their existence.
In short, he was somewhat of an enigma, whom but few understood, and none could properly appreciate on limited acquaintance. During all this interview his apparent calmness was
a concealment of feeling. After leaving the presence of his
father, it burst forth with additional violence, in consequence

of being for the time restrained. This mighty tempest, though heart-rending while it lasted, was of short duration; like the tornado, prostrating in its violence, but continuing only for a brief period. The vessel having arrived in port, with a sorrowful heart he prepared to leave it. Pursuing his way a short distance, he paused, and, turning about, gazed long and wistfully backwards. Resuming his sad and uncertain course, he cast behind home and friends, and looked hopefully forward to the future. What pleasing reflections does that one word "home" give birth to! Let it be grand or humble, it is ever associated with the dearest memories of life. It is one of the few things, that, amidst the changes of life, we still remember with joy; and the memory becomes more and more endeared to us as time increases the gap between it and ourselves.

The old homestead, the tree that first shaded us, the stream we first angled in, and the landscape that first greeted our infant eyes, make their impress upon our minds, the bright and pleasing hues of which are as lasting as life itself.

Pausing in the highway of life, memory leads us back to that blessed place, when youth and innocence were our happy lot. It is our earliest impression, and the last to fade from our memory; and when we have acted our part in the great drama of life, though we may have been successful beyond our most sanguine expectations, fortunate beyond desire, gained the admiration and applause of the world, and the satisfaction of ourselves, we still look back and find no place so like paradise as our first home, and no moments so productive of happiness as those spent within its sacred walls. This wayward and unhappy son had alienated himself from those endearments that he was fated never to experience on earth again, and sundered one of the most sacred obligations of humanity, — the sympathy between parent and child. From all these he wandered, to commence a new and doubtful career, to enter upon business where there is so much uncertainty, selfishness, and deceit. He was determined, persevering, and ambitious, — qualities that always befriend us, and which often prove more efficient than personal influence: the latter only directs the road to fame, while the former guide us to the goal. He was proud that all his impulses were honorable, proud that he had never been guilty of any thing for which he should feel self-abased. He was cast entirely upon his own resources, and it afforded him consolation that he was conscious that his abilities were fully adequate to the emergency. The wide world was before him; and he was at liberty to choose his own way through it, to carve out his own destiny, to make for himself a name, honorable in the coming time. The youth was wandering through the streets of a strange city, with the aimless manner of one who walks that he may commune with his own thoughts and fancies, alone in a crowd, solitary in the midst of a multitude.

During all this time the gloomy and obdurate father suffered the most acute pangs of remorse. It was not until after the separation that he learned to estimate his son properly for those shining qualities which he had passed by with such cold indifference. The treasure is never so dear as when lost, and the father felt now that he would sacrifice any thing to regain the love of his alienated child. Every effort was made to induce the son to return to the vessel, but without effect; and after repeated disappointments the humiliated and unhappy sire departed on his ocean journey.

Of intervening time occurring from his landing in the United States to his advent in Pittsburg, I can gather no reliable information. On his arrival in the town, he was highly impressed with the importance of the location, and beauty of its surroundings, situated at the confluence of the two important rivers, Allegheny and Monongahela, one flowing from the north, and the other from the south, forming the still more important Ohio. Its future as a manufacturing-point was fully settled in his mind. Judging from its position, with an ample water-communication extending to the Gulf of Mexico, surrounded with immense deposits of superior bituminous coal, and mighty forests of excellent timber, it required but little effort of the imagination to prognosticate what it is to-day, — a manufacturing city second to none in the Union. Impressed with these views, he resolved to settle, and make it his future home. Endowed by nature with talents of no ordinary ability, he was soon afforded an opportunity of bringing these qualifications into employment.

Gen. James O'Hara and Major Isaac Craig, men of note, whose interests were closely identified with the growth and prosperity of Pittsburg and surroundings, both holding high positions under the General Government, connected with the quartermaster's department and manufacturing interest of the West, having entire confidence in him as a gentleman, and his ability as an expert accountant, tendered him the responsible position of confidential clerk and general agent for the transaction of all business with the quartermaster's department and glass-making. Isaac Craig, Esq., grandson of Major Isaac Craig, has in his possession quite a number of interesting relics of the olden time. Among them are manuscript copies of letters written by the subject of these memoirs to government officials and officers of the various frontier military posts, running through a period of years from 1790 to 1807.

In accordance with his preconceived opinion, that Pittsburg was destined to become an important manufacturing and commercial centre, he acquired considerable real estate in localities which proved the wisdom of the selection, as they are now considered among the most valuable within the limits of the two cities. These purchases, however, owing to a limited capital, involved him in pecuniary embarrassment, which compelled him to part with piece after piece, until all was disposed of except the sixty acres now embraced within the limits of the Fifth Ward of the city of Allegheny.

For the inheritance of this portion of the estate, his children are wholly indebted to the care and management of an affectionate mother, who determined, during the lifetime of her husband and since, that this at least should be preserved intact for the benefit of her children. With this purpose in view, she persistently refused every attempt at alienation of the property. After her death it was divided by a decree of the Orphan's Court equally among her six children then living.

The father had frequently written to the son, deploring their unhappy estrangement. These letters the latter persistently refused to acknowledge. They were forwarded unopened to the office from which they were mailed, without comment. There was one, however, — the last, it is supposed, that was written, — which came into the possession of his wife during the absence of her husband on a visit to the North-West on business connected with the quartermaster's department, marked *important;* and not knowing where it could reach him, she opened it, and thus became aware for the first time of a history, which, owing to her husband's reticence, was always a mystery to her. On his return, however, and being made acquainted with what had occurred, he exhibited no gentle evidence of his disapprobation. True to his previous resolution, he continued inexorable to the last, and would not rest satisfied until he had exacted a promise that the information obtained from the letter should not be followed up. Without reading it himself, he consigned the letter to the same fate as the others, carefully noting on the outside the circumstances attending its opening.

How unfortunate that this letter was not retained! It was an acknowledgment by the father of his error; an abject apology for his unnatural and inexorable conduct; a piteous overture for a reconciliation which the proud and unrelenting son would have done well to consider, and would have afforded a starting-point in tracing up the lost one.

Many of the items upon which these memoirs are based are so vague and indefinite that the writer has been compelled to draw upon his imagination in order to supply what might be deemed otherwise incomprehensible to the reader. The main facts, however, are true, as they have been handed down to me by others.

Of the father's subsequent history, there is but little known. It is supposed he was lost in the harbor of Curaçoa in the West Indies, during the prevalence of the great earthquake which occurred near the close of the eighteenth century, the tidal wave of which overwhelmed and destroyed the shipping in the harbor, and the inhabitants residing near the seashore.

DEATH OF HON. ORMSBY PHILLIPS.

THE following papers were clipped from "The Pittsburg Dispatch," issue of Nov. 13, 1884 : —

Hon. Ormsby Phillips, one of the owners of "The Dispatch," died at his residence on Ridge Avenue, Allegheny, yesterday morning at nine o'clock. For the past three weeks Mr. Phillips had been seriously ill; and although not entirely unexpected, his death was a severe blow to his grief-stricken family.

The deceased, with whose prominence in the community every citizen is familiar, was born at Jefferson Barracks, a few miles south of St. Louis, on Oct. 2, 1829. His father, Major Asher Phillips, served in the war of 1812; and his grandfather was Oliver Ormsby, an early settler on the South Side. At an early age, Mr. Phillips, with his parents, removed to Louisville; and he was educated at the schools there, and at the Western University in this city. At the age of nineteen he took charge of a telegraph-office in Louisville, and soon after came to Pittsburg. Here he was one of the coterie composed of Messrs. Robert Pitcairn, Andrew Carnegie, Henry Phillips, and David McCargo, who were employed in the first telegraph-office opened in this city. Later he formed a partnership in the iron-foundery business with John and W. J. Anderson, and subsequently engaged in the manufacture of glass in the firm of Phillips & Co. In 1862 Mr. Phillips was commissioned captain of Company C, Fifteenth Regiment of State Militia, and served until the regiment was discharged. In November, 1881, he became a partner in the Dispatch Publishing Company, and filled the position of business manager until his death.

Mr. Phillips filled several important public positions during his lifetime. In 1867 he became a director in the Western Penitentiary, and served as secretary of the board until May last, when he was elected president. In this position Mr. Phillips labored assiduously for the best interests of the institution, and the impress of his unselfish efforts will live long after him. He was one of the early directors of the Morganza House of Refuge, and also served many years in the same office in connection with the Western Pennsylvania Hospital, and the Insane-Asylum at Dixmont. His traits of character and disposition seemed to especially fit him for the work which his association with the institutions named involved. It is not surprising that Mr. Phillips was also prominently identified with nearly every charitable enterprise of a public nature. He seemed to throw his whole soul into such work, and his energy contributed largely to the success which invariably attended such enterprises. The Sanitary Commission Fair saw Mr. Phillips among its promoters. He was elected mayor of Allegheny City in 1874, as an independent candidate. His opponents were D. L. Smith, Republican, and the late Peter Farley, who was killed a short time ago on the Fort Wayne Railroad at Wood's Run, the Democratic candidate. Mr. Phillips's election was due to his personal popularity; and for this reason it is not to be wondered at, that, during the riots of that same year, Allegheny City was remarkably free from acts of lawlessness. Since 1867 Mr. Phillips was one of the trustees of the Dollar Savings Bank. He was also a director of the Boatman's Insurance Company, and a vestry-man of St. Andrew's Church. In all these varied fields of labor the deceased brought the force of his own individuality prominently into play. He enjoyed the high respect and esteem of the entire community, and his loss will be keenly felt outside the circles of a grief-stricken family and a host of friends.

Mr. Phillips was married on Oct. 17, 1859, to Miss Annie S. Bakewell, daughter of the late John P. Bakewell. She with five children survive him: the latter are Messrs. Bakewell and Henry Phillips, Mrs. Sarah Phillips, wife of Professor Phillips of the Western University, and Misses Annie and Margaret Phillips. He also leaves a brother, Dr. T. A. Phillips of the East End.

In Memoriam.

At a meeting of the Board of Inspectors held this morning, the following resolutions were adopted, and ordered to be published in the daily papers of the city : —

WHEREAS, In the wisdom of an all-ruling Providence, we, the Board of Inspectors of the Western State Penitentiary, have been called to record the death of Hon. Ormsby Phillips, who since 1867 has been an active participant in all of its councils ;

Resolved, 1st, That, in making this minute, we gladly recognize his noble qualities of head and heart, which were shown in his urbane consideration of the opinions and feelings of others, and his uniform Christian courtesy toward all made his companionship genial, helpful, and valuable.

Resolved, 2d, That in the position of secretary of our Board, an office which he filled for seventeen years, he was careful, faithful, and accurate. And his long experience and intimate knowledge of the institution admirably fitted him for the presidency of the Board, to which he was called last May, at the death of President T. H. Nevin.

Resolved, 3d, That in carrying forward the change from the old prison, and the responsible work of the erection of the new building, his hand never failed in the patient and judicious performance of his part of the allotted duty; and because of his familiarity with the demands of the circumstances, and his spirit of wise economy in all things pertaining thereto, we shall greatly miss his able counsels, and thus do deeply regret his loss.

Resolved, 4th, That in his death the official management of the prison has not only been bereft of much knowledge and many characteristics of mind which will be difficult to replace, but all the prisoners who knew him have lost one whom they could truly call a friend. His voice and efforts helped to throw open the dark double doors which had so long closed them in solitary confinement. His advice to them was always plain, direct, and earnest, and along the line of the acquirement of manliness, self-control, and reform.

Resolved, 5th, That whilst the State has been deprived of an upright conservator of its interests, and these cities and this community of an exemplary citizen, it is upon his family, where his goodness and gentleness and real depths of affection and heart-life were best shown and known, that this blow has fallen heaviest; and hence to them, one and all, we wish to be permitted to convey our sincerest sorrow and sympathy in this hour of sudden bereavement.

WILLIAM ROBINSON, JUN.

ALLEGHENY, in pursuance of the Act of the General Assembly of the Commonwealth of Pennsylvania, approved April 10, 1840, was created a city; and Gen. William Robinson, jun., had the honor to be chosen its first mayor. He was born on the seventeenth day of December, 1785, in the old family mansion, on the west side of Federal Street, on out-lot No. 36, in the "Reserve Tract opposite Pittsburg."

The old homestead was removed a few years ago, and its site is now covered by substantial three-story brick buildings. He bore the reputation of being the first white male child born north of the Allegheny River.

During his life he took a prominent and active part in politics, and in every thing appertaining to the growth and prosperity of his native place. Possessed of abilities of no ordinary kind, endowed with a liberal classical education, a graduate of Princeton College, and having read a full course of law with the late James Ross, he was eminently qualified for all the duties of life; but, unfortunately, his haughty and dictatorial manner kept his friends at a distance, and seriously interfered with his political aspirations.

In his early youth he became familiar with the aggressions of the Indians, with whom his parents had many fearful encounters in defending their humble homestead. With the Chief Cornplanter and his band, who remained on the upper waters of the Allegheny, he kept up a friendly intercourse until his death.

In 1806 he unfortunately became involved in the notorious scheme of Aaron Burr for the conquest of Mexico, having been led with others to embark in the undertaking through a mistake as to the principal object to be attained. On the death of his father he inherited considerable property lying within the present limits of the city of Allegheny, a part of which he laid out in lots, and called it "Buena Vista," and named its streets after the battles of the Mexican war.

Gen. Robinson for many years was interested in commercial and industrial pursuits. He acquired the title of general by virtue of a commission in the State Militia.

In the internal improvement of the western part of the State, his enterprise and personal influence were beneficially exerted; and in the construction of the Ohio and Pennsylvania Railroad (now P., F. W., & C. Railway), he largely invested his means, and was chosen its first president.

He was one of the projectors of the first iron-mill in Western Pennsylvania, and a corporator in the first bridge erected over the Allegheny River.

He was the first president of the Exchange Bank of Pittsburg, and at one time was a member of the State Legislature.

He was elected to the select council of Allegheny continuously from 1849 to 1856, and was chosen its president.

He died on the twenty-fifth day of February, 1868.

THOMAS SAMPLE.

THOMAS SAMPLE was the next in order to assume executive honors in Allegheny. He was elected mayor in 1841. His regular business was that of a tanner and currier: his tan-yard was located on the west side of Middle Alley, between Water Alley, now Park Way, and Gay Alley. He was a man of sterling character, rather eccentric in his habits and disposition, and had an ordinary education. He was for several years magistrate in the First Ward, and had his office in the tannery. He died a few years ago, on his farm near New Castle, Lawrence County, Penn.

A very singular incident occurred during his official career as magistrate, connected with the atrocious murder of a farmer, committed by a negro tramp, on the Beaver road, below Economy, Beaver County. It appears the farmer was on his way to Pittsburg, driving a two-horse team: overtaking the negro on the road, he generously invited him to take a seat in the wagon. Shortly after, and before reaching Economy, the negro treacherously murdered him, by beating out his brains with a stone, which he had previously provided for the occasion. Secreting the body under a culvert, he continued on with the team towards Allegheny. He staid over night in Sewickly, at the stone tavern. Before retiring to bed, he endeavored to remove all tell-tale evidence of his crime by casting the bloody straw in the wagon on the manure-pile. In the morning he proceeded on his way to Allegheny, and put up at the old Pennsylvania tavern, on the north-east corner of Ohio and Webster Streets, the site of which is now occupied by St. Peter's Church. Here he offered the wagon and horses for sale.

The body of the unfortunate farmer having been discovered shortly after the murder, parties living in the vicinity trailed the fugitive to Allegheny.

Just before dark the negro discovered that pursuers were on his track, and immediately shifted his quarters to the old tavern-stand on the corner of Federal Street and River Avenue. To this point his pursuers trailed him : but before they could arrest him, he fled to the river ; and in his attempt to cross it on the ice to the Pittsburg side, he broke through, and was drowned.

The body was recovered the next day, and deposited in the old town-house on the south-west Diamond Square, where it lay awaiting the action of the coroner. To the amazement of the authorities, the body suddenly and mysteriously disappeared.

Subsequent events pointed directly to Mr. Sample as the principal party engaged in the "taking off."

The boldness of the transaction created quite an excitement at the time ; and it continued without abatement until it leaked out that the object in surreptitiously removing the body was to skin it, and tan the hide, in order to solve the problem as to the quality of material manufactured out of the cuticle of the "genus homo." Razor-strops and watch-guards were fashioned out of the novel leather, and distributed among the curious.

Mr. Sample was considered somewhat of a genius in his way. To his insatiable disposition to solve the various problems of law, physics, and mechanics, may be attributed this seeming violation of the laws of humanity and good order.

It was generally conceded that he was actuated by no other motive than the one above indicated. In view of the high estimation in which he was held by the citizens generally, he was unmolested. He died in Mahoningtown, Lawrence County, Penn., Aug. 11, 1876.

WILLIAM BARCLAY FOSTER.

WILLIAM BARCLAY FOSTER was the third mayor, having been elected in 1842, and again in 1843. He was one of the oldest and most highly esteemed citizens of Allegheny County. His political proclivities were of the Democratic order, and he was warmly attached to his party. He was a gentleman of culture and refinement, and was much admired for the qualities of his mind as well as for the goodness of his heart.

He was born in Berkeley County, Va., Sept. 7, 1779, and died in Allegheny, July 27, 1855. He was married in Chambersburg, Penn., to Miss Eliza Clayland Tomlinson, who was born in Wilmington, Del., Jan. 21, 1788, and died Jan. 18, 1855, six months preceding his own death. They had nine children.

One of his sons, Stephen C. Foster, gained quite a reputation as a musical composer: his beautiful and pathetic ballads are the admiration of the musical world. He lived respected and died lamented on the 13th January, 1864.

His grandfather, Alexander Foster, was a native of Londonderry, Ireland; emigrated to this country in 1728, and settled in Little Britain township, Lancaster County, Penn. James Foster, the father of the subject of our sketch, removed to Berkeley County, Va. He was a soldier in the patriot army, served through the whole of the Revolutionary war, and highly distinguished himself at the storming of Yorktown. After the close of the war the father removed with his family to Washington County, Penn., and settled near Canonsburg. He was chosen one of the first trustees of Jefferson College in 1790. The son, William B. Foster, came to Pittsburg, April 20, 1796, and went into business with Major E. Denny and Anthony Beelen in 1806, for the purpose of general merchandizing, on the north-west corner of Market and Third Streets. In 1812 he was appointed commissary of the Pennsylvania Brigade in the Black Hawk expedition, and in 1814 and 1815 he was appointed commissary for the United-States Army, and expended over fifty-eight thousand dollars of his own means for the use of the government. He loaded the steamer "Enterprise," Capt. Henry M. Shreve, with supplies and munitions of war, for the army under Gen. Jackson, which opportunely arrived at New Orleans, Jan. 5, 1815, three days before the battle of the 8th.

In 1814 he laid out the town of Lawrenceville from a part of his farm, and sold to the government the thirty acres on which the United-States Arsenal was erected.

In 1821 he was appointed register and recorder for Allegheny County. He was elected three times to the Legislature of Pennsylvania, first in 1824, and last in 1829.

He was appointed the first collector of tolls on the Pennsylvania Canal at Pittsburg, and was continued in that position for seven years.

In 1832 he was appointed to make up the statistics of the United-States Judicial District of Western Pennsylvania preparatory to a revision of the tariff.

The writer cannot recall to memory any special event that marked the period of his administration as mayor. He was always credited with the faithful performance of its duties, and enjoyed in an eminent degree the confidence and respect of his fellow-citizens.

JONATHAN RUSH.

JONATHAN RUSH was the seventh mayor-elect of Allegheny, having been chosen in 1849. He was born in Morris County, N.J., on the twenty-second day of May, 1801, was the second son of Jacob and Susannah Rush, and a descendant of one of the oldest German families in the United States.

The subject of this sketch served an apprenticeship to the hatting business, in Morristown, N.J. On the completion of his engagements, in 1826, and moved with the marvellous and glowing tales of the Western World, he left his native place, journeyed westward, and finally settled in Pittsburg. He was employed in the hat-establishment of Mr. James Wilson.

He was married in 1829 to Miss Sarah Campbell, formerly of Offwick Valley, Huntingdon County, Penn. In 1835 he removed with his family to New Lisbon, O., but returned in the following year to Pennsylvania, and from that time (1836) dates his connection with the town and city of Allegheny. It was during his administration as mayor of the city, that the great fire, and firemen's riot, of the 16th July, occurred.

His fearless and determined action on that occasion was, doubtless, the means of saving a large amount of property, which otherwise would have been involved in the general ruin. His action proved him to be a man of indomitable courage. Although an ardent Whig, he seldom took part in politics. Notwithstanding this fact, he occupied a number of important positions in the government of the city, having been elected treasurer, and served in that capacity during the years from 1851 to 1853; after which he was chosen assessor of water-rents, and in 1854 and 1855 was also appointed collector of water-tax.

The duties of these several positions he discharged with

ability and fidelity, and his mild and unassuming manners procured for him a host of friends.

He was a member of the Cumberland Presbyterian Church of Allegheny, of which he was one of the founders, and always maintained the character of a devout Christian gentleman.

He died on the thirteenth day of May, 1863.

HENRY SHAFER

WAS born near Pittsburg, of German parentage, during the French and English war. He was employed, in the interest of the English, at Fort Duquesne, as an expert hunter and scout, enjoyed the confidence of the officers of the fort, and was frequently complimented by them for his zeal and indomitable courage in watching the movements of the hostile Indians, and reporting promptly to the commandant of the fort in time to checkmate them in their raids. He also contributed valuable services in supplying the fort with meat and game.

In the year 1790 he built a log cabin on the borders of a small stream which empties into the Monongahela, at a point on which was located the ship-yard where the first steamboats were built at Pittsburg, and where the viaduct of the Pittsburg, Cincinnati, and St. Louis Railway crosses the Monongahela. The stream is generally known as " Suke's Run."

His humble cabin was located on the north side of the run, near the site now occupied by the celebrated " Round House."

In 1794 he purchased a small farm north of the Allegheny, to which he removed. Here he lived for over ten years. This property is now occupied as a city of the dead, — " Hilldale." In the latter part of the year 1804 he disposed of his property, and took up his residence with his children, in Elizabethtown, Allegheny County, Penn.

He died at the home of one of his children, in Elizabethtown, full of .years, in 1849.

JOHN SHAFER

WAS born in Pitt township, on the north side of Suke's Run, Aug. 18, 1794, and followed the occupation of a fisherman. He was united in marriage, in Ross township, May 15, 1817, to Miss Emily Short. They had ten children, — five sons and five daughters. One son and three daughters are still living; viz., —

Sarah, widow of the late William P. Macky, born April 25, 1818, married June 11, 1849.

John, born Sept. 19, 1820. Emily, widow of the late A. H. English; born April 11, 1838, married May 25, 1856. Harriet; born March 30, 1842.

Eliza Jane; born Jan. 24, 1820, died Dec. 1, 1842.

Mary Ann; born June 17, 1831, died Feb. 1, 1860. The other four sons died in early youth.

Mr. Shafer was highly esteemed for the probity of his character. With the enterprise of youth he united the careful considerations of age. His life fully justifies the confidence reposed in him by his many friends. Although he had passed his threescore years and ten, he retained in a remarkable degree his mental and physical powers.

In every relation of life he proved himself a man of unswerving honor and integrity. He would consent to nothing, no matter what the inducement might be, which would tend to lower himself in his own estimation, or that of others. His standing was of a higher order; and when he believed himself right, no power on earth could divert him from the dictates of his own judgment.

He died at his residence on Beaver Avenue, city of Allegheny, Sept. 28, 1867. His widow survived him eight years. She was born in Ross township, on the bank of the Ohio River, Oct. 14, 1800, and died at the family residence on the 29th of May, 1875.

MARTIN SHORT.

MARTIN SHORT was born in the city of Dublin, Ireland, in the year 1750. He was apprenticed at an early age to learn the blacksmith-trade. The relations between him and his master not proving of an amicable nature, he "sought other fields and pastures new." Secreting himself on board a German vessel about to sail for the United States, he made arrangements with the captain to work his passage to Baltimore, for which port the vessel was cleared. Arriving at that city, he was induced by the captain to remain on board in the capacity of cabin-boy, and continued as such for several voyages across the Atlantic. While thus employed, he acquired a knowledge of the German language. At the age of seventeen years, and upon a subsequent arrival of the vessel at the port of Baltimore, he left it, and obtained employment in a ship-yard, in which he was engaged until he enlisted as a soldier of the war of the Revolution.

After the close of the war he settled in Hannahstown, Westmoreland County, Penn., where he was united in marriage to Miss Mary Shocky, a German girl, whom he had met and wooed on board of the vessel, during one of his voyages across the Atlantic.

About the year 1800 he removed to Allegheny County, and settled in Ross township, in the part now embraced within the limits of the Fifth and Sixth Wards of the city of Allegheny, where he resided until his death, which occurred on the 19th of January, 1842, in the ninety-third year of his age.

He was the father of a large family of children, thirteen in all, — two sons (Adam and Valentine), eleven daughters. The only ones of whom there is any authentic information, and who survived him, are, —

Sarah, who intermarried with Harry Faulkner; Elizabeth, who intermarried with James Fletcher, born 1800, died 1875; Emily, who intermarried with John Shaffer; Julia, who intermarried with Henderson Donly; and Valentine, who was married to Polly Sellers.

All the above were born on the north side, in the territory now embraced within the limits of the city of Allegheny, except Valentine, who was born at what was then known as Tom's Run, near where it empties into Chartiers Creek, on the 17th of January, 1792. He died in 1883.

Mr. Short was an active participant in the glorious siege of Yorktown, battle of Bunker Hill, surrender of Lord Cornwallis, and many of the sanguinary encounters which marked the period of the nation's struggle for independence. At the momentous crossing of the Delaware, amid snow and ice, he had his feet severely frozen, the effect of which he felt to the day of his death.

On the uprising of the Indians of the North-West, and commencement of hostilities, he again enlisted, and participated in the disastrous defeat and rout of the army under the unfortunate but brave Gen. Arthur St. Clair, Nov. 4, 1791, by the combined Indian forces led by the celebrated Indian chief "Little Turtle." In that engagement he was severely wounded with a rifle-ball over the left eye, and was left on the field, where he was found by an officer, who bound up his wound, and generously cared for him until they reached a place of safety, both barely escaping the roving bands who scoured the woods for stragglers of the routed army.

At the expiration of his term of service he was honorably discharged, and returned to his home in Allegheny County.

In 1802 he was employed by Messrs. Denny & Beelen in the erection of their glass-works on the north side, on the bank of the Ohio River immediately opposite the head of Brunot's Island, and subsequently in the works of Messrs. Craig & O'Hara, on the south side, opposite the Point of Pittsburg.

He died poor, but highly respected, and was buried with the honors of war in the Methodist graveyard, the site of which is now occupied by the Union Depot. On the occasion of his interment, the Pittsburg Blues and other military organizations took quite a prominent part.

JOHN WOODS.

JOHN WOODS, an old settler on the north side, was born of Irish parents at Elkhorn Creek, James River, Va., in 1750. He came to Allegheny County, and settled at Peter's Creek, and was there married to Sarah Stephenson in 1780. She was born in Sussex County, Del., in 1752, of Scotch descent. Miss Stephenson was remarkable for her physical strength as well as for her strong mental powers. She was just the woman to mate with the hardy pioneer, and bear the rigors of a comparatively unknown country, and circumvent the hostile intentions of the nefarious Indian foemen.

He settled in Ross township at the mouth of Wood's Run, April 1, 1794.

They had twelve children, — six sons and six daughters, — born in the following order; viz., Fanny, Elizabeth, Ellen, Susan, James, John, Joseph, Rebecca, Sarah, Pressly, Jeremiah, and Peter.

Mr. Woods died at the old homestead at Wood's Run, Sept. 2, 1819. Mrs. Woods died at Racine, O., in May, 1844.

REV. ALLEN D. CAMPBELL.

ALLEN D. CAMPBELL, D.D., was born at Chorley, Lancashire, England, March 15, 1791. In his youth he came to the United States with his parents, who settled in the city of Baltimore, Md.

His father was a man possessed of more than ordinary ability and large attainments in spiritual matters, and was for many years a ruling elder in the Associate Reformed Church. The subject of this brief memoir was naturally of a vivacious and ardent temperament ; and, until enlightened by divine grace, the strictness of the parental management was highly distasteful to him.

He graduated at the University of Philadelphia, then under the care of Rev. Drs. Gray and Wylie. For these eminent educators he manifested a strong attachment, second only to his love and veneration for his theological instructor, the Rev. I. M. Mason, D.D., who exercised a wonderful influence over his pupils.

He was licensed by the presbytery of the Associate Reformed Church of Philadelphia in 1815, and was appointed by that body to preach in the vacant churches in Western Pennsylvania.

In the spring of 1817 he was married to Miss Nancy W., the accomplished Christian daughter of the late Benjamin Bakewell. In the following year he was ordained by the presbytery of Monongahela over the churches of Meadville and Sugar Creek, where he labored devotedly until the synod of Scioto separated from the church east of the mountain. He refused to go with them, and united himself with the presbytery of Red Stone of the Presbyterian Church.

In the fall of 1820 he removed to Tennessee, which brought with it new scenes of labor in the charge of the First Presbyterian Church of Nashville, where for seven years he labored faithfully in his Master's work, amid many difficulties, and much pain and suffering from frequent attacks of illness. Whilst here, he found many warm friends. To Gen. A. Jackson he was particularly indebted for his unceasing friendship, and kind hospitalities received at the Hermitage.

The friendship thus begun was maintained by each as long as they lived. During the exciting political campaign, in which his friend and patron was conspicuously before the public as a Presidential candidate, he devoted himself, especially after his return to Pennsylvania early in 1827, ardently to correct the calumnies circulated about the old hero, and spared no pains to present his friend's good qualities in the most favorable and truthful light.

In the latter part of the following year, the family removed to Allegheny County, to their pleasant home overlooking the beautiful river, where he lived until the day of his death, which occurred Sept. 20, 1861.

Although for a while he had no settled charge, his labors were undiminished. Prior to his leaving Tennessee, the project of establishing a theological seminary in a locality more accessible to Western students had commenced to agitate the attention of the church. Of this measure, so important and imperiously demanded by the growing interest of the West, he became the firm and zealous advocate, in view of which the General Assembly of the Presbyterian Church, at their session held July, 1825, at Chillicothe, O., appointed him a director of the contemplated seminary, which was two years after located, by authority of the General Assembly, on the common ground in the Reserve Tract opposite the city of Pittsburg.

A modest commencement was effected by the reception of four students, who were instructed in theology by the Rev. Joseph Stockton and Rev. E. P. Swift.

The subsequent election of the Rev. Dr. Janeway and inauguration in October, 1828, seemed to argue auspiciously for the future of the infant institution; and the warmest hopes were entertained for its growth and prosperity.

In proportion to these flattering hopes was the disappointment experienced when Dr. Janeway resigned his position in consequence of existing doubts in his mind as to the legality of the title by which the land was held on which the seminary was to be erected.

In the midst of gloom and despondency, growing out of this state of affairs, Dr. Campbell tendered his services as agent, to visit England and Scotland for the purpose of collecting theological works : this offer was promptly accepted, and proved eminently successful in its results, securing to the institution a library of over two thousand volumes.

This labor of love, involving the hardships and dangers of a trip across the Atlantic ocean, and an absence of over eight months from the comforts of home-life, and considerable expense, was performed gratuitously.

His intercourse with Dr. Chalmers, Edward Irving, and many other pious and talented ministers of Great Britain, was a source of profit and pleasure throughout his subsequent life.

He was subsequently induced to give up his charge of the Fourth Presbyterian Church, located on the north-east corner of Penn Avenue and Mechanic's Street, Pittsburg, where he had labored for many years under discouragement, and devote his entire time to the interests of the Western Theological Seminary.

The duties of his position as general agent, and instructor in church government and discipline, he discharged with rare fidelity. His official relation to the seminary terminated in 1840, yet he was to the close of his life the untiring advocate of what he deemed for the best interest of the institution.

During the memorable controversy of 1837, which demoralized and sundered the Presbyterian Church, he was by no means inactive or a neutral spectator. Eminently qualified by his previous training, he championed the cause of orthodoxy and ecclesiastical order as against the cry of bigotry and exclusiveness raised against those who dared to battle for what they deemed the truth; and his candor and straightforwardness elicited the admiration, even of his opponents.

He was a true lover of his adopted country. The condition of affairs during the late Southern rebellion caused him much unhappiness.

His loyalty to the national cause, no one could doubt. As an evidence of the interest he took in the nation's cause, he accompanied a regiment of Home Guards, of which he had been appointed chaplain, in their parade through the cities of Pittsburg and Allegheny, July 4, 1861. His desire was to accompany them into active service, nor would any thing have prevented him from so doing but the consciousness that the state of his health was too uncertain to bear the rigors and hardship of camp-life.

He was peculiarly happy in his marital relations, and owed much of his usefulness to the faithful and accomplished companion of his life. The asperities of his ardent nature, and impulsive utterances and actions, were wonderfully tempered by her dignity, intelligence, and habitual serenity of mind. To her literary ability and profound thought, the Church at large is eminently indebted.

Her ample means enabled her to feed the hungry, and relieve the distressed. Instead of surrounding her home with the display of wealth and the profusion of luxury, every thing was simplicity itself. She died Aug. 10, 1862.

Dr. Campbell and his amiable wife were both proverbial for their liberality and hospitality: their home was ever open to both friend and stranger, and their purse to the claims of benevolence. Many a theological student and struggling Christian minister have abundant reason to remember with gratitude their many acts of kindness.

They had seven children, — one son and six daughters, — named respectively, Benjamin B.; Ann B., wife of Rev. John Kerr; Euphemia, wife of B. P. Bakewell; Jane H., wife of William Bakewell; Ellen, wife of B. Page; and Sarah.

REV. JAMES RODGERS, D.D.

SOME men are born, live their life, and pass away, leaving behind them a monument far more lasting than the shaft of granite; "footprints on the sands of time" which cannot be washed away, and which serve to encourage many a poor, stranded fellow-being to start afresh instead of succumbing to what is called destiny or the inevitable. James Rodgers, a citizen of Allegheny, hewed his own monument, reared his own shaft, and was honored and beloved by all with whom he came in contact. He was an Irishman by birth, having been born near the town of Oneagh, Tyrone County, on the twenty-second day of December, 1800. His father, William Rodgers, was a member of the Irish Presbyterian Church. The family consisted of one daughter and three sons, of which James was the second born. When but seventeen years of age, he, having been educated as a civil engineer, left his home for Belfast, and then sailed for New York. Leaving New York, he went to Meadville, Crawford County, Penn. Here he made the acquaintance of the Rev. Daniel McLean, to whom he appealed for advice as to obtaining employment at his profession. At that time the services of civil engineers were not greatly in demand; and Dr. McLean advised him to open a school, which he did. He succeeded so well in his vocation, that he sent for his parents, and purchased a farm, upon which he settled them. He taught until about 1821, when he retired to his farm, and applied himself to the study of Latin and Greek; and three years later he entered the Western University. He graduated with honor in 1827, and then entered the Theological Seminary of the Associate Church at Canonsburg, Washington County, Penn. At the close of the fourth session (1830), he was put on trial for licensure by the presbytery of Allegheny; and the following September, by the presbytery of Miami for ordination.

In October he was licensed and ordained, and appointed to the Miami Mission, which included a few vacancies in Missouri, Indiana, and Illinois. While there, his beloved mother died; and, having completed his mission, he returned home, being then thirty-one years of age, and in the full vigor of his manhood. Soon after his return, he received a call from the united congregations of Noblestown and Ohio, which he accepted, entering at once upon the performance of his duties. In 1832 he met his wife, Miss Eliza, youngest daughter of Mr. Thomas Livingston, and was married. He then settled in Noblestown, the distance between his two congregations being about eighteen miles. About this time a number of families applied for organization in Allegheny City. In 1837 they succeeded, and Mr. Rodgers was called upon to minister to their spiritual welfare. After considerable debate at the meeting of the Associate synod in session at Philadelphia, neither of his congregations wishing to part with him, he was installed. His first sermon was preached in a large hall on Federal Street; his new congregation being poor, and unable to build. At that time Messrs. William Bell & Blackstock operated a large cotton-factory, which employed many hands; and, seeing the want of a desirable place of worship for a congregation made up of toilers, they purchased a lot on the second bluff above the river, between Federal and Sandusky Streets, upon which was erected a large, substantial brick building, which was finished in 1839, and is now the Second U. P. Church. These gentlemen intended to present the property to the congregation, which, through the labors of Mr. Rodgers, soon became prosperous; but, alas for human plans! it was not to be so. The firm became embarrassed, and the property was about to be levied upon by the sheriff. Through the perseverance and indomitable energy of Mr. Rodgers, however, it was finally saved.

In 1845 the Board of Jefferson College conferred the title of D.D. without solicitation upon Mr. Rodgers, and certainly was the title never more deservedly bestowed. In 1850 he commenced a series of lectures on John Bunyan's "Pilgrim's Progress," which have since then been published in book-form. After finishing this course of lectures, he took a rest from his labors, —

having increased the membership of his church from 270 (1840) to 430, — by taking a trip to Europe, staying two months. About this time his health became slightly impaired, suffering very much with a soreness of the throat. As he was chairman of the Board of Domestic Missions, he was appointed to visit the churches in the Far West, thus enabling him to take a rest from his duties. At first he improved, but soon the symptoms reappeared; and he arrived at home completely prostrated, and was compelled to take to bed. He was never after able to fill his pulpit, and sent in his resignation; but so beloved was he by his congregation, that they rejected it, his pulpit being filled by substitutes. He a second time sent it in, and after much persuasion it was accepted, thus closing his career as a minister of the gospel; the event taking place early in 1860, after having been in the ministry for thirty years, and of the Associate now the Second U. P. Church of Allegheny for twenty-one years and eight months.

Being now without occupation, he was, not long after, called to take charge of the book-store of the Board of Publication of the U. P. Assembly. He appeared to be the man for the place, and the concern thrived under his administration. His health, however, grew worse, and early in July Dr. Rodgers found it necessary to go home as a result of indisposition; and after an illness of about three weeks, on the 23d of July, 1868, death claimed him, thus closing a long life of usefulness and goodness. He faced death as only a brave and good man can, — fearlessly. A wife and three children survived him, — Thomas Livingston, Elizabeth, and William B. Rodgers.

REV. THOMAS SPROULL, D.D.

By Rev. J. W. Sproull.

THOMAS SPROULL was born in the northern part of Westmoreland County, Penn., about a mile and a half from the village of Freeport, on the fifteenth day of September, 1803. His parents, Robert Sproull and Mary Dunlap, were natives of Ireland; the former of County Tyrone, and the latter of County Derry. His father, the youngest of three brothers, unaccompanied by any friend, came to America in 1784. According to his own record, "he embarked in the ship 'Congress' from Londonderry, in the twenty-second year of his age, July 23, 1784, and landed at New Castle the 11th of September the same year." For about ten years he remained in the eastern part of the State, when he removed to the neighborhood of Mercersburg, Franklin County. There he met, for the first time, his future wife. With her mother, five brothers, and one sister, she had come to America about seven years later than he had. They were married on the twenty-fifth day of February, 1794. That same year they removed to Westmoreland County, locating on a farm near the one they lived on at the time of his death.

Westmoreland County was then regarded as the frontier. Stories of Indian massacres were familiar, and, indeed, the fear of the red man had not entirely died away. It was still common to conceal valuables, and go armed to daily labor. Greensburg, the county-seat, was twenty-eight miles away; Pittsburg, the chief market for the products of the farm, about thirty. Usually produce was taken to Pittsburg in canoes by river, the time occupied during a trip being three days. The nearest post-office was Freeport. The mail-carrier also supplied subscribers with the weekly papers. Few sounds were more welcome than the tooting of his horn, as almost the only means of hearing from the outside world those pioneers had was the weekly paper. School-facilities were very meagre. A pay-school for three months in the winter was the only opportunity for a long time parents had to secure an education for their children.

The subject of our sketch manifested a strong desire to obtain a thorough education, and availed himself of every opportunity to increase his store of knowledge. The circumstances of his parents were such that he had largely to depend on himself. When sixteen years of age he was so far advanced as to take charge of the winter school. In 1826 an opportunity was afforded him to prepare for college at a private academy taught by Rev. Jonathan Gill, a Covenanter minister, near Turtle Creek. In 1828 he entered the junior class of the Western University. Having been advanced a year, he graduated in 1829, and subsequently taught in the same institution.

His ancestry on both his father's and mother's side were Covenanters. It is not strange, that, early in his life, his attention was devoted to religious subjects, nor that, when he made a profession of religion, he identified himself with the Covenanter Church.

Early in life he had made up his mind to be a minister. After leaving college he studied three sessions under Dr. Black. He was licensed to preach by the Pittsburg presbytery on the — of April, 1832, in Pittsburg, and on the 4th of April, 1832, was ordained at New Alexandria to the ministry as a missionary.

In 1833 the Covenanter Church was divided on the subject of civil government. Dr. Black identified himself with what was subsequently known as the New-Light branch, and, being deservedly held in high esteem, was able to control a large majority of the members. At the first meeting of the adherents of the old side, but thirteen were present : subsequently others connected with them. In 1833 they called Mr. Sproull to be their pastor, and on the 12th of May, 1834, he was installed. That relation continued until Oct. 13, 1868, when, being required to give his whole time to the seminary by direction of synod, it was dissolved. From that congregation, there have been organized five distinct congregations, — Pine Creek, Wilkinsburg, Allegheny, Pittsburg, and Central Allegheny. During his pastorate it was the largest, wealthiest, and strongest in the church. Indeed, no other congregation in the body has ever attained so large a membership, or wielded so powerful an influence.

.In addition to performing his duties as pastor, during the greater part of his ministry he discharged also those of professor in the Theological Seminary. In 1838 he was elected professor in the Western Seminary. In 1840, the Eastern and Western Seminaries being united, he was continued in that position. Resigning in 1845, he was re-elected in 1851; and again resigning in 1868, he was re-elected the same year, with the understanding that he would obtain a release from his congregation. He was also one of the editors of " The Christian Witness " for two years, and for nineteen years was either editor or co-editor of " The Reformed Presbyterian and Covenanter."

He has also published a large number of sermons, lectures, and pamphlets. In 1882 he published his " Prelections on Theology," a volume of four hundred and fifty-five pages, which has been favorably received.

The title of Doctor of Divinity was conferred on him by Westminster College.

On July 1, 1834, he was married, by Rev. John Crozier, to Magdalena Wallace, third child of John Wallace, Esq., of Pittsburg. Of their twelve children, seven reached maturity. The oldest, Christiana Wallace, married Professor Newell, who was licensed by the Covenanter Church to preach the gospel. The second, Rev. R. D. Sproull, was for some years pastor of the Reformed Presbyterian Church of Rochester, N.Y., but subsequently of the Presbyterian Church of Providence, R.I. The third, Rev. J. W. Sproull, was for some time pastor of the Monongahela Congregation of the Reformed Presbyterian Church, and afterwards of the Central Allegheny, and is one of the editors of "The Reformed Presbyterian and Covenanter." Mary Magdalena, the next, is the wife of Rev. C. D. Trumbull, pastor of the Reformed Presbyterian Church of Morning Sun,

Io.   Thomas Alexander, the next, was pastor of the Reformed Presbyterian Church of New Alexandria until his death, on the 8th of April, 1878.   William Oliver, the next, is professor of Latin and Arabic in the University of Cincinnati.   Theophilus, the youngest living, is a member of the firm of Myers Shinkle & Co. of Pittsburg.   All received a college education.

ALEXANDER YOUNG.

ALEXANDER YOUNG, Sen., was born in Lanarkshire, near Glasgow, Scotland, in 1784.

He came to the United States in 1819, and settled in what was then Ross township, Allegheny County, on the bank of the Ohio River, on an out-lot of the Reserve Tract, immediately above the mouth of Strawberry Lane, in April, 1820. From here he removed to the mansion and large farm of the late Thomas Cromwell in 1822, and in April, 1823, to Ferry Lane (now Beaver Avenue), a short distance west of Island Lane (now Washington Avenue).

In 1826 he purchased from Marguerite S. Parke the ten-acre out-lot, No. —, lying on the river-bank on both sides of Beaver Avenue, upon which he erected a substantial frame dwelling, opposite the mouth of Western Avenue: the building is still standing, one of the last of the landmarks of the olden time.

April 1, 1839, he removed to a large farm in Lower Burrell township, Westmoreland County, upon which he resided until December of the following year, when he returned to his former residence in Allegheny County, where he died on the sixteenth day of February, 1841. Having made no will, his large estate was divided under the intestate laws of the Commonwealth.

Mr. Young was educated a farmer; his teachings and experience in the old country were brought into use here; and he was considered one of the most thorough, extensive, and successful market-gardeners in Allegheny County.

He was, in the strictest meaning of the term, a self-made man, starting in life without any of the appliances of wealth, and but meagre opportunities for acquiring an education: by his courage, forethought, indomitable perseverance, and integrity of character, he acquired considerable wealth, and attained a most respectable position in the community in which he had cast his lot.

Endowed by nature with a generous disposition, he was charitable without ostentation, and strictly honorable in all his relations, while at the same time he was earnest, resolute, and determined.

He was united in marriage in Lanarkshire, in the year 1814, to Miss Elizabeth Smith, who died in Allegheny, March 24, 1872, in the eighty-fourth year of her age, in the full use of her mental faculties, beloved by her children, and highly respected for her many Christian virtues.

They had seven children ; five survived them, — two sons and three daughters ; and two died in infancy.

Alexander Young, D.D., L.L.D., the eldest, was born in Lanarkshire, June 4, 1815 ; was educated for the ministry ; graduated, was called and ordained pastor of the Reformed Presbyterian Church of St. Clairsville, O., in 1842, the pulpit of which he occupied with marked acceptance for sixteen years, from 1842 to 1858. In 1855 he was chosen professor of theology in the Associate Reformed Theological Seminary at Oxford, O. Subsequently, he was elected to a similar position in the Theological Seminary at Monmouth, Ill., occupying at the same time the pulpit of the first U. P. Congregation, and subsequently that of the second congregation of the same place.

He also, during the sixteen years of his connection with the above, filled acceptably various professorships in the Monmouth College.

On his return to Allegheny County, in 1874, he was elected professor of Pastoral Theology and Apologetics in the United Presbyterian Theological Seminary, in the city of Allegheny.

During the thirty-three years of his teachings in Ohio and Illinois, he never failed to meet a class, at the hour appointed for recitation, on account of sickness.

Elizabeth, the eldest daughter, was also born in Lanarkshire, Jan. 31, 1817 ; is the widow of the late Abraham Patterson, builder and contractor. He was for several years a member of the councils of Manchester and borough of Allegheny.

Stephen was born in city of Pittsburg, Penn., Nov. 24, 1819; is a farmer, and occupies a part of the farm in Westmoreland County.

Jennette was born in Ross township, Oct. 22, 1829; is the wife of Mr. B. Kennedy, journalist, for many years connected with the press of Pittsburg and Allegheny.

Agnes was born also in Ross township, Feb. 11, 1830; is the wife of J. T. Simpson, who at present manages a mill and farm at Sampler Station on the Pittsburg and Western Railway.

CPSIA information can be obtained
at www.ICGtesting.com
Printed in the USA
BVOW11s0147200317

478895BV00020B/461/P